PENGUIN BOOKS
FACING THE MIRROR

Ashwini Sukthankar was born in Mumbai in 1974 and grew up between Papua New Guinea and India. After studying comparative literature at Harvard University, she moved back to Mumbai, where she is a writer and an activist.

D0890588

Facing the Mirror

Lesbian Writing from India

Edited by Ashwini Sukthankar

PENGUIN BOOKS

Penguin Books India (P) Ltd., 11 Community Centre, Panchsheel Park, New Delhi 110 017, India
Penguin Books Ltd., 27 Wrights Lane, London W8 5TZ, UK
Penguin Books USA Inc., 375 Hudson Street, New York, NY 10014, USA
Penguin Books Australia Ltd., Ringwood, Victoria, Australia
Penguin Books Canada Ltd., 10 Alcorn Avenue, Suite 300, Toronto, Ontario M4V 3B2, Canada
Penguin Books (NZ) Ltd., 182-190 Wairau Road, Auckland 10, New Zealand

First published by Penguin Books India (P) Ltd. 1999

Typeset in Palatino by Digital Technologies and Printing Solutions, New Delhi

Printed at Chaman Enterprises, New Delhi

Trying to analyze lesbianism is much like the party game of pin-the-tail-on-the-donkey: a large cut-out of the animal is propped up, and turn by turn each child is blindfolded, given a paper tail and told to pin it to the correct spot on the rump. Excited screams; bold guesses; random circles; nervous touching; unmapped strides; a wide rim of jeers; and maybe at the end, no more than the accidental puncturing of a paper eyeball.

V.S.

Musings of an Immaculate Soul: Listen to the inner voice. Acknowledge the moments of troubled fear and anxiety and let them drive you to achieving your fragment of peace. Take a stand, as a person with your preferences—no, it's not the only aspect of who you are, but acknowledge it to yourself and you'll be able to seek new heights in all the other parts of your life.

Shaila

When you are paid to write, and you write about your love for women, sometimes you feel that you live your love at every moment of every day. Sometimes you feel like a prostitute. Either way, it's an enriching feeling.

A.S.

In my early years in Bombay, the need to find other lesbians was dire. However, there weren't any. Or so it seemed. Women traveled to freer countries just to be able to love a woman. Those who could not do that fell for any available sari. The results were disastrous. Each one ended up used, abused, and went to see psychiatrists who had attitudes. Lesbian love was termed 'abnormal'—whatever that means. Imagine, having to see a shrink because you could not find a woman to love.

Sweetpea

Contents

Passages

✦

Home

🌿

Worlds

Differences

❧❧

Connection

❧❧

Love

❦

Editor's Note

In early December, just weeks before the publication date of this book, the Shiv Sena launched a frenzied assault on screenings of Deepa Mehta's film Fire. Some lesbians in cities across India chose to be visible, as lesbians, at protests against the Sena violence—though individuals connected to the film claimed that it was not a lesbian-themed work, we wanted to emphasize that the attacks on it were impelled by homophobia.

We were accused by segments of the media of having 'hijacked' these protests by the mere act of being visible, or of having 'derailed' the 'larger' debate of artistic freedom and democratic rights simply by being present. And a simple placard that declared its bearer to be 'Indian and Lesbian' earned an entire community much censure for alleged militancy and cultural anarchy.

One longs for the luxury to be impatient with the question of whether or not lesbianism is part of Indian tradition. Those of us who live out the twin truths of being Indian and lesbian know what we are and where we came from, and are too busy with the day-to-day struggles of our lives to yearn for lost utopias when women's love for women was celebrated on temple wall paintings and in ancient scriptures.

The reaction to our living presence has been painful to witness, a further reminder that the 'culture of tolerance' in which we live is fictitious. But it reinforces our belief in this book, which reflects on and represents our reality today. We will not be shamed into pretending that we do not exist.

Acknowledgements

I am grateful to the editors at Penguin India, especially Smriti Vohra, whose sensitivity and dedication will be appreciated by each of the contributors to *Facing the Mirror*.

Many thanks to Sandhya Luther for designing the cover, and to Catherine Sluggett for her illustration.

'Closeted in a Triangle' is used by permission of *Naya Pravartak* (in-house journal of Counsel Club, Calcutta); 'Looking Different' and 'Dyking Around' are excerpted and reprinted from *Bombay Dost* (quarterly magazine of the Humsafar Trust, Mumbai).

The executrix of the estate of Sagitta allowed me to use the poems 'Declamation' and 'Rekindle Hope All Ye Who Enter within These Gates'.

Thanks also to Javid Syed and to Prabha Khosla for easing a little of the financial burden of putting this book together.

Introduction

The question is inevitable and sceptical. '*Are* there any lesbian writers in India?'

Are there any lesbians in our country who have been published and feted, their sexuality acknowledged? Of course not. For Indian lesbians, putting our words into public space has so far meant having to manipulate brutally the dimensions of who we are. You could ask the author of a well-known novel of the 1960s, whose book was only published after she went back over the manuscript and painfully changed her swashbuckling heroine into a man. When I approached her to be a part of this compilation, she said apologetically that she had not written a single word in over thirty years. 'Write as a lesbian?' she asked incredulously. 'Sorry, forgotten how.' After many hours of coaxing, she did produce a small piece, 'Always in Due Course', which appears here under her pen-name, Barley. 'I'll call it fiction,' she said, and added, 'After all, it would be appropriate to call it that.'

No lesbian in this country needs to have that comment explained; we are accustomed to having our lives be a myth.

Our status as myth means that many people truly believe we don't exist, and it means inhabiting the domain of their ignorance, which is neither acceptance nor condemnation. It means being able to live together and spend time with each other, as long as the sexual root of the relationship is never discussed with anyone. It means that it causes no comment when women meet together in public, or in groups—but only as long as we act 'normal'.

It means that, even if we don't live outside the law, as gay men do in our country, we live between its lines. Section 377 of the Indian Penal Code[1] makes homosexual acts between men illegal but it does not technically have lesbianism in its purview, since the legal definition of intercourse requires penetration. When it was suggested to Queen Victoria in 1885 that 'Macaulay's Law' (so called because it was originally framed in 1861 by Thomas Babington Macaulay) should be extended to address female homosexuality, she was horrified, refusing to believe that such acts between women were possible.[2] The story is a cornerstone of lesbian dark humour, a wry commentary on the advantages of not being taken seriously.

A very similar kind of legal logic was in operation when the then British Government put Ismat Chugtai on trial for obscenity after her short story 'Lihaf',[3] about a little girl who witnesses a lesbian love affair, was published in 1941. The charge was dismissed because, as Chugtai's lawyer argued and the judge in Lahore agreed, the story could only be understood by a mind familiar with lesbianism anyway, so there could be no question of the author having intended to corrupt the innocent. The virtuous reader, after all, would be unable to conceive of anything so improbable as love between two women.

Both of these examples would seem to suggest that being a fiction has been useful to the Indian lesbian, and that invisibility has been our best friend.

But the invisibility conferred on us by the law—our special share of the country's colonial legacy—does not necessarily result in lesbians being 'legal', and therefore having legal recourse to fighting discrimination and harassment. On the contrary, invisibility means that the fact of our existence is still more shocking when it is revealed, and the very law that seems to ignore the reality of lesbian existence is employed to crush it out. The threat of Section 377 is used by families to coerce daughters to leave lesbian relationships, it is used by employers to justify firing lesbian employees, it is used by mere acquaintances to blackmail and persecute.

The spectre of Section 292, the obscenity law, poses the same menace to our public voice as 377 to our public lives.

The choice, then, is stark: either to remain within the realm of secrecy marked out by the law and reinforced by society, or to start claiming public spaces, with the explicit hazards that accompany them.

This is not to discount what we have created between the many layers of silence. Lesbian existence cannot be confined within a discourse of catastrophe. Many of us have been able to hold on to our belief in the voice within, to nourish it and give it shape and form through writing or oral narrative which testifies to our own realness. We share those words with trusted friends, and indulge in sly humour at the expense of the straight world which does not suspect that we flourish under its very nose. The spaces we create with and for each other are precious, powerful and sustaining.

But silence is no protection against the relentless pressure to marry. A secret bond between two women does not automatically confer on them the right to share a life, a home, a child. Silence is a zone we inhabit on sufferance. Easily invaded, easily demolished, it leaves us at the mercy of people who can simply choose whether or not to know and care.

Difficult, therefore, to insist that lesbian desire is private, without a public face and repercussions, and that what we do in bed is nobody's business but our own.

The course of lesbian visibility in India has been like scattered fireworks—an isolated episode here and there which consumes itself in its own sensationalism and leaves no trace of the life that was its context. In recent memory, this includes media spectacles such as lesbian suicides—digested with prurient relish and then forgotten—or lesbian marriages, which are undone as soon as they have taken place with friends and families immediately issuing denials. When Neeru (alias Dinesh) Sharma married Meenu Sharma in Faridabad in 1993, both sets of parents fell over themselves to insist that nothing had actually happened.'"Neeru and Meenu just posed as a newly married couple for fun,"' the mother of one was quoted as saying.[4]

According to the researcher Giti Thadani, the fact that lesbians are still harder to pin down in the more distant past bespeaks an equally deliberate erasure, with the mutilation of sculpture that depicts slesbian love, and the deliberate misinterpretation of texts describing it.[5] She also points out that the terms historically used to describe women who love women—such as sakhi and saheli—have been purged of their eroticism over time and reshaped into harmless descriptions of female friendship, so that today we find ourselves banished from language itself, literally at a loss for words.

So much for the idea that it is entirely of our own volition that lesbians are neither seen nor heard! Who would *choose* to hide? It's like violence from within—a schizoid dismembering, the self ripped into its public parts and its private parts, in every sense of the phrase. But what an effort it was for us to convince *ourselves* of our own existence, let alone others. Living without a history of your own kind is like living without the reassurance of a reflection in the mirror. Every lesbian who claws her way into self-awareness in a society that insists upon heterosexuality, has surely experienced the horror of that complete alienation from herself, the perilous feeling of being the only one. 'Maybe she is like me,' we've all thought, looking with longing and fear across a room, a bus, a street. 'But what could I possibly say to her? What if she's not?'

Even those of us in touch with each other are always in the process of learning to live as lesbians, grasping at identity as we go. Sandhya, one of the contributors to this book, calls it 'inhabiting a room which doesn't exist'; Flora B., another contributor, compares it to 'walking along the edge of a cliff without a map'. So many experiences feel like firsts, because all the women who have gone through them before have left no record behind. We ask ourselves: Am I the first lesbian to face the death of a lover and to have to hide the grief from everyone around me? The first to want a child and to wonder how two women can bring up a family? The first to question the idea of monogamous relationships?

For all these reasons, we share our lives in these pages. We did not necessarily have a collective goal in mind, but certain impulses came up again and again. We put pen to paper so that one less woman might have to experience the isolation we did. So that the anger and the passion which chokes us might begin to mean something beyond itself, the emotional energy set free from our individual, distinct lives to help other women chart theirs. So that we might make a shared language for the feelings which have been robbed of their name. Claim a public niche beyond the ignorance which has been our licence to live, beyond general tolerance to the acceptance that presupposes understanding. Challenge those who would say that our lives have nothing to do with theirs: 'I want to tell them, I wear the face of your loved ones,' the contributor Anasuya asserted. 'I could be your mother, friend, wife. I want to tell them, I am both lesbian *and* one of you, like it or not.' And so we try to articulate the many connections of shared faith, shared blood, shared experience, writing of similarities without hiding the many points of difference.

Many fear, legitimately, for the space that could well be destroyed as lesbians become visible: the sakhi space where, in the gender-segregated Indian world, women can live and be together in relative freedom. Liberation is far away; until then, surely, the existing, makeshift territories should not be surrendered. 'In all this talk of breaking the silence, what will happen to the women who walk hand-in-hand on the street? What about the women who live with each other quietly, without being interrogated by anyone?' But muteness is an option only for women who can pass as heterosexual; it is of no use to those whose androgyny speaks for them, and are therefore easy targets for discrimination. So, while increasing visibility will certainly make individual lives more difficult in the short term, beyond invisibility and obscurity lies the prospect of solidarity and community.

In any case, the domain where sexuality can remain undefined relies on an unquestioned silence for its existence, and that silence is slowly being perforated. Fewer and fewer lesbians can claim that they pass a day without having a co-worker or casual acquaintance ask about boyfriend prospects or weekend engagements. Let us remind ourselves that this is the era of website pornography and glossy magazines which, in exquisite detail, describe twenty easy ways for a man and a woman to orgasm simultaneously. It is not enough, today, to remain silent in order to avail of that traditional space—we are forced to lie.

For most of us, then, the question is not whether to relinquish the safety of silence, but how to negotiate an alternative. It is in the hope of finding one that we write, and that we write together naming ourselves lesbians.

But what does it mean to write as a lesbian? In the face of what has already been articulated, it's a political act of courage and conviction. It's writing with the whole self, with personal integrity in every sense of that phrase—bringing to the words an awareness of all the parts of which we are composed, without any exclusion or censorship.

And yet, when we talk of 'Indian lesbian writing' the term is in conflict with itself; the very theme which tries to draw this book into a whole is challenged from within by the words and lives of the women who wrote for it.

Indian.

There would be no need at all to discuss what it means to be Indian, were it not that the cultural basis of lesbianism is always disputed. A letter to the editor of a newspaper objected to an article on homosexuality with the complaint that this aberration was linked to 'the loss of our social values, moral code of conduct and above all, our Indianness'. The author defended the Indian Penal Code, which makes homosexuality illegal, with the words, 'The IPC is correct; it is a fragment of society which is wrong.'[6]

It did not seem to bother him that the entire IPC is a relic of the days of colonialism, a hodgepodge of legislation arbitrarily designed to rout out crimes which were supposedly specific to India, ranging from human sacrifice to the devadasi tradition and 'professional sodomy'.

So, since we must dwell on this point, in the context of this book, to be Indian is to write with a knowledge of this country, and to relate to its particular freedoms and restrictions and proprieties from that perspective.

Lesbian.

Even the terminology of desire is problematic. Some reject the word 'lesbian' for its white or Western connotations, preferring samyonik (a term we have constructed from the Sanskrit roots sam = union and yoni = female genitalia), or saheli. Others find it too politically loaded, and prefer terms such as 'woman-identified' or 'woman-centred'. Is 'lesbian' a word which excludes in other ways? Some of us identify as bisexual.

But we name ourselves here as lesbian, though it is such a difficult word, and unsettles even those of us who live out our love for women every day. We find it hard to claim the identity which accompanies that love, and we are intimidated by the social outrage it will bring. We trip over its syllables, stammer, find the sound sticking in the throat and try to work around it with gentler but specific alternatives like 'gay', 'not straight', 'woman-loving' or 'dyke'.

Nevertheless, we want to claim it here particularly *because* it is so uncompromising.

By contrast, study the current conversations around homosexuality in India, and you will see how rare it is to find a strand of the debate which says exactly what it means. Review after review of Deepa Mehta's film *Fire* described the love and desire between the characters Radha and Sita (Nita in the Hindi version) in terms of emotional bonding and loneliness, not once using the word 'lesbian'. A whole page of articles on homosexuality appeared in a newspaper under the bewildering headline 'Liberalism: Can We Handle It?'[7]

Other meditations on homosexuality might effortlessly wield the appropriate terminology, but seem to find it next to impossible to attach the correct meaning to it. Thus, despite all their broad-minded progressiveness, they evade having to engage with us in any thoughtful way. For example, a recent article breezily referred to Lesbos as an 'ancient Greek poetess [who] spent most of her life dallying in perfumed bowers'.[8] That a journalist could so easily conflate an island named Lesbos and a lesbian named Sappho need not surprise us; however, it should serve as a timely example of the need for us to intervene in the face of facile and irresponsible misrepresentation.

In this context, it is not difficult for lesbians to disappear into the gap between a word and what it signifies. On the other hand, when we name ourselves we can see ourselves for who we are: a group of women utterly diverse in terms of region, class, community, age, marital status, but with this one thing in common. Our love for women—that which marks us as different from the rest of the world, which brings us together, and which must be voiced if it is not to be lost.

Writing.

The pieces that were produced for this book are the abiding public affirmation of lives far too often lost on the sidelines. It might not be writing in the purist's sense, but then whose life is exemplary literature, after all. Women sent in poems scribbled on scraps of paper and hidden away for years, extracts from journals, love letters—astonishing artifacts in a world which consumes and discards the written word like any other mass-produced commodity. Other women asked if they could record their narratives on tape for us to transcribe, since they were either not literate, or had spent so many years using the written word as a shield of prevarication, that writing to reveal and express had become impossible. Again, it might be argued that this genre, whatever it is, is not writing. But for the purposes of this compilation, 'writing' signifies the gritty imperfect media through which the body, with its yearning and its suffering, spoke out; the process through which our lives, put into the tangibility of words, could be made public. Some pieces were translated from regional languages—by other lesbian- and bisexual-identified women, of course: a translator has to be wholly faithful to her author's tongue, the nuance and the music of it, and we could not expect such fidelity from someone with a different erotic awareness.

Somewhere in the convergence of all these nebulous realms—of 'Indian', 'lesbian' and 'writing'—in the free confluence of fiction, essay, poetry and memoir, this project resides.

The very fact that the contributions exist between categories, impossible to classify, makes this book more than the sum of its parts. The diversity of our points of view, the range of our experiences, the dissension we choose not to hide, help us escape any simplistic attempt to define lesbian life. For that reason, it is all the more important to point out that each of us speaks only for herself, never for lesbians in general. We have had far too many experiences of people trying to come to reductive conclusions about 'what we are' to subscribe to any monolithic descriptions of our community.

Indeed, that was the initial impetus for me to do this project—that in the recent flurry of media scrutiny of lesbian lives, in the torrent of articles with their neatly summarizing 'Glad to be Gay/Sad to be Gay' headlines[9], we looked at ourselves and saw indistinct shapes distorted beyond recognition. The few of us willing to be interviewed were approached with questions that demonstrated the interviewer's keen desire for the easy stereotype. 'So do you play the role of man or woman in your relationships?' 'Do you ever wear saris?' 'Was your father a strong influence in life?' The results of such a discouraging process were equally absurd. One article declared in tones of excited discovery that 'Lesbians are highly sensitive, not only can they be caring and highly possessive, they sometimes behave like people in love', and went on to sum up the collective lesbian psyche with the observation that the 'naturally narcissistic streak in women makes them admire other women and their bodies, as an extension of themselves.'[10] We were fetishized, made the symbol of Western debauchery, of feminist independence. We were living our lives with no other motive, it seemed, but to defy patriarchal tradition, to be fashionable, or to spite philandering husbands. Recently, an article in a women's magazine quoted, by way of authority, a prominent psychiatrist who spoke on lesbians in India with all the confidence of those who presume to know us. What could make a woman 'choose' lesbianism, the journalist wondered inanely. The psychiatrist asserted in response that 'it is not only unhappiness but also the general suppression of sexual appetites in our society that contributes to homosexuality.'[11]

Again and again, our lives were boiled down to pornography or caricature, with few exceptions. This would not have been so destructive if we had any other source for reflections of ourselves, but as it happens, we were utterly dependent on the mediation of those who offered to speak for us and interpret us.[12]

We found ourselves scrounging for subtext in movies like Kamal Amrohi's *Razia Sultan*, with its lingering kiss between two women, or trying to decipher neighbourhood gossip about a woman murdered by her husband because he insisted that her friendship with another woman took her out of the house too much. There were books and magazines from the West, but even the women with access to them knew that the niches we have to carve out for ourselves here are very different—not lesbian cafés and bars and bookstores. We have to shape our own spaces, piecing them together out of nothing more than thin air and the willingness to take a risk.

I think of Amita and Naseem, who met me in Mumbai six years ago in a small coffee house, knowing nothing more about me than the three-line letter I had written and sent to *Bombay Dost* magazine. They made themselves vulnerable to the possibility that I might have been a journalist hoping for a steamy exposé of the lesbian underworld, or a bigot with a mission to exterminate homosexuals. Their act of courage showed me how women with few resources could create a world for each other. At that point I was living outside the country—and thought I would have to continue to do so, in order to live as a lesbian. But after meeting Amita and Naseem, I realized I did not have to choose that exile.

This was not the picture the media showed me. Apart from the interview-based articles, there were sensational stories focusing purely on the cataclysmic aspects of our lives: couples hanging themselves, or stealing money for a sex-change operation. And of course, no article on homosexuality in India could appear without the obligatory reference to Oscar Wilde and 'the love which dare not speak its name'.

But who labeled it unspeakable, why should our love not find its voice? For the sake of the lesbians who looked at the stories and could not connect with them, who flinched as they read the pathologies of guilt, shame, death and rupture and doubted their own chances of survival, the time had come to make ourselves heard. We had to share our respective strategies for existing in India, with respect to India, with everything that these entail both as idea and in the practice of our daily lives.

I reached out to women I knew and women I had never met before, writing letters and meeting them in person. A few promised immediately to write. Supriya was someone I had known since childhood in her persona as a domestic worker. Even as a child I must have known she was like me in some subtle unrealized way, feeling the truth of it before I analyzed it years later, spoke to her and heard the story of her carefully concealed relationship with her husband's first wife. When I asked her to write for this compilation, she agreed at once. 'If I let this chance go by, how will anyone ever know how I have lived?' she demanded. 'Tired of the Broom' was taped, transcribed and translated from Marathi. It is an oblique challenge to those who insist that only women with the luxury of wealth and access to the West could possibly be decadent enough to love other women.

Others chose to write of themselves through fiction, a genre which, as Qamar Roshanabadi put it, comes naturally to people who live on the margins. 'Gays are so habituated to experiencing the world as a pageant, a sport with strange rules that they cannot participate in,' she explained. 'For me, immersing myself in creating a reality forces me to reassess that feeling of distance, of removal . . . I'm shaping the clay, but my hands *are* the clay.'

From the perspective of women who write for a living, in

workplaces that completely deny the lesbian, perhaps writing for and of themselves was particularly hard. Gauri, a copywriter accustomed to 'trumpeting on about heterosexual family bliss in three languages to sell vegetable oil', was initially at a loss when asked to narrate something of her own experience, on whichever topic she wished, without any directions from anyone. 'I can't do that,' she laughed. 'You'll have to give me a brief.' Journalists, too, described having to struggle to express their personal truths in a field which demands that they write for the abbreviated attention span, and prioritizes 'objectivity' to such an extent that any individual views must be suppressed ruthlessly. For example, Kokum recounted having been asked to do an article on homosexuality by an editor who had no idea of her sexual orientation—'the usual Gay But Not Happy type of piece', she explained dismissively. Under the circumstances, the task of writing for this book felt strange and awkward, since she was suddenly allowed to be aware of herself thinking, breathing, desiring. Ultimately, she lampooned the style and substance of the daily reportage she generally produces, in her piece 'A Lesbian Crime Reporter Takes a Day Off'.

And then there were the many women who did not, or could not, write. For some, the task of reflecting on themselves as lesbians was beyond the realm of consideration, so common had it become to describe themselves to others, even think of themselves, in ingenious ways that side-stepped sexuality: single woman, career woman—even, one lesbian offered half in jest, someone who had taken a vow of celibacy.

Other women were occupied with issues more pressing than, or in conflict with being lesbian—such as commitments to spiritual practices or leftist ideologies—which made sexuality 'incidental' or 'not a priority'. Puja, whom I met at a handicrafts fair looking after a stall run by a deaf women's group, derives her sense of belonging entirely from that community. Her piece, 'A Different Love', spells out why she privileges one identity over the other. And there were several women who did not want to write under a pseudonym. Almost all the other contributors have done so, because the circumstances of our lives do not allow most of us to use our real names. But these women felt that having to write under a pseudonym would defeat the purpose of making public, that it would be, instead, another mode of concealment—'as if I didn't have to do enough of that in real life,' one protested. Many believe that until lesbians can write under their own names, without fear, Indian society is not ready for such a work.

However, a number of those who accepted the inevitability of pseudonyms described it as a kind of ironic freedom, allowing them to delineate an absolutely private space in which to explore and enjoy their hidden selves. 'What is my "true" name anyway, when it functions as the label for a walking lie?' demanded the woman who appears here as V.S. 'I live between a mask and a face. You could seal that distance with a hair.' Of course, in all of this we are never allowed to forget that the primary motive of the pseudonym is safety, a shield to deflect the light. No editorial device distinguishes the real names from the pseudonyms here—we reject the notion of a hierarchy which valorizes the ability or desire of individual women to be 'out'.

Several women had questions about whether this project of compilation was a good idea, suggesting that perhaps the sharing of our creative energy should be restricted to our community. A particular concern was whether the writing with erotic content should be so widely accessible. Certainly, those of us who had ever been involved in lesbian organizing could not help but have qualms, given the eager flood of letters our groups tend to receive from heterosexual men who believe that lesbian sexuality is, by definition, a storehouse of pornography for them. A common refrain in such letters is that 'two women together are a work of art'. Art? By which artist, and for what spectator? The underlying assumption is that women are put together by the hand of men, for men to view—a theory confirmed by the fact that all of these hopeful characters write respectfully to a nonexistent 'Dear Sir' when seeking addresses for 'lesbian girls'. But all of us who wrote for and were involved in this book were clear that this compilation was by lesbians and primarily for lesbians. It was obvious that our writing would be open to misinterpretation by people brandishing their own agendas, but none of us were ready to exercise self-censorship for such a reason.

The women whose writing appears here are largely middle class, English-speaking, from the major metropolises of the country. The almost complete absence of working class women and women from rural areas renders this whole collection incomplete. We would have liked to make this project a more strongly activist effort, as Maya Sharma suggested when we approached her for a contribution, by trying to contact the many women who were divided from us by language, class, region. But that work was far beyond the scope of this project. We hope someone will take it up and seek out other traditions of lesbian relationships, and trace women dragged into the spotlight for a hideous moment and then forgotten, like Leela Shrivastava and Urmila Namdeo, the two police constables from Bhopal whose attempt to get married to each other in 1988 resulted in such media frenzy.

So who are the women representing themselves here? We are all lesbians, as pointed out above, but what that means is not necessarily obvious.

Even for the contributors at ease with the word 'lesbian', and the definition—however enigmatic and fickle—that accompanies it, the identity clearly means a variety of things beyond the basic sense of being a woman who is drawn to other women. Certainly, for some it signifies purely the erotic. Sangeeta, who described herself to me in her letters as 'a housewife from Haryana', does not present her life with her husband as being in conflict with her passionate involvement with a woman friend, portrayed in her piece, 'A Hot Movie and More'. She writes in the blunt sexual language of commercial pornography—a style which we could, if we chose, find degrading of women in general and lesbians in particular. However, the fact that such a piece was authored by a self-identified lesbian and brought into a lesbian space cast my own position on pornography into question: When we write erotica and make it public in this manner, are we merely replicating the ways in which society objectifies us, turning our lives into sexual commodities for the entertainment of men? Are we unable to think of being sexual with each other without a male voyeur validating us? Or on the contrary, are we confident enough of the autonomy of our desire to be able to display it without being concerned about the unintended viewer who might see it and respond to it in ways equally unintended? Whatever the answer, there is no question that lesbian communities need to find ways to accommodate the occasional lover of women, for whom lesbianism is a sexual event, not a whole life.

For Naseem, lesbianism is in part a deliberate stance adopted in opposition to patriarchy. In 'Reflections of an Indian Lesbian', a paper presented originally in 1991 at the Asian Lesbian Network conference in Bangkok, she points out that there is a political weight to the identity over and above the private fact of our sexual practices. Those of us who agree argue that the kind of self-awareness that is needed to acknowledge our own sexuality, in the face of patriarchal oppression, should bring an awareness of the oppression of other groups too, a questioning of the ways we continue to practice discrimination on the level of community or class, despite the heightened consciousness of our own marginalization. On the other hand, many lesbians feel that when we make an identity political we exclude individual women who are not invested in these beliefs, and introduce the possibility of division and isolation all over again. As Rita, an upper middle-class woman from Mumbai remarked plaintively, 'I just want to *be* gay, I don't want to attend conferences about it.'

For other women, 'lesbian' indicates the totality of woman-centred lives, which we lead for and with each other, as seen in Mallika's short story 'Milli Dreams of a Women's World'.

At the same time, there are a number of contributors who make the rest of us examine the ease with which we call ourselves lesbian. A.G., one of the women who wrote in these pages, realized over the months which followed, that she was no longer comfortable identifying herself as gay. 'But having been through all that, now I don't feel quite straight either,' she commented subsequently in a letter. Nevertheless, her writing is included here, a testimony to her questioning.

Sophie, who writes in 'Will I Ever Be Free?' that she is determined to get a sex change one day, is also uneasy conceptualizing herself as a 'woman-loving woman'. This issue is a painful one, given the context of all the stories we hear of lesbians who think they must have themselves surgically sculpted into men because there seems to be no other way to love a woman and be loved in return; who feel they have no choice but to be alienated from the flesh into which they were born in order to fully experience their sexuality. Many lesbians believe that the only thing these women need is counseling and a supportive community. But at the same time, we can't ignore the ways in which gender and sexuality are both distinct and yet impossibly fused. Whether we identify as lesbian, heterosexual or somewhere in between need not have anything to do with where we place ourselves on the scale of masculinity and femininity. It is also true, however, that a number of lesbians will testify to being relentlessly accosted on the street with the comment 'Are you a boy or a girl?' because their appearance challenges the stereotype of what a woman should look like.

Questioning our own labels can be surprisingly positive. We need to explore the tension between knowing ourselves to be 'lesbians' and 'women', and probing the places where those definitions seem to fray, if we hope to arrive at an understanding of the complexities through which a genuine sense of identity emerges.

I confronted my own assumptions when I received an anonymous telephone call a few months ago, at two in the morning, from a seventeen-year-old girl. Her very first question to me was: 'Why are you a lesbian?' We have grown accustomed to such questions from the straight world, but from each other? 'I—don't know,' I stumbled, the practised litany of nature and nurture hushed in my throat. 'I know why I am,' she told me. 'I was raped by my boyfriend and his friend last year. It made me an insomniac. You know, it can make someone a lesbian, too . . .' Can it? I wondered through my anguish. I still don't know. Most of us are eager to assert that we were 'born this way', drawn to women as naturally as plants to sunlight, while others talk about embracing lesbianism as a free choice, to live out our basic conviction that women are central to our lives and our happiness. It is a bleak notion that there might be some of us who come to this identity from an unyielding space of pain and destruction. There are no easy answers. What can we do except embrace the reality, which is simply that we exist today as women who love women. From that assurance we have to glean the language with which to speak the unthinkable.

Passages, the first section of this book, describes some of the slippery, uncertain transitions in our lives. We try to look at ourselves outside the freezing light of sensation—our lives in motion, at the crossroads of decision, on the threshold of excruciating awareness. Some of us chart our personal histories through time, as Shikha, Mina A. and Veronica have done. Others focus on significant moments of change—Queenie remembers her 'First Time' with another woman, while Rajkumari writes in 'Learning and Waking' of leaving her marriage to start life afresh.

The pieces which appear here are not just about our first inklings of our sexuality, however. We chronicle many other rites of passage. Sagitta, who died several years ago at the age of eighty, wrote 'Declamation' for her partner of many decades; this poem announces their love to the world—seas, forests, skies—without telling another human being. In 'Words, Yours and Mine', Mani and Palash write of their decision to leave their respective homes in a bid to be together; they describe the plan they had made to kill themselves, and how they changed their minds. Suicide and elopement are two favorite themes of media representation of lesbians—but these events have a very different aspect when seen from the other side of the distortions, framed within the larger picture of our lives.

There can be no disguising the pain of change, the terror of confronting the unknown. Transformation is as much about the fracture of old ideas and patterns as about discovery and new beginnings, but the pieces here speak, for the most part, of the euphoria of possibility.

For many lesbians, the sphere of household and family is an unpredictable composite of sanctuary and prison. While it might offer refuge from the assaults of the outside world, it can just as frequently be a coercive realm of financial dependence, the incessant pressure to marry, a grim monitoring of sexuality. The pieces in *Home* reflect that constant tension and duality. Domestic existence is most frightening where the boundaries between self and family are violently collapsed. In 'Coming Home after Tuition', Balarama Bai, a survivor of incest, describes this experience and the way it propelled her to question her heterosexuality later in life. Since our notion of who we are is so closely bound up in the dynamics of family, it is not surprising that other pieces in this section reflect, humorously or otherwise, on where lesbians come from. Molly/Manju, for example, uses the trope of family to write a fantasy of her own genesis in 'With Respect to Marriage', describing her tale as 'an exploration of multiple strands of ancestral inheritance: Gujarati, Catholic and Lesbian'.

The rigid model offered up to us as the 'traditional family' is constantly reshaped by lesbian reality. Almost all of us have parents and some of us have children (from heterosexual marriages or through adoption)—how do the people bound to us by ties of blood accommodate themselves to the double lives we lead? Amita's story 'Foreplay' describes two women struggling to balance their commitment to children, parents and to each other; in 'One and One Is Three', Radhika, mother of an adopted son, remembers the process of having to untangle child custody without recourse to legal help when her relationship with her lover came to an end.

One of the most poignant stories, speaking volumes about the complex ways in which we interact with the families of our lovers, half-ignored, half-acknowledged, is one that was never written down. A lesbian in Mumbai remembers having received Diwali cards year after year from an old friend of her mother's, inscribed 'To Mary and Another'. Her lover's family, in turn, would derisively refer to Mary as 'paleli ladki'—a house-pet. 'But when Ayesha got married,' she recalls, 'they begged me to go to Madras with her and look after her.

Twenty-three years on the outside looking in, and then suddenly I was in and I didn't know if I wanted to be.'

Worlds brings together the wider backgrounds of lesbian existence. Some women reflect on the anxieties of performance ... the parts we play at work. For some of us, our work is linked closely to our sexuality—Giti Thadani, for example, was one of the founders of Sakhi, a lesbian archive and documentation centre in New Delhi, and her piece 'Silence and Invisibility' is based on her research recovering and uncovering lesbian histories from archaeological sites and ancient texts. But for others, the gulf between the work persona and the private one is so vast that it is amusing, as Rashmi recounts in 'Some Funny Business', a description of quite literally hiding your sexual self next to your skin. There are stories of the repercussions of having sexuality figure in the workplace, from the stark fact of losing one's job, as Preeti points out in 'The Score', to Gauri's hopeful ideal of being able to use it to sensitize colleagues about sexism and homophobia, narrated in 'The Bi-Line'.

This section also dwells on worlds across time—Julia reconstructs love and loss in a previous birth in her poem 'laipai'—and across cultures. For those of us who have experienced the West with its bright lure of greater freedoms, Zebunissa Makhfi's comment on her feeling of 'being spliced between two unrealities' cannot but ring true—each world we straddle seems almost hallucinatory when we're away from it, and yet we're haunted perpetually by the question of where our home really is, if acceptance as a gay person comes from a place which often despises us as Indian. Her poem 'Cherokee Driver', for example, is concerned with the fundamental irony of 'Indian', as in desi, and 'Indian' as in Native American. 'My lover used to laugh about that,' the writer remembered. 'She would say to me, "Hey, I'm as Indian as you are!"'

Love across geographical distance is also the theme of

several pieces—Pia's 'Fateful Encounter' describes her first sexual experience in Kenya; K.K.'s 'To One Who Went Away' is a collection of letters to a girlfriend working in Dubai; Angina d'Pectoris's 'The Pugglee and the Budmash' uses a sardonic Anglo-Indian vocabulary to make a statement about squandered passion.

How can a community preserve its sense of togetherness given the divergent perspectives and lifestyles which threaten to fissure us? *Differences* addresses some of those issues. We cannot afford to gloss over the points of possible rupture, rendering the sexual outlaws or the radical fringe invisible as we ourselves are rendered invisible within society as a whole. After all, as Sherry Joseph's recent article on the Indian gay and lesbian movement pointed out, 'if forced conformity is to be resisted, it must be by representing human lives as multiple; selfhood as several; communities as voluntary and various.'[13] Accommodating our own nonconformists is a process many balk at, given how much each of us has longed to 'fit in'. We try to manoeuvre between those who call lesbianism a sickness of the mind, and those who try to find our deviance scrawled on our bodies. We listen to mental health professionals who try to locate poor male role models and 'ugly mannish influences' in our lives; we also cringe when we remember what happened when Bhopal police constables Leela and Urmila were accused of lesbianism. They were made to undergo a full medical examination, which, to quote the Director-General of Police of Madhya Pradesh, 'found nothing.'[14] The actual words of the report: 'Poorna roop se mahila hein.'[15] On both fronts, lesbians are not considered to be women. Faced with the stereotype of the lesbian as 'man trapped in a woman's body'—the unhappy creature who hates men and yet wants to be one—we are so easily alienated from ourselves, our emotional needs manacled in self-doubt, our erotic ones paralyzed and negated. And with still greater ease, anxious to demonstrate our own normality, we shun those of us who 'look different' as a liability. We accuse them of wanting the privilege of being male and heterosexual, whether by passing as male or actually getting a sex change.

Why do we accept society's easy categorization of us as either masculine *or* feminine, male *or* female, when an examination of any individual's life will show how those categories are insufficient? My mother, entirely confirmed in her heterosexuality, can recall having felt moments of discomfort within the confines of gender. 'When I was three, four years old,' she mused, 'I saw a Sikh boy with his hair tied up in braids, urinating. And I thought, how wonderful, a little girl who can pee standing up! Why can't I do that?'

Gender identity can be a realm of performance and expression rather than a narrow trap, as I realized when I first met Sophie, who is transsexual-identified, and hopes one day to become Sean, both legally and biologically. She showed me photographs of the roles she had played in TV serials, image after image of herself heavily painted with make-up, her hair long, her body clad in half-buttoned garments. 'It must have been hard,' I sympathized, 'having to feel so unlike yourself to make a living.' Sophie was silent for a moment. Then she smiled with typical self-depreciation. 'Actually, it was kind of fun,' she admitted. 'You have to try everything once before you die. Of course, now I've decided to give up acting... until I can come back as a hero!' Gender difference—whether that of Sophie or Miss Kokilaben, who describes what it feels like to be 'Born in a Man's Body', demonstrates how convenient societal definitions of 'man' and 'woman' are incapable of containing anyone.

Other differences with which we have to reconcile ourselves include sexual practices such as sadomasochism—a debate suspended between larger considerations of the general censorship of women's lives on the one hand, and the culture of violence against women on the other—or lifestyle choices such as multiple relationships. 'The River', Shaka's letter to two women whom she loves, and Anasuya's poem 'Threesome' touch on both the intensity and the difficulty of living non-monogamously. These are only a few of the many issues we deal with when we try to come together.

Even more than the individual bonds of love, however, it is the groups, the networks, the friendships between us, described in *Connection*, which society finds disturbing. In 1992, seven students at a government high school for girls in Thiruvananthapuram formed the Martina Navratilova Club, and were chastised by a remarkably severe punishment: complete expulsion. As one newspaper put it, 'the girls were united in a strong mutual bond, which was more than just a physical relationship. The institution head [. . .] felt lucky at being able to prevent the growth of the group.'[16] The ominous trend, as far as the principal was concerned, was quite clearly the fact that lesbian sexuality was not restricted to secret, shameful encounters, but became the basis for an alternative social structure.

The blame, of course, fell on the family. School authorities explained that 'most of the girls were children of estranged lower middle-class parents, with the father being alcoholic in almost all cases'—as though fragmentation and dysfunction at home could account for the girls trying to create disturbing bonds among themselves. Class is always used as an othering device to divide women—usually it is alleged that lesbianism is an upper-class Westernized phenomenon, but the discourse is surprisingly versatile and can be adapted to attack 'lower-class', 'poorly educated' women if the need arises.

Women-centred lives extend far beyond sex. All of us, not just politically motivated lesbians involved in gay activism, need validation from a larger world. I have received letters mailed without a return address, written as though groping in darkness, from women who say that they just needed to let someone know that they exist.

The women's movement has not always been able to accept lesbians, as Amita points out in 'A Decade of Lesbian Halla Gulla'. But, as many heterosexual women have begun to note, lesbian experience is closely woven within wider feminist concerns and can be understood as such if we consider sexuality to be something more than the sexual act, and intrinsic to one's very being. As Nivedita Menon writes, any act of interference in the realm of sexuality, whether through violence, the attempt to control reproductive rights or the refusal to accept any sexual orientation other than hetero-sexual, places in peril one's very sense of self.[17] The same patriarchal forces which urge survivors of abuse or incest to feel guilt and shame, are in operation where alternative sexuality is concerned.

Lesbians have also sought to make connections with gay men—with varied success, since our concerns do not necessarily overlap. Lesbians have to deal with complete invisibility and combatting social pressure to marry, while gay men need to focus their energy on the AIDS epidemic threatening their community and the unambiguously criminal status of male homosexuality under Section 377. Nevertheless, when *Bombay Dost* magazine was started in 1991, it was through the joint efforts of three gay men and three lesbians; in the early nineties the Red Rose meetings in New Delhi—so called because the table at the coffee house would be marked with a single flower—also combined the presence of gay women and men. Although our attempts to organize together in recent years have been limited, we all recognize the need to build coalitions as well as to find our separate spaces. In any case, the friction has never prevented our friendships from developing. Both Ruth Vanita, in her poem 'The Unconsumed' and Ann Urning's 'Jogtrot' dwell on such bonds.

The groups that we have created, as lesbian and bisexual women, have been involved in a variety of work. Examples include Sakhi in New Delhi, which has documented and archived our histories and served as a resource centre, and Sangini, a help-line and support group in the same city; Stree Sangam of Mumbai has, since 1995, organized two nationwide retreats, co-sponsored a conference on lesbian, gay and bisexual rights in India, and networked with women all over the world. 'Dyking Around', a report of the first retreat—the first time we gathered from around the country as lesbian and bisexual women—appears here. Many women who are new to organizing assume that because we are all lesbians, because we understand the pressures of each other's lives, we should be able to work together without tension. Shalini's poem 'womonlove' alludes to some of the heartache of disagreeing with, and being hurt by, the women who are our chosen family.

Here, we also depict our more informal connections. Gauri's 'XX' is a rumination on the kind of easy familiarity lesbians often develop with ex-lovers. The theme is much-discussed in our communities. Mary, whose lover left her to marry a man after having spent more than two decades with her, once pondered aloud on ways to describe what she shares with Ayesha: 'It's quite an amazing life we led together. It might not seem fulfilling to a lot of people because of the way it—I wouldn't say ended. After all, when I look at what we have today, I don't think we've done too badly.' This section also includes Kristen's 'My Best Friend Is Gay . . . and So Am I!', a lesbian college student's light-hearted recognition of how lucky she is to have found camaraderie when so many others like her are completely isolated.

Love is a selection of writings on what some would say defines us as who we are. The tone varies from poetic celebrations of lovemaking, like Julia's 'The Forest Fire', to Soraya Patel's tongue-in-cheek 'Louse'. Sandhya's poems 'All Cherished Loneliness is You', written after the death of her lover fifteen years ago, find a place here, as do Samira and Jay's letters to each other, 'Stealing the Stolen', which chronicle an affair between two women already involved in other relationships. The book ends with Qamar Roshanabadi's 'Vande Mataram!'—a satiric, patriotic manifesto that proudly stakes a claim to all manner of passionate traditions.

In part, this book celebrates creativity and coming together. But it is also a grieving, for the women who did not have the freedom to write, for the stories which will never be shared. Three months ago I came to know that Seema, whose piece 'Toward a Lesbian World' appears here, attempted suicide and was in a coma. I have not heard from her since then. She led a very restricted life in the Middle East, wheelchair-bound, pressured by family to stay in a marriage she had not wanted to contract in the first place, forbidden any access to the phone by her husband. She could only contact me in secrecy.

So finally, this is a tribute to writing as a record of our lives, but also a reminder that no text or script can be a substitute for the actual feat of living. We can never let ourselves forget that the story is not enough, and that there are some silences too immense for words to bridge. Perhaps sometimes, only the silence can speak our truth.

Ashwini Sukthankar
Mumbai, December 1998

Notes

[1] 'Of Unnatural Offence: Whoever voluntarily has carnal intercourse against the order of nature with any man, woman or animal shall be punished with imprisonment for life or imprisonment of either description for a term which many extend for ten years and shall be liable to fine.' (Indian Penal Code, Section 377).

[2] Terry Castle. *The Apparitional Lesbian: Female Homosexuality and Modern Culture.* New York: Columbia University Press, 1993. p.67

[3] Ismat Chugtai. 'Lihaf (The Quilt)', trans. Syed Sirajuddin. In *Women Writing in India*, vol. II. Eds. Susie Tharu and K. Lalitha. New Delhi: Oxford India, 1993. pp. 129-38

[4] Soma Wadhwa. 'Parents deny marriage between girls'. *Pioneer*. New Delhi: July 22, 1993

[5] Giti Thadani. *Sakhiyani: Lesbian Desire in Ancient and Modern India.* UK: Cassel, 1996

[6] Ghaiyur A. Ahmed. Letter to the editor. *Pioneer*. New Delhi: Feb. 3, 1994

[7] *Sunday Times*, New Delhi: Nov. 22, 1998

[8] Ashok Banker. 'Do Gays Have More Fun?' *Mantra, The Magazine for Men*. Aug.-Sept. 1998. p. 13

[9] For example, Punam Thakur. 'Glad to be Gay: Indian homosexuals start to come out of the closet'. *Sunday*. Aug. 16, 1992. Or Soumitra Das. 'Sad to be Gay'. *Sunday Statesman Review*. Calcutta: April 18, 1993

[10] Deepa Gahlot. 'Gay is a Sad Word'. *Femina*. Sept. 8, 1992

[11] Davinder Mohan, quoted by Sumita Sengupta. 'Eves and Erotica', *Savvy*. Aug. 1998

[12] We had hoped that the media might have been more sensitive to lesbian issues in the wake of Deepa Mehta's film *Fire* and the Shiv Sena attacks on it in December, 1998. On the contrary, we were treated systematically to:

Inflammatory rant: . . . unnatural sex has been growing apace. However, the consequences of this trend will be nothing short of calamitous. The neglected and traumatized children of such 'parents' would tend to end up as morons, lunatics, criminals or all the three combined.' K.R. Malkani. 'Any rational being will concede that homosexuality is unnatural'. *Sunday Times*. New Delhi: Nov. 22, 1998. Shallow flippancy: 'A lesbian is [. . .] a regular guy except she's a girl.' Jug Suraiya. 'Ire vs. Fire'. *Sunday Times*. New Delhi: Dec. 20, 1998 Peremptory dismissal: '. . . we must come up with our own solutions to our problems. We cannot import and adopt our values from the west, believing them to be universal. [. . .] In the case of the recent controversy about Fire, I don't think there was a need to use slogans like "Lesbian is Indian." Lesbianism is just a way of life, not a part of culture.' Ebrahim Alkazi in an interview with Nikhat Kazmi. 'The Ulysses of Indian Theatre'. *Times of India*. New Delhi: Dec. 19, 1998 Self-righteous homophobia: 'No wonder the militant gay movement, which has hitherto operated as website extensions of a disagreeable trend in the West, could now come out into the open and flaunt banners in Delhi suggesting that "lesbianism is part of our heritage." It is plainly not. Thievery, deceit, murder and other IPC-defined offences have a long history. That doesn't elevate them to the level of heritage.' Swapan Dasgupta. 'Fire Next Time: A debate hijacked by conflicting weirdos'. *India Today*. Dec. 21, 1998

[13] Sherry Joseph. 'Gay and Lesbian Movement in India'. *Economic and Political Weekly*. Aug. 17, 1996

[14] B.K. Mukherjee, quoted by Saisuresh. 'There was no marriage', *Illustrated Weekly of India*. March 20, 1988

[15] Mira Savara. 'Who Needs Men?' *Debonair*. April 1988

[16] 'Lesbian Trends in Kerala Schools'. *Indian Express*. Madurai: Jan. 29, 1992

[17] Nivedita Menon. 'Destabilizing Feminism'. *Seminar 437*. Jan. 1996

Passages

Hero

Veronica

I was brought up by my aunt because my parents were facing financial difficulties. She was quite well off, so it was a comfortable life. Right from childhood I liked to play with boys—cricket, kabaddi, gulli danda—and I liked to wear jeans. My aunt was strict, the kind of tough stepmother-guardian you see in old Hindi movies. She wanted me to have long hair and wear frocks. I hated it. One day I took her scissors and cut my hair, so badly that my father had to take me to a barber to get a boy-cut. My aunt was so angry, she beat me with a stick, but I felt so free and happy, I didn't care. She made me stand in a corner all day as a punishment, but I kept sneaking off to the mirror and admiring myself, flicking my hair back with my hand like a filmi hero.

My cousin lived in the same house, she was in her twenties. She said one day, unexpectedly, 'I think you are a lesbian.' I was nine or ten years old. I said, puzzled, 'What is a lesbian?' She said, 'A lesbian is a girl who is not interested in boys.' I said, 'I like boys, I play with them all the time.' She said, 'That's what it is, you are like a boy.' I said, 'Is it bad to be a lesbian?' My cousin answered, 'No, it's not bad, God has made you this way. But for your sake, I hope you don't really turn out to be a lesbian, because the world will give you a hard time.'

I didn't think any more about what she had said. I was too young to understand. She got married and left the house. My aunt shifted to another place. I went back to my parents, though they were still having financial problems. Life was difficult for this reason. But I was happy in the all-girls convent school I was sent to. I was a tomboy, a tease, very popular.

3

In Class 5 I fell in love with a girl in Class 8. Her name was Sandra. Suddenly I remembered my cousin's words, and I realized what I was involving myself in. But I couldn't stop myself. I was diwani over Sandra. Each morning in school the first thing I did was to find her and hug her. We were supposed to call the senior girls 'didi'. I couldn't do that with Sandra, though I used this form of address with all the other older girls. They remarked jokingly, 'Didi kya, Sandra is your jaaneman.' I found it strange that everyone took my obsession to be natural. No one ever commented that it was abnormal.

Sandra reminded me of Zeenat Aman, my favourite actress. I fell for her when in a school play she danced to the tune of 'Chura liya hai tumne jo dil ko . . .' I wrote her name on my hand, and all over my notebooks. She had beautiful long straight hair, lovely eyes, she was quite a pataka. She was a boarder, I was a day scholar. Boarders were not allowed to buy anything from outside the school. I used to spend my pocket money on snacks like churan, papri, aampapad for Sandra. The other girls said, 'She is just using you.' I was very hurt.

One day there was a school inspection. We had to be in full uniform, clean, ironed, shoes polished etc. I loved wearing ties. With my collar in place and my blazer buttoned, I thought I looked a real hero. But before the inspection I lost my tie in some free-period masti, we were acting scenes from movies and I was playing goonda, a total villain. I looked everywhere for the tie, but I couldn't find it. Sandra was the prefect on duty. She gave me a real yelling. I felt terrible. I didn't care about being punished, but I couldn't bear the fact that she was angry with me. Then as the bell went for assembly she took a brand-new tie out of her pocket, pulled my collar up and knotted the tie, perfectly. Don't ask how my heart was beating . . . she said, 'Don't lose this, it is a present from me.' I was so happy, I felt my feet had left the ground. I showed all the girls the tie, saying, 'See, Sandra has given this to me.'

She left the school after the Class 10 board exams. Thinking about her departure, I was in very bad shape. I desperately wanted to give her a gift I but had very little money. As a boarder she also got very little money, but she gave me a school bag and a geometry box. I had made her a card for Valentine's Day. I still remember the words inside it: *Some love one, some love two. I love one, and that is you*, with the word *you* standing up from the paper as a cut-out. At my friend Shikha's suggestion I gave Sandra a red rose. Shikha also stole a beautiful embroidered shawl from her sister's dowry, and gave it to me so I could give it to Sandra.

Sandra was very touched. She said, 'I'll always keep the shawl.' We exchanged addresses and she wrote in my autograph book. Then she said, 'Come to the dormitory with me.' She put the shawl in the suitcase by her bed, and suddenly she caught hold of my hand, pulled me towards her and kissed me on the lips. She held me in a long hug. I remember that kiss till today, my first kiss. I almost lost my senses. I didn't know where I was or what was going on, but the emotion was so powerful and the sensation so beautiful.

I spent the evening in the dormitory. The boarders hid me behind a wall whenever a nun came by. They played and chatted; I sat holding Sandra's hand. Finally I had to leave because it was getting near the boarders' bed time. The girls said, 'Come on, Sandra, give Veronica a kiss.' She kissed me on the cheek. The next day I saw her with her sister in a ricksha outside the school. I got on a cycle and followed them to the bus stand. She was holding her luggage and looked sad. I could cycle very fast and well, even do tricks at full speed. So I started to ride after the bus while it was still moving slowly. Sandra saw me and kept staring through the window. I followed the bus as long as I could, till I almost had an accident. A rickshawala yelled at me, 'Abbe chhore, kya kar raha hai, dekh ke nahin chala sakta?'

After Sandra left the school, I became really depressed. Nothing and no one could console me. Later on I came to know that while I had been pursuing Sandra so innocently, Shikha had sneaked into the dormitory and had had sex with Sandra's younger sister! Shikha was a Hindu, but if she fancied Christian girls she would go with us to church and even sing in the choir, though her voice sounded as if a flute was cracking . . . she tried to cheer me up, but I felt increasingly miserable because everything in the convent reminded me of Sandra. Luckily, things changed and I was soon placed in a new environment that distracted me. But after many years, when by chance I saw a picture of Sandra in *Stardust* magazine—she had won a beauty contest and was being crowned by a film star—I immediately cut out that photo and kept it.

Our new principal changed some of the convent's rules. The Christian students used to get concessions in school fees, but the nun insisted that we pay full fees and also arrears! The parents of Christian students protested, but she did not listen. People went to the parish priest and complained. He approached the principal but she would not listen to him either. Then she started allowing boys from a neighbouring school to enter the convent grounds, to use our basketball court and games field. Naturally some chakkar started between the boys and the girls. Many orthodox parents didn't like the idea of coeducation. The priest told them, it is better to put your daughters in another school. My parents put me into a Hindi-medium school, all girls, for one and a half years.

All the subjects were in Hindi. I had a very tough time with my studies. But the girls were wonderful, not snobbish like the convent girls . . . I was very popular. I flirted with the other students all day long in real filmi style, using dialogues . . . They loved it as much as I did. There were other girls there from English-medium schools, but the Hindi-medium girls didn't pay them the kind of attention they paid me. Maybe my lesbian nature attracted them, though none of us had the words to describe this aspect of our friendships. I sensed some other girls were 'like me', but I never discussed my feelings with them, or with anyone. All through school I felt I was 'different' in some basic way from the other girls, but it was never a source of tension for me because I had accepted myself for who I was.

Our class teacher was very old. Her relatives had been killed at Jallianwala Bagh, so she hated anything associated with the English. She gave me hell because I came from an English-medium school. In our monthly tests I failed miserably in every subject except English, where the standard was so low, I could have taught the teacher. She continued to find ways to humiliate me, she slapped me and threatened to fail me in the final exams . . . I don't know how I would have managed without the help of the other girls. They even came to my house and gave me tuitions in the evenings. Somehow I passed the exams. The teacher accused me of cheating, but there was nothing she could do.

My home science teacher liked me a lot. One day I took her a garland of chameli. She said, 'Put it in my hair with your own hands.' She had a plait down to her waist. She gave me a hairpin and said, 'Pin the flowers so they don't fall out. At night I'll take them out and sleep with them under my pillow.' I found this a bit strange but it didn't make me uncomfortable at all, because of the atmosphere in the school. The girls didn't have any idea about lesbian sex. Any girls who were very close would just make each other their 'behen'—that was the term we used.

When I was in Class 8 I fell in love with a girl in Class 9. She had such beautiful eyes, I wanted to drown in them. Even though I'm a Christian, I went to the temple with her and performed all the rituals along with her. We wrote daily love letters and shairi—I remember some still—*Chandni chand se hoti hai, sitaron se nahin/Mohabbat ek se hoti hai, hazaron se nahin*. I found all this emotion very natural. I felt I was in love with all the girls of the Hindi-medium school. They used to compete for my attention; they were jealous of each other and tried to spend time alone with me. I would break all the rules—clowning, flirting, eating in class, throwing chalk, reading comics—but no one complained, nor was I punished. The girls helped me with my homework, and even paid my fees once when I couldn't afford it, because of some family problems . . . they helped me to cheat so I could pass my exams . . . I really missed these wonderful girls when I was sent back to the convent school. I felt deprived of the affection I used to receive every day. I found the convent girls cold and selfish and arrogant. Worst of all, the nuns constantly punished me for speaking in Hindi, which had become a natural habit.

Looking back on all this, I am amazed at the extent and quality of my innocence. I never went beyond hugging or kissing in school. I couldn't even really imagine what could come beyond that. Later, when I was sixteen, I became friends with a very good-looking girl—she was slim, with long straight hair and big eyes, and she was very 'mod', as they say. She wore miniskirts, and used make-up, eye shadow, lipstick. She plaited beads in her hair and wore anklets all the time.

At Christmas I had gone to her place, and I said, 'I don't have any gift for you.' She said, 'If I ask you for something, will you give it to me?' I said, 'Okay', and she said, 'Kiss me.' So I did. Soon after that I was at her house one day, and she said, 'I don't want to play any more carrom, let's enact scenes from movies. Pretend it's a suhaag raat; I'll pull my chunni down like a ghoonghat and you lift it.' I enjoy this type of dramebaazi, so I agreed, and lifted her chunni, singing 'Kabhie kabhie . . . ' Then we kissed, and I had sex for the first time.

She knew everything . . . I kept wondering, is this right, is this normal, but internally I had already accepted myself as a lesbian. The initial doubts and guilt about my sexual nature do not trouble me any more. If God has made me this way, I can not help it.

(*as told to V.S.*)

Glossary

Abbe chhore, kya kar raha hai, dekh ke nahin chala sakta? – (lit.) Damn you, boy, what are you doing, can't you look where you're going?

behen – sister

Chandni chand se hoti hai, sitaron se nahin/Mohabbat ek se hoti hai, hazaron se nahin – (lit.) Moonlight is from the moon, not from the stars / You can love only one person, not a thousand

chunni – long scarf

Didi kya, Sandra is your jaaneman – (lit.) What sister, Sandra is your beloved

diwani – obsessed, crazy with love

dramebaazi – histrionics

ghoonghat – when a garment or other piece of cloth is used to cover the head and face for modesty

pataka – firecracker

suhaag raat – wedding night

My First Time

Queenie

My parents are very orthodox and strict disciplinarians. I was not allowed to mix with boys of my age. Being the only

9

daughter, I was protected and looked after very well. By the time I was eighteen years old, I was full bodied, with well-developed breasts. My sexual instincts were aroused. But I did not have any outlet other than masturbation.

At this point in time, a young couple—the husband was twenty-eight, the wife twenty-six—came to live in the flat opposite. They were friendly and gregarious. Hailing from Kerala, they had just moved to Tamil Nadu. Aunty had a very big bosom and fleshy lips. She was extremely pretty and voluptuous. I was drawn to her, and after college I would go to spend evenings in her house till Uncle's return from office.

In Aunty's house, I used to read film magazines. One day, she gave me soft porn magazines like *Debonair* and *Fantasy*. While I was looking at the breasts of the semi-nude models, Aunty sat near me and asked whether the breasts in the photo were bigger than hers and mine. First I blushed at that question. Then I haltingly told her that the model's breasts were bigger than mine, but smaller than hers. Aunty laughed and said, 'You have not seen my breasts, how can you say they are the biggest?' I did not have any answer except to stare at her. She removed her sari and I had a full view of her enormous breasts. Suddenly there was a knock at the door and Uncle came in. I went back home. Aunty's breasts cupped in a tight blouse hovered before my eyes, and I could not sleep at all.

Next morning, Aunty came to my house and requested my mother's permission for me to stay over that night, since Uncle was going on tour. My mother readily agreed. My heart leaped with joy. After dinner, I put on a nightie and went next door. Aunty was in her nightie with the first three buttons open and her breasts protruding. In the centre of the table lay a pornographic book of lesbian pictures. I became excited, seeing two women sucking each other's breasts and licking at pussies and kissing each other. Aunty put her hand on my shoulder and started caressing my upper arm. She pulled me towards her and held me in a tight embrace and kissed me all over my face and finally on my lips. I opened my mouth and welcomed her tongue. She started removing my nightie and massaged my breasts. I did the same to her. Aunty's breasts were bigger than mine and the tips were hard. I wanted to taste them. Sensing my desire, she put her breasts in my mouth and I eagerly sucked them to my heart's content. Aunty kept playing with my breasts and then her hands went down to my pussy. We adopted a position by which both of us could lick the other's pussy; we inserted our fingers in each other's vagina and we achieved orgasm at the same time.

I am grateful to Aunty for giving me this experience. She initiated me into this beautiful relationship, which continued for two years until Aunty and Uncle shifted out of our town.

I started to long for another such relationship and I have been successful in that regard from time to time. I made my fifteen-year-old maidservant lick my pussy. My mother's friend, who was about thirty-five years old, succumbed to my charms and used to offer her breasts for my sucking and her pussy for my stroking.

No man with his swollen penis can give me as much pleasure as a woman's lips, mouth, breasts, fingers.

Older

Soraya Patel

I

I needed the money badly. Textbooks cost the world (and we are supposed to be a country of starving millions). Millions?

Maybe. Starving? Well, I was. I was in the café in college, brainstorming with Maria. We were trying to generate ideas on how best to make some money.

An invincible cord connects Maria's brain and stomach. Normally when the former gets activated, so does the latter. My fingers searched my pocket and discovered the scalloped edges of a two-rupee coin. I prayed that Maria's two crucial organs would choose not to make contact. However, the gods weren't listening.

Maria's orbs come to rest on the damned sandwiches. Forgetting that I was financially challenged, she asked me if I too wanted one. Ah, the ignominy of the situation! I decided to go on a 'diet'. She nodded, and that's how I went home with two rupees and a plan.

The sandwich had accelerated her thinking process and we both remembered the two jazz ballet classes I had attended years ago. Maria had a friend who had a friend who needed girls for shows. Dance? Could I hold my own in front of girls who had been dancing their entire lives?

But by this time hunger had knocked the sense out of my brain and I grinned at her like the Cheshire Cat. Maria placed the vital phone call. I was to audition the next day.

II

Back home, and nourished by a banana, the full horror of the situation hit me. A hot shower, and I was trying desperately to appreciate myself as I toweled down.

Stretch marks spattered my thighs—concealer would do the trick and hide them. But what about my toothy smile, sleepy eyelid, chewed nails that begged for glue-on falsies? My thighs! Never mind the rest, but with legs like these I did not look like I was worth the pay.

Why couldn't I be thin? Like Chinky, my drug addict brother who frequently disemboweled my piggy bank with childlike enthusiasm. Skinny bastard, never put on an ounce but whatever nourishment he partook of went straight to his nails. They were long, hard, yellow and had streaks of black under them. They were his favourite weapon.

He'd shriek and dig those talons into you if you refused to part with your money. The network of scars on my arm bore ample testimony to this fact. Mostly I wished he were six feet under.

My plans for a parlour makeover dashed, I pulled out a rusty razor to do my legs. Subsequently, lost in thought about the future, I cut my thumbnail.

I burst into tears. I was disgusted with my body. I didn't like even one small thing about myself. My nerves were frayed to the point of snapping. And how I needed this job.

III

The audition was a disaster. There was this bald man who smoked and catwalked. The women were sexpots. None of them smiled back and all of them had these fake accents and put-on pouts. As for me, I wanted to bolt.

Baldie made me sweat and he kept shaking his barren head. I got nervy and slipped in a pool of my own sweat. The wide grins like those in toothpaste commercials got to me and I left the room howling. I was so embarrassed and ashamed.

Back in the greenroom, I sank onto a bench. The tears came out in heaves. Visions of failing the year for want of textbooks gnawed at my brain. I saw myself, a wine glass of pesticide in my hand . . .

The cat who had led the spiteful remarks stared down at me. 'You've come to laugh at me. Get the shit out,' I spat, as my arm shot forward to push her away. She smiled. I scratched her, and she had all the more reason to laugh as my false nail came undone. This was too much. I collapsed in a fresh set of tears.

She casually draped her long bony arm across my shoulders and said it was not the end of the world. I said it was, for me. I gulped and cried some more. I hugged her, just for comfort. She ruffled my hair. I'd have blubbered in front of anyone. When Grandma was alive, I'd tell her everything. She died two years ago leaving a gaping emptiness in my heart.

Like water breaking through a dam, the words rushed out. The pressure of studies, the lack of money, Chinky's fatal attraction to my wallet and . . . I knew I was making an ass of myself. Chances were she was bored and had tuned me out and of course I couldn't stop myself. I wanted badly to shut up, but I couldn't and she got up and walked out.

She came in again.

'You got the job.'

I stared stupidly.

'Smile,' she snapped.

I said I couldn't but muttered something about being thankful. I stood up laboriously and she caught my arm and led me to a basin. With mascara streaked down my face, I looked like either a tragedy or a comedy, depending on your point of view. I washed up.

IV

I was like a big stupid animal. She did everything for me. She picked up the remnants of that disastrous audition—towel, stretchpants, T-shirt; helped me out of my tacky get-up and into my jeans and shirt. Stuffed the rest into my bag.

She opened the door, steered me out, ignored my feeble protests and piled me into a cab. Once in, she appeared harried and preoccupied and I was too scared to ask our destination. So I was as meek as a lamb.

I was about to say something, but she flung me a forbidding look and I stayed silent, regretting my earlier flood of confidences. She was staring hard out of the window, her face a patchwork of exasperation, fatigue, irritation and amusement.

We stopped at a restaurant. She ordered me out. My mind protested, my legs obeyed. I decided that it was undignified to make a scene, and in any case I was too tired.

She ordered lunch . . . for two. That's when the tears really came.

V

I wordlessly chewed on something that looked like the aftermath of a rail disaster. I hadn't any appetite. I wasn't really sure what to make of it at all.

There was silence. Then she began to talk. Parents divorced, no siblings. A trained dancer.

Later that night I slept well.

VI

Life is in turns good, bad, good . . . it goes like this, in a cycle, you know. The previous day was good, even if a bit weird. Next day was awful. Chinky was in a rage. He scratched, kicked, and we thrashed each other. I was so furious, I couldn't speak. I fumed through the lectures at college. We had dance practice at two that afternoon. I longed for my siesta. But I needed to see Piya.

I sort of liked her impersonal brand of caring; it was rather comforting.

She was in the greenroom. I noticed how she wasn't thin, but she wasn't fat either. She had straight lank hair.

Whenever I looked at her I lost my breath. Warmth crept up my face and ended below my eyes. I had never felt this strange, ever.

I brushed it aside as she smiled wistfully at me. When the smile was replaced by a frown, I swallowed hard. Chinky's handiwork must have been showing on my face. But Baldie was oblivious, prancing around like a demented monarch. He yelled profanities at me. I fought my tears as Piya pacified him.

VII

We began what was to become a daily ritual in the months that followed. We perched ourselves atop the wall that circled the big tree with its generous branches that seemed to embrace the air. As the wind played with the leaves, a kind of calm enveloped us. I guess it was the comforting foliage. Or maybe it was something else.

I felt like I knew her. Really knew her. I did my Jerry Lewis act for her and she cut up completely. I loved that warm soft smile.

Each time I spy a tree I am seized by an inchoate yearning to climb it. On the way back from practice I succumbed, scrambled up and mentally continued my tete-a-tete with Piya. Some people make you feel completely yourself. You don't worry about your hair, your nails or how you sit . . . you know.

But there has to be something askew when all seems right. She had very long nails and she would run them up my neck, and I'd feel so strange . . . I wanted to get up and run away, far far away.

VIII

I wanted to push her off and run where she'd never see me. I had no idea why, and that upset me further. She had only been kind and understanding because she was a good human being. There was no ulterior motive.

Why then did I feel uneasy?

I was edgy and irritated. Maria noticed. I said it was Chinky. I decided to avoid Piya by playing aloof. She'd get the hint—I was no longer interested in us being friends. I felt guilty, though. After all, I owed my job to her.

Baldie was shrieking like a violated virgin. Sometimes I

wanted to set his pants on fire so he'd yell more . . . he was so irritating and comical. I had to cup my hand over my mouth.

Piya's smile spread across her face. I turned away, my face deadpan. Her smile faded. She looked confused. I took perverse pleasure in behaving like this. It was my way of hitting back for the discomfort she caused me.

I did not know a particular sequence of steps, so Baldie (who had at some point decided that Piya was my guardian angel) ordered her to teach them to me. Damn.

We were ejected from the room. I wanted to cry. I had butterflies dancing in my stomach. She walked her slow, quiet hip-walk towards me.

She stared. Wanted to know if I was all right. I said I was fine. She knew I was lying. For my sake she played my game. She looked a bit upset. I kept getting the hand movements wrong.

She motioned forward to correct me. I don't know why, I flung myself on her and then pushed her away. And then I ran. In the greenroom I did not wait to change. I just jerked out my bag and fled, my chest pounding.

IX

I couldn't eat. I kept playing with my food. Finally I flushed it down the pot. My mother was her usual nosy self. I had enough questions of my own that seemed to emerge from my darkest recesses. I did not need her interrogation.

I had locked up forbidden emotions as a child. But I remembered guilty images. The shame, the pain, the rage—till one day I turned my back on it all and thought it was over.

Piya called up—the phones safely separating us. I tried to sound casual. The afternoon boohoo, I said, was the outcome of failing a test. She laughed. I did too, but it was hollow.

X

We had a show on Saturday. We practised like hell, till our

17

bones were sore and our muscles tortured, but our spirits remained high. Piya and I were full of jokes. Baldie screeched less. It was past seven and we all filtered out of the changing room, completely drained.

I had lost my eyeliner. I was hunting for it. Komal was throwing on her shirt. I turned and looked the other way.

Nude women were getting to me now, unlike in the past, when somehow I looked but did not really look. Komal said 'bye'. I was sprawled on the floor scrabbling for the tube under the cabinet. I got up and stripped off my tights. Ouch, my thighs hurt. I had a stubbed toe, too.

Piya sauntered in. Alarm. I was too tired to think or control myself. We said hello and she sat next to me. She bent down and caressed my bruised foot. I wanted to get up and move away, but my legs felt like lead. And after what seemed like forever, I stared into her eyes, gasped and leaned forward and kissed her. For one moment I thought I was losing my mind. The kiss was different. We both knew it. It was more than just friendly. A deep, lingering kiss.

I knew I'd never be confused again. I knew I'd never again feel strange. I could not protest. I did not want to. We weren't simply friends. I knew it now. We'd lost the innocence forever. Like a snake that had shed its old skin, I had slipped off my childhood.

As I looked into her eyes, I felt in control for the first time since we had met. We held hands and I did not want her to go. I felt no guilt. I felt new. I felt that nothing could disturb me.

XI

My mother was yelling. Chinky had slit his thigh because she'd refused him money. Blood all over. The neighbours were around, helping. Chinky was violent. Mother was on the rampage. I was an easy target for her litany of complaints. I was a moron, another mouth to feed, ungrateful, she shouldn't have had me or Chinky.

That she shouldn't have had Chinky is indisputable. But me?

She slapped me. Angry, hurt, bitter, I slapped her back. I tried to get into the bedroom. She tore at my shirt. I was blind with tears of fury. My mother yanked open my drawer and hysterically flung clothes at me. I picked them up and tried to get them back into the drawer. She slammed it shut on my fingers. I screamed. She told me she should have had an abortion. She told me to leave the house for good.

I ran out of the room, out of the flat and into the dark night. It was raining. I only had five rupees. I phoned Piya.

She was waiting at her door, worried. I was crying and dripping wet. We held each other.

I was too tired for food. I had a shower and dropped exhausted into her bed.

XII

Somewhere between then and the first blush of dawn I lost so much and grew so much more. The taste of each other as our moment happened. I seized it, engraved it into memory so that I could return to it, over and over.

What I cherish most is the fact that for the first time I felt my body could be a source of happiness.

The everyday process of growing up had never been easy for me. Everything about my body would irritate me. I hated myself, I hated life. My body bore the brunt of that anger.

I was diagnosed as anorexic when I was fourteen. It never really left me. Anorexia is the guest that refuses to go and has to be treated hospitably. I have long spans of normalcy punctuated by bouts of starvation and self-loathing.

Piya made me feel so special I forgot about myself completely.

The next day I left for home. Mother was calm.

After practice that day, Piya and I lingered in the room.

The show was fine on Saturday. On Monday, I bought one textbook.

XIII

Cookie and Pritam had the ice placed round the coffin. In a complete daze, Mother went through accepting the flowers and condolences. I was shocked that I felt nothing. In a few hours the earth would cover Chinky, my brother, dead of a heart attack. I was scared to touch him. My cunning, sulky brother had nothing to do with this sleeping child.

Drained, hollow, I walked away from the cemetery. My aunts helped Mother into the car and drove home. I rang up Piya.

XIV

After Chinky's death I grew withdrawn. Piya moved to another troupe, citing differences with Baldie. I left too. She never seemed to fully comprehend my anguish, or the anger, the isolation and the weariness. My mother sank into her own depression.

Piya and I simply drifted apart. Just as there had been no clear beginning, there was no clear end.

I graduated. Gave my textbooks to Chillie's sister. A year after Chinky's death I found a new job. I hardly saw any friends.

Mother had aged. I looked older, felt older.

And I couldn't date. I just got bitter every time someone asked me out. Life was a robot's routine: work—home—TV—bed.

XV

Months since I had seen Piya. Was it still possible to love her?

Paying the bills made me feel older—a dry, tired feeling.

The freshness that had revived me when I first slept with Piya, the half-tearful, half-joking, half-adult, half-child I had been, responsible for someone else's body and emotions, was a precious memory. That was the sweetest growing up I did. After that, reconciling myself to maturity was a real chore—wrinkled and laborious.

I paid the bills, got a better job, learnt about banks—finally.

Growing up has no timetable . . . some things change you, others don't.

XVI
The train was jampacked. Our unsuspecting eyes met. We looked away and then I turned back, to stare, to claim. But she was lost in the suffocating sea of heads, of bodies.

After a long time I felt better.

Wanderer

Rekha

I graze all over these arching slopes.
Up your breast I climb,
Plant my lips on the pinnacle.
The pink trail of teeth proves I am the first
To come this way.

I skate from hipbone to hipbone.
Descend past your navel

To the whirlpool's rim.
My tongue, slow, cunning,
Writhes to the crevice,
Falls stunned in the wet valley,
Turning there like a child in its bed.
You devour my fist
Up to the knuckle.
The earth heaves
Again. And again.

Usha

Mita Radhakrishnan

Usha was God's gift to mankind, most specifically to me. From the moment I saw her, I was enthralled. Totally, utterly overcome. She entered my life as a 'new girl'. There I'd been, nine years old, in fourth standard, carrying on with my life as usual: school, classes, my friend Roochi who had a hole in her heart and had to have an operation, my pal Nadeem who would surely be a famous artist when he grew up . . . Nine turned to ten, and from fourth we went to fifth standard. We were in Army Public School—or Defence Services Public School as it was known then—and consequently, every year, 'new' boys and girls joined while old ones left, as parents were transferred in and out of Delhi. That made the start of every year especially interesting. Us 'old' ones got to act like dadas and throw our weight around. The boys did; the girls were just mean in a sissy kind of way that I didn't like. I preferred to be a bit of a dada and I could, because I was in with the boys in those days.

She immediately stood out. She was different. I took one look at her, with her fair face, her beautiful hair arranged just so—in a mod style that was surely her own idea and not her mother's—and with the most breathtaking grey-green eyes I had ever seen. My heart stopped. Speechless, I simply couldn't play the dada anymore. I can't remember what happened after that—I'd like to think I took her hand and bowed to her utter beauty. Probably when I found I could talk again I asked her what her name was . . . Usha. I kept saying it over and over. Can you imagine my ecstasy when she took to me too and we became 'best friends'? Usha and I were inseparable. We did everything together that we possibly could. I think we even sat together in class. She was a Malayalee like me, and that gave us an added secret special connection in a world of North Indian Hindi-speaking children.

What did two little ten-year-olds talk about so endlessly? I can't remember much now, except that we both had elder brothers with whom we fought and whom we found odious. One thing is sure—whether it was family or school or whatever, we never ran out of things to say. I remember going to Usha's house in Sector 8, R.K. Puram, once, when her parents had invited me and my parents over for her birthday party. I was curious to see where she lived and I remember wishing very much that her parents were richer so that she could live in a bigger house. I think our mothers were quite happy with and a little indulgent of our friendship—it was quite obvious that we came first on each other's list of priorities, even before them! We probably got on their nerves sometimes, the way we went on, grabbing the phone after coming home from school and then calling each other again just before going to sleep, to say good night before we met each other the next day. Once, we talked nonstop for three hours.

I don't think I had the words or the understanding then, at ten, to say that I was in love with my best friend. We held hands, but then all little girls did that. All I knew was that my world began and ended with Usha. Everything and everybody else was secondary. How often I'd have the urge to throw my sweater over monsoon puddles so she could cross over without getting her feet wet. I lived so that she would never be hurt, never fall, that her beauty would always remain unblemished, that she would always be happy. That was my life's dream.

There were other birthday parties and other friendships, but Usha's eclipsed them all. One of my old pals who continued to be in my life was Manish. He was known as a troublemaker and always seemed to be doing badly in class—but he was my mate. We used to treat each other to vegetable burgers and Thums Up at the canteen. He always managed to get plenty of cash from somewhere or the other, while I was very prudent with the ten rupees I received as pocket money. Manish was my main connection with the boys and my dada side. Often Usha, Manish and I used to go to the canteen together.

When we moved to the next class, somehow our sections got changed. I was in Section 6C while Manish and Usha were in 6B. This meant I could only see Usha during assembly, recess, PT period and after class. That drastically reduced our time together. Then something else changed. Quite soon, long before it became the subject of school gossip, I realized Usha and Manish were 'going out'. I think I must have known from the moment Manish replaced me in her heart. I can only remember an awful wrenching pain inside me. The whole year I ached as Usha dolled up for Manish every day. I remember watching them as they went to the canteen. They were very daring, even holding hands. We were all eleven years old. It was a scandal. The whole senior school was agog. I defended Usha valiantly. I couldn't bear anyone making remarks about her. Besides, Manish was my friend too. Usha was obviously in love with him. I loved her, and I did the only honourable thing to do—I pulled back.

But when Manish came over to treat me at the canteen like in the old days, I was too overcome by jealousy to accept. I remember brushing his hand off my arm and hissing that I didn't want his burgers anymore. He probably couldn't understand why I was so angry. I didn't have words for anything I felt. No one knew. My heart was one big knot about to burst. I kept quiet and tried to make new friends in my section. Usha became more and more distant.

I somehow realized that I felt for her what Manish did (or should it be the other way round? That Manish had started to feel for her what I'd been feeling all along?) and that was not how it was supposed to be. But I didn't have the space to think about that because the pain was just too great. I tried to cover up by reading Star Comics and pretending to like boys. Inside, I repeated her name over and over. My beautiful Usha.

Then one day, she stopped coming to school. Nobody answered the phone any more and I remember trying to find her house again, this time by myself, eleven years old, feeling very small and quite scared crossing the big Ring Road. All the flats looked the same. I kept hoping to see Usha on one of those little balcony-verandas. I heard bits and pieces of the story from other friends. She had fought with her elder brother in the eleventh standard and he told his parents about her and Manish. Her mother withdrew her from school the very next day and we never saw her again.

They say that the first love is always special. I know that I truly loved a girl when I was ten: a pure love that existed before words could distort and limit it. God gave her to me for a time and then took her from my life. After many lovers, now I'm finally with my soulmate, the woman with whom I would like to spend the rest of my days. The Divine has brought us together. She tells me about Gislen, her first lover, from when she was fifteen and in a Catholic school in France, and I tell her about Usha, and we smile.

➤✦

Learning and Waking

Rajkumari

At the age of forty, to awaken is painful because the eyes have become accustomed to darkness, and sudden light hurts. The pain is like glass smashing inside the skull.

I was very young when my grandfather had his stroke, and he was never the same afterwards. 'Learning to walk is easy for babies when your body is soft enough to take the falls,' he said. I remember the look on his face, almost at peace. 'Learning once was enough for me and anyhow it is too late for me to learn again.' He refused to get out of bed because he said he did not like stumbling with each footstep.

At seventy it is less difficult to say no to life, folding yourself up and away like cold-weather clothing that does not belong in the sunlight. At forty I could not stay in bed merely because I knew one day that I was not in my place any more. I had burst out of my circle and started flying loose outside the closed systems of belonging. Externally I was no different from what I was before. But my mind was aching with the shock of a new birth.

When I was born, what I looked into from the horizon of my Ma's arms was not this strange life. My big wet eyes threw me twenty-five years down the well of waiting time, into a scene where I would also lie in a bed, hips torn apart, a little baby girl on my stomach. My journey ended in that vision.

The anger of those days of change will never leave me. The rage thrashes inside my head like a fish pulled from the sea, not knowing where to go and how to get out of this net. My fault or theirs, I still wonder. They are also sullen and unforgiving in their abandonment. Ma seethes in her old age of wearing saris that are scrubbed smooth as water with repeated washings. When I separated from my husband she crawled to me again and again on her knees, crying for me to relent. My daughters could not speak, their words turned into vomit or tears, and my heart, which is the heart of all mothers, is still in rags. I swung from hating them to loving them, hate to love, love to hate.

How to describe why this life began to disgust me? My husband began to look and smell like a brute in the bed where three months earlier I had still wanted to touch him in the darkness. My daughters were so like him, more man than girl with their thick legs and sharp teeth. This is true vision after wiping the dust that clouds the eyes of all the fools walking upon this earth.

Or is it the curse of madness?

I went to a psychiatrist on my own. I looked at his stupid shining face as I talked and talked about what continues to sit heavily on my head like a bloated vampire: thoughts of wanting the cleanliness of women, and fantasies of their hands with small and soft hairless fingers. Drenched in thick sweat, I lay in bed always waiting for the same nightmare. I would be strapped into a chair with my feet glued to the ground and an electric knife would cut into me from above to remove my face from my head. Fingers poke into the bleeding brain to probe the roots of my desires, which are pulled out like small white worms.

This life of strange mixes. I sometimes wish only that it could be over. Then this body could be poured out into the dry earth with everything else—gushing rivers which never find the sea, flowing past fields which poison their own harvest, under skies in which the birds suddenly find that they cannot fly and fall screaming to the earth.

Buffaloes and Men's Cologne

Shikha

I've always been attracted to women and have had crushes and flings since the age of twelve. But I didn't know the word 'lesbian' in those days. I was very innocent in that respect. I didn't read much, I was completely involved in sports and outdoor activities. I used to fancy the women I saw—I was aroused by even a casual touch.

My father was a senior army officer. He used to take the family to a hill station in summer. There was a nurse I liked a lot, she used to come and give us our checkups. A sweet pain went through me whenever I stared at her. I used to wait for her to come to my father's house. She found me cute and petted me, making me sit next to her. I thought she found me good-looking; that made me feel great. I saw a Hindi movie that was playing nearby at least a dozen times so that I could enjoy the romantic songs and dialogues, imagining the nurse as my lover—not specifically as a man or a woman, but in a general sense as someone I desired. The next summer, when we came to the hill station for the holidays, I found out that she had got married. I didn't enjoy that vacation at all. I could see she was in her own world, she was not the same person who had liked me and enjoyed my company . . .

Soon after that my uncle came and took me to his home near Delhi. He had a daughter, she was about twenty-five. I was thirteen. I remember the way she entered the drawing room full of huge windows—she was very attractive, a better version of the actress Zeenat Aman. She looked directly at me. We exchanged glances as my uncle introduced us. He said, 'Take Shikha and show her around.' We went to a neighbour's place and watched some videos. I kept looking at my uncle's daughter. I found her so sexy. She was wearing a sari and she had such beautiful long hair, she could sit on it. In the middle of the room, with other people nearby, she suddenly murmured, 'Please fasten my bra hook, it has come undone.' She led me to the bathroom. I lifted the back of her blouse and did up the hook. My heart was beating very fast. I moved my fingers lightly on her skin.

We walked home. She pointed out a famous Radha-Krishna temple on the way. She said, 'Are you scared of the dark?' I said, 'Yes, sometimes.' She caught my hand and gripped it tight. I didn't want her to let it go. I was in such a daze of ecstasy, I couldn't think clearly. As we approached the house she released my hand. I wondered why she couldn't keep holding it. Our parents were chatting in the drawing room. The atmosphere was very relaxed, but I was in a strange heightened state.

We slept in the same bedroom, this woman and I . . . In the middle of the night I woke up in her arms. She was caressing me all over. She thought I was asleep, and I let her think so. I was sexually innocent, in my own mind. She fondled my small breasts and kissed me on the mouth. The next morning when I woke, she was no longer next to me. I went to the bathroom and looked at myself in the mirror. I felt as if something wonderful had happened to me. That day I had a bath three times, I wanted to look fresh and clean for her . . . Later we met in my mother's room. My cousin smiled, but said nothing.

All day I was impatient, I almost felt as if I was getting a fever. But she could not even hold my hand, her father was constantly there. At night we went to sleep immediately, we were both tired. Again in the middle of the night I woke in her arms, she was fondling me and undoing all my nightdress buttons. I started coughing for some reason. She got nervous, buttoned me up, shifted to the other side of the bed. She did not approach me again. The next day she was distant and silent. I could clearly feel the difference in her manner, and I was puzzled. The whole day we had someone or the other with us. In the evening her father said, 'Take Shikha to see the buffaloes at the back of the house.' There were about six-seven animals tied up in the small garden full of mud and cowdung. She sent the man working there on some errand. Then she caught my hand, saying, 'Be careful of these buffaloes.' We stayed like that for a while. My excitement and happiness kept growing by the minute. When we went back to the house she released my hand.

On the third night again I woke to the sensation of her kissing me and unbuttoning my clothes. Her hands went to my crotch. I found it a little strange but I was enjoying her touch, I didn't want her to stop. She put my hand on her own genitals. I let it be there, but I didn't know what to do with it. She manipulated my fingers, thinking I was asleep, or maybe she knew I was only pretending . . . I don't know if she had an orgasm or anything like that, I couldn't tell what pleasure she was getting. Both of us fell asleep after a while.

The next day we went to Delhi. We broke journey on the

way with her relatives. They lived in a small flat, and had three young kids—we slept in the drawing room, all piled up together. I was very disturbed to see other children hugging her. I desperately wanted to be alone with her somewhere. I was really struggling with my feelings. The next night we reached home. There was a power cut. My sister said she would sleep in our double bed with our cousin, and told me to sleep on a folding cot next to the bed. My cousin lay on the side of the bed near the cot. She was talking to my sister, but her hand kept stroking me and casually she asked once in a while, 'Are you asleep? You must be very tired, we've traveled all day.' I was thrilled. I caught her hand, I was ready to push away my fear and let her know that I knew about her, about me, about us. Then there was a horrible moment when the electricity suddenly came back on. We jerked our hands free as if we had received a shock of 220 volts. I tried to sleep while she chatted with my sister. I had a transistor I used to listen to, dreaming as the old romantic Hindi movie songs played; I wanted to console myself with this music but my sister wouldn't let me switch it on.

The next day more relatives arrived, the house was full. My cousin went away in a light blue Ambassador car. I remember the look she gave me as she left without saying anything, without my telling her anything. For weeks after that I was very shaken and depressed, overwhelmed by a sinking feeling. I kept going over my memories of those nights when she had touched me; I kept spinning fantasies so that I would somehow be able to recapture her presence and acknowledge everything that had never been said, and never would be.

In college, women fancied me a lot and I would return their interest, but I didn't have much freedom to actually reciprocate. I contented myself with minor crushes. At that time I was doing a course in a polytechnic. I really fancied one girl in the hostel. She was gorgeous, with wonderful long hair; she reminded me of the actress Supriya Pathak. Her relatives were forcing her to get married. The night before she left I was in her room with her and two other girls who were asleep. We were whispering to each other, the lights were off. I kept urging her to resist family pressure. I got onto her bed, and we had just started to kiss when some other hosteler came in and put on the light, saying, 'Oh, you're leaving tomorrow, don't sleep tonight, stay awake and talk to us.' We immediately moved apart. There was a horrible violence about that moment of instant separation. I was so frustrated and angry and miserable, I felt as if a hundred and ten people had come between us.

Those days a lot of ragging used to go on. I was protected by an NRI woman from America who really pursued me. I slept in her room sometimes. I was from a restricted middle-class family while she was very rich and mature; we were opposites by nature, but the attraction was very strong. We developed quite a reputation. I used men's colognes and enjoyed the compliments I received. I became the cigarette supplier for the hostel. Smoking was forbidden but we smoked secretly on the roof. I wanted all the pretty and smart girls to chase me, demanding cigarettes.

The Dussehra holidays came, and this NRI woman didn't have anywhere to go, as her family was in America. I went home as per the rules but came back early, without really understanding why. There was no one else in the hostel. I still remember the sight of the long rows of empty beds in the dormitory; the luxury of having space and being alone, of choosing a bed—and most of all, having three days alone with each other, three uninterrupted days to make love. But the warden spoiled it for us when she came on the second day and suspiciously demanded why we were not at our local guardians' houses. My lover was so angry, she painted graffiti on the hostel walls and pasted a drawing of the warden's face onto a bikini-clad woman from the centrefold of a tabloid newspaper. She put the poster up in the hostel and we really enjoyed watching the warden rant and rave and try to rip it down. There was a huge brass gong in the hostel that was used to announce mealtimes and regulate the daily routine. It was indispensable. We stole it, put it in a big black bag and smuggled it out, and sold it to a kabariwala for Rs 375. With that money we bought food and soft drinks for a Dussehra jam session we had in the hostel. We invited the warden also—we laughed as she ate the chips and pastries and sandwiches. The next day there was no gong to control our timings, so we all overslept and no one knew when it was time for meals—there was total confusion. It gave us a lot of satisfaction. I realized how compelled I was by my lover's rebellious nature. She was defiant and possessive. I remember the way she made coffee for me every night. During the ragging, some seniors had yelled at me, 'Wipe that smile off your face!' but she had rescued me so coolly, saying, 'You can't do anything about that smile, Shikha, why don't you come and have a cup of coffee with me instead?' That was my first cup—after that there were many more!

During lovemaking I felt consumed, lost in the world of our two bodies. My involvement with my partner was always total, whoever I was with. My actions came from the heart. I was not anxious, nor did I feel guilt or shame or doubt. There was a certainty about my convictions. I wanted to enjoy the present. I avoided discussing my feelings with my partners because I felt it would bring tension into the relationship. All my lovers were straight women who enjoyed the sexual satisfaction they got from me, that they failed to get from men. I did not think of myself in terms of sexual categories; I was unfamiliar with the meaning of the word 'lesbian'. Initially I thought it was a sort of mental imbalance, an illness or psychological disorder. My concept of myself as a gay person changed after I became involved with a woman who openly identified herself as a lesbian. Even after the hostel when I was working small jobs in offices, I had never considered myself a 'lesbian'. I thought lesbians must be weird sexual creatures.

The first time I was called a 'lesbian'—by a heterosexual friend who was annoyed that I did not spend time with her instead of the other women I found attractive—I was unprepared for such a vicious accusation. I was ready to hit this friend but other people calmed me down, saying, 'She's mad, she doesn't know what she's saying, let her be.' I felt really insulted, because I considered 'lesbian' to be a term of abuse. The peculiar thing is that even though I was having sex with women, I still thought I was the only one of my kind. I could not have imagined that I'd ever embrace the label 'gay'. I never thought that the word 'lesbian' would one day sound like sweet music to my ears.

(*as told to V.S.*)

The Gate

Anasuya

An ant drags a feather, in its jaws it seems so heavy.
What is the weight of honour?
When I fall from grace,
will my honour drift lightly,

or shatter, like illusion?
I hear in my heart forgotten voices.
High sweet pledges of love.
Stirring now like unborn babies
waiting in a blood-lined womb.

A girl,
eyes lined with kajal.
The careful outlines blur
as tears soak my eyes.
She was waiting
to walk with me to school.

I call her with my eyes
but hers sweep past.
Seeming not to recognize
me, hidden in the lined middle-aged.

She-devil's eyes.
Knowing this time
the worth of promises.
        Waiting for me
                to speak . . .
                        to move

to cross old Lakshman's silly line.

Am I mistaken?
Is it only myself out by the gate,
waiting for a me she knows will come?

➤❮

Coming to Women

Preeti

Growing up, I always *knew* even though I never labeled it. There are hundreds of theories about what makes one gay, and they all boil down to this: either you are born with it, or it's the result of social and sexual conditioning. I always wonder why people choose to make it an either/or. It *is* something you're born with, to a certain extent—you have a predisposition—and then certain influences trigger you this way or that way.

When I was a kid reading fairy tales, I always identified with the prince. Not because I considered myself masculine, or wanted to be a boy, but because I also had feelings for—well, in the fairy tale it was a beautiful woman. But looking back, I see that I was in love with the *idea* of femininity and tenderness and caring. Once I read a story where there was a love triangle, the usual story about the 'other woman'. And I thought, if my husband ever fell in love with another woman, I would surely have tremendous sympathy and compassion for her, and would try to understand what she was going through. I would surely end up loving and accepting her. So this was how, at a very early age, I started longing for anything that was soft and gentle.

I never had any guilt about this, to me it was the most healthy, the most normal way to feel. I have always been an extremely demonstrative person—if I feel something, I have to express it, and I naturally express it physically. So the boundaries between physicality and sexuality are a little blurred: if I have a feeling or an emotion it manifests itself in the form of a need to touch, or stroke, or caress someone—a young child, an adult, sometimes a man. Not that I want to molest children or have sex with men. But I'm sure that if I felt like *this* about a man, I would be as accepting of those feelings. It's just an accident that I am this way. Sexuality is part of the continuum of one's emotions, and maybe if my family life had been different, if my father had been an affirming male role model, I might have swerved the other way instead.

My father could be considered a most unmanly man—he's not macho, and in many ways is unlike most Indian husbands. But sometimes I wonder if it might have not better to have had a 'typical' male figure in the house, because then it's very clearly delineated who's the man and who's the woman! For all the external loving that my father expressed to my mother—and theirs was a love marriage—he was never really there when she needed him, and I slowly began to realize that there was only so much you could get out of any man, in terms of support and understanding. If I had started out with that knowledge, maybe I could have worked out some kind of a makeshift relationship with a man.

Even at the age of nine, I was observant. My mother had just had a retarded child who needed a lot of care in the early years. She was looking after this baby on her own. But even if my mother had spent the day with my sister in the military hospital, my father would still come back from work in the evening demanding that she cook some very exotic meal. Which she would do, despite the fact that she was terribly tired physically, and emotionally distraught. I used to be aghast at all this and think, how insensitive can a human being be? I came to the conclusion that it didn't make much difference that my father was a much softer man than most. It didn't give him any more insight into how my mother felt, having to raise a retarded child, and having to run the house on a slim budget. He made all the token gestures, but the internal support just wasn't there. It was finally my mother's responsibility, it was literally her baby.

37

I remember feeling profoundly helpless. I wasn't old enough to be of use, but I was old enough to be aware of what she was going through. I started feeling such disgust with men when I realized that ninety-nine per cent of them are not even aware of women's tremendous capacity to endure. It seemed to me that women live in a completely different universe.

When I was about eleven, we had a maidservant, a very wild, very sexual, and—although this is not politically correct—a very cheap woman. She was sleeping with a lot of men in the army area where we were staying; even at that young age, I was aware of this. She would take my sister downstairs, apparently for a walk, and go sit in the park instead. Once when I happened to pass by, I saw my sister wandering off somewhere while the maid sat in a corner under a tree with a man who was fondling her. I told my mother about it and all hell broke loose; *her* concern was for the child, since this woman was obviously not looking after her properly. But when it was openly discussed in the family, my father's reaction horrified me. He shouted and screamed, accusing the maid of being a whore and being a bad influence on the house; he slapped her and then picked up a hot iron as though he was going to brand her with it. I remember rushing towards him and grabbing the iron from his hand, yelling 'You can't do that!' And then I had a flash of intuition: I suddenly realized that his gesture was not a moral response to our maid's loose character; my father himself was sexually attracted to her and was fighting that impulse. He was not the sort of man to sleep around, he was a very conventional, virtuous Indian male in that respect. The only way he could cope with his feelings for the maid, as a respectable middle-class man, was by being violent.

This incident made me really loathe my father. But as I went through college, I found that double standards were at the very core of heterosexual relations. It was either sexual hypocrisy or emotional hypocrisy—a man pretending to understand a woman, pretending to love her, when really it all came down to hard-core sex for him. The emotion was just the gilding of the pill, even in the most tender and sensitive and demonstrative relationship. It wasn't that I had any hangups about sex—I grew up completely and totally and unabashedly sexual. But I felt that men sugar their desire, and put a lot of fancy frills on it in order to hook women into giving them what they want. I thought women understood sexuality to be an extension of feelings as much as it is a physical act. The wooing and the courting between men and women is a major piece of bullshit, and this very cynical view was one I developed at an early age.

I come from a traditional middle-class background, and while there was openness to us mixing with the opposite sex, there was no discussion about the facts of life, we were just left to find out in our own ways. When I was twelve I used to be very close to a male cousin who was five years older than me, and I remember I was sitting with him one day listening to the Beatles, and he was talking. He was telling me about this girl and how she had been wearing shorts when they last met, and how her long legs attracted him. He said that the two of them were going past a hospital when she suddenly turned around and said to him, 'Oh, I should go in for a checkup.' My cousin started giggling in a silly sort of way, and told me, 'So I asked her, "Why, have you been up to mischief?" and she said, "I think so. I've missed my period."' The blatant way in which he expressed that . . . I was very bewildered and innocent, and I felt as if glass had shattered inside me.

And that made me conclude that men are so odd, they are so irresponsible when talking about sex or being sexual. This lack of consideration made me angry and vengeful. I had been living in a very romantic world and it didn't make sense, this flippant way of talking about things. On another occasion, the same cousin told me that he'd forgotten to buy condoms . . . It opened up a window in my head, showing me men's typical crass, gross way of thinking about women, the complete opposite of my idealized vision.

When I was in my last year of school, there was a much older woman in my class—she must have failed frequently!—who grew very fond of me, and used to take me to her house. Once she went out of the room and left me to browse around, and I came across copies of *Penthouse* and *Playboy*. Thrilled, I started flipping through them—of course I was aroused! But just then she came back and grabbed the magazines from my hands, saying, 'This is not for you.' I said, 'But why?' She answered, 'You're too young. When you're older that's a different thing, but right now you should not be looking at these.' I *was* very young then—I finished school when I was all of thirteen. But much later I linked these two events in my mind and thought, how strange, a woman cared about the effect that open sexuality might have on my mind, and was concerned, whereas a man had shown complete insensitivity. So I grew more and more inclined towards women as the years went by.

I always had a powerful need to express my feelings. Unfortunately we're brought up in a society where touch is frowned on, and physical contact is equated with sexual interest. When I was younger, the innocence with which I approached men would get me into a lot of trouble. In college, when I was doing the party scene, I didn't realize that a lot of the guys were trying to 'get' me, so to speak. Because of the openness of my nature, they used to think, well, here's an easy lay. I would get attacked by these men, under the cover of darkness and loud music, when all I was looking for was friendship.

I suppressed a whole lot of negative feelings where men were concerned, but it's like trying to control water—you put up a block somewhere and it'll emerge elsewhere. I started realizing that I was so much more comfortable with women because I didn't feel sexually threatened or degraded by them. If it had been at all possible for me to have grown up in a society in which men didn't exploit women like this, I might not have been a lesbian at all. My abhorrence was not necessarily a revulsion towards the male sex, but towards the lecherous mentality of the men I had met. My attitude was not based on gender, initially—I was looking for gentleness and softness anywhere I could find it. I shut myself off from men because the way they treated me as a mere object really assaulted my feelings.

The only difference between me and the typical Indian woman is that even though she too experiences all this, she still enslaves herself and goes through all the damaging shit—men are lucky that there are women out there who will treat them like gods until the end of time. But if a woman has developed even a small amount of self-awareness, how can she tolerate male chauvinism? It's not necessary for a lesbian to be a feminist, but if you're a feminist it's logical to be a lesbian. If you understand yourself on this level and you've realized that your capacity to think and feel is intimately connected to your being a woman, how can you not be gay?

I was fast becoming aware that I had passed my threshold of endurance. Through my recognition of the complete callousness of men towards women's real feelings, I started making a connection with the attraction for women I had experienced right from childhood. My lesbianism wasn't a political stance, it was the outcome of my natural development.

Over and over I found that when I talked to men about whatever upset and hurt me, their capacity to understand was zero. And one day I just gave up. It was much easier to be around women and much more comfortable, since you didn't have to work hard at trying to make them understand, you didn't have to try to be someone else, nor did you have to pose and pretend.

At the age of twenty-five I said, to hell with all this heterosexual nonsense, and felt a sense of complete freedom. Suddenly, I came into my own.

(as told to A.S.)

Meeting Myself

Julia

Blame it on the Brits!

If you are one of those washed, cleaned, ironed and packed-in-stiff-brown-paper-packet Indians brought up in English-medium schools from the days of the Raj, you'll have learned by now that in addition to having introduced us to the wonders of their administrative abilities, their insatiable hunger to rule the world and to stay connected by rail, road, air, water, the Brits also robbed us of our robust, rustic nature and replaced it with the cold suppression of all emotion. Thus a passionate Indian, even fifty years after Independence, can never feel free to express the gushing warmth of the heart nor the tropical heat of the muladhar chakra, without feeling a little ashamed. Better still, reject it altogether!

Home from boarding school for my winter holidays, I gazed in rapt silence through the clear windowpane of my room at this young Khasi woman playing hopscotch with her daughter. She was fabulous! Long, wild waist-length hair, brown eyes, a healthy young body and a laugh that came from her heart. She was married and lived with her husband and their daughter Rita in the house next to ours. Her name was Mem.

Longing mixed with my guilt as I stared at her breasts moving up and down under her dress as she jumped from square to square. She became conscious that I was watching her. I looked away but not before I saw her pick up a shawl and wrap it around her body. I drew the curtain as she walked off. I felt a little hot behind the ears and was quite sure she felt the same. I locked my door and went and stood before the tall mirror. Slowly I removed the navy-blue blazer of my uniform and loosened my tie. I took a deep breath and pulled it off my collar. Hastily I unbuttoned my snow-white shirt and stopped . . . the sight of my bra filled me with pride. I posed before the mirror, smiling to myself, tossing my head from side to side and enjoying the newness of my emerging breasts. I unstrapped my bra and cupped them with both hands. I thumbed my pink nipples. Hmmmm . . . what fun! I threw my shirt, tie and bra on the bed and pulled down my navy-blue pleated serge skirt. Blue knickers welcomed my wandering eyes with their bold frills and flare. I rolled out of them and stood naked in my black shoes and white socks before the mirror. Hair was beginning to grow on my pubes. I began to count—one . . . two . . . three . . .

The houses in Shillong are quite primitive. The bathroom can be used only to take a bath. Often there is a commode, but to defecate you have to go outside the house to the furthermost end of your compound where a toilet will have been built purely for this purpose. The clothes-washing area is also outside the bathroom in another little specially created space. Our house is like this as well.

Presently I ejected myself from the toilet and was delightfully surprised to see Mem washing clothes in the adjacent area. Her buttocks moved back and forth, up and down as she squatted on the platform and bent over to rub and scrub the garments. I was engrossed in the movement of her buttocks and mentally trying to visualize the cleft between them when I was jarred from my reverie by her daughter calling out to me.

I rushed to pick her up. I stood a foot away from Mem, my hands nearly brushing her shoulders. She stopped what she was doing as if pinned by my energy. 'Ballai, Khaun,' I said in Khasi. 'Yes, darling?' I kissed Rita's cheeks as if I was extending the kiss to her mother.

Mem stood up and rushed inside her house. She had noticed the crack in my voice as I spoke to Rita. I had seen a strange sparkle in her eyes as she looked slyly at me before running into the safety of her home.

The movie theatre was jampacked with Khasi men, the smell of cheap whiskey on their breaths. They came with prostitutes, not to see the movie but to have sex. Heavy necking was going on, and as soon as the lights went out, the women began to manually masturbate the men. Some even allowed the men to finger-fuck them.

It was my first date with Mem. The five o'clock show was *Summer of '42*.

Mem had never been to school. She could not speak English. We spoke to each other in Hindi. When I asked her to the movie she felt so shy, she blushed and giggled all at the same time.

The man sitting next to her began to make passes at her. Uncomfortably, Mem edged closer to me. My blood rushed to my groin. I picked up courage and held her hand. It was wet with perspiration. I wiped it with my handkerchief. Then I put her hand on my thigh. She didn't resist. It became increasingly difficult for me to see anything on the screen. I was completely blinded by the cascade of emotions inside me.

I pushed open the bathroom door not realizing she was inside.

The naked body of a woman can freeze you.

I stood on the threshold like a statue, looking fiercely at her open mouth, her neck. My eyes caressed her shoulders . . . She grabbed the towel and draped it around her body, covering her breasts as if to hide them from me. With one hand she covered the dark mound as if to protect herself from me. Her eyes didn't leave mine . . . fear, anticipation, desire, helplessness written large within them.

I raped her with my gaze.

Then turned away, shutting the door behind me.

She came into my room as if drawn to it against her will. I sat calmly pretending to read a book as she examined everything, giving each object a little attention.

Then she turned to me.

Instinctively I became aware that this was the last day of my virginity. Panic and increasing wonder gripped me as she came and sat beside me. With one twitch of her hand she pulled away the book I was pretending to read. I buried my face in my palms. She began to laugh!

I looked up at her, and from then on I don't remember how I reached the other shore.

Lying next to me, she resisted everything—from the first kiss to stroke after stroke of my hand, to each successive orgasm. The more she resisted, the more I wanted her, the more powerful I grew in my first act of love as I penetrated each barrier within myself. At last when we lay with nothing but our naked skin between us, we broke even the physical boundaries that defined our selves as separate. Intertwined, we moved our thrusting hips in rhythm. We groaned, devoured by passion, our bodies shuddering in orgasm again and again . . . until our mouths were desert-dry and bloody . . .

Years later, as I sat at the feet of my Master, I heard someone ask:

'Beloved Bhagwan, who is this "other" we seek?'

My ears filled with his answer.

'The "other" is you. In the "other" you see that side of yourself which you cannot see otherwise. The "other" mirrors your own reality.'

I thought of Mem—simple, natural, pure.

Me, myself.

Glossary

muladhar chakra – the root chakra; lowest of the seven energy centres, located at the base of the spine

The Point of Madness

Flora B.

The Darkness had paled to grey. A pinpoint of light, way above, beckoning her upward like the Star of Bethlehem. She tried to push away the clinging blackness, but it slipped past her hands and wrapped itself around her mind again. It had the sticky viscosity of molten wax, suffocating her. It tried to seal off that drop of light. She flexed her mind, compressed it like a spring and leaped for the light, clawing through the Darkness and tearing the fleecy black from her path. For a dizzying instant of mad terror, her mind slipped and almost tumbled into the gaping, yawning abyss below. Then, with a last violent effort, she burst through the triumphant ring of light like a circus lion bounding through a flaming hoop, and landed in a garden of exquisite lucidity.

The sharp edges of the flower petals gashed her, the blunt mangoes gleaming balefully through the leaves pounded her like fists. The colours burned across her mind, scouring away the coarse residue of blackness. She stretched tentatively to get accustomed to her body again. After these periods where her body was squashed into a few cubic centimetres of cerebral pulp, it was a relief to feel herself expand and diffuse through the flesh into each toe and fingertip. She felt the heat gathering under her braid of hair. She heard the gardener's rasping saw as he sliced through branches to prepare for the monsoon.

She eased herself from the reclining chair where her lover's practised hands had placed her. She could hear her whistling somewhere in the garden. It must be Friday, since the family had allowed her to visit. There was a bowl on the grass next to the chair, crusted with the remains of creamy dal and rice. Her lover must have been feeding her body while her mind writhed helplessly. She sighed, and tried to put the bleak terror behind her.

But the Darkness was not easily vanquished. It took her by surprise the very next night, ambushing her unwary mind and smothering it in heavy black. Her body crashed from the dining room chair onto the floor, twitching and retching violently. But this time the Darkness had a new density, a dull grotesque weight. It echoed with silent screams born in the centre of her brain and radiating out to soak into the black. In moments of terrible clarity she saw her unresisting body sway with a sickening rhythm to the slap of waves, heard her own mouth churn words her mind was powerless to control. She heard herself scream a name over and over. Disturbed faces billowed over her. Then a heavy tide of Darkness flooded her with an angry roar, drowning out the world.

It seemed like a hundred years before the Darkness receded, leaving her mind limp, exhausted, with all memory ripped away. She had just enough strength to seize the passing moment, gathering a few faint impressions. A window letting in sunlight and sun-warmth showed blue sea and blue sky. A vase of flowers released a spray of colour and wisps of perfume. A thin fog of soothing piano music filtered in from somewhere. The walls were a dignified white that stood aloof and did not crowd in on all sides like the yellow colour of her old bedroom . . . her old bedroom?

Her mind whipped around and snatched at that little scrap of memory, but it unraveled and fell to pieces the moment she grasped for it. She shuddered with angry sobs and dry screams of frustration. A bell shrilled, ownerless feet tramped through a rising forest of Darkness. Someone grabbed her arm and pierced it with a sharp sting. A mask choked her. But it was too late. She curled her mind into a ball to prevent the brutal Darkness from assaulting her.

But there was no Darkness. Instead there was just beautiful, vast, blissful Oblivion. For a few dragging seconds, she was wary. The repellent Darkness was skilled at assuming many different forms to beguile her into submission. Then she felt her mind relax and unfold in a narcotic stupor. There was no sound. No movement. No thought. No emotion . . .

Then a dazzling light cracked the smooth surface of the Oblivion. A cruel talon reached into her nest and winched her lacerated mind back into her body. As always, she felt her eyes opening first. Then one by one her limbs began their demands. Her aching ankle shrieked for help, while her mouth complained about the taste of the cereal they had been feeding her. The glare and the noise became intolerable.

It took even longer than usual to accustom herself to the world beyond her mind. Whirling white masses slowly resolved themselves into faces. Clots of syllables gradually congealed into words. Figures in crisp white thronged about, exuding a smell of antiseptic. One face in particular touched off a little burst of frustrated memory. The peculiar twist of the nose, the faint double chin below the soft cheeks and the long curling hair—the way it all fitted together just escaped her groping thoughts. The face was pushed away by angry hands and everything dissolved briskly, leaving the agonized, bewildering flavour of thwarted desire. She felt her yearning body quiver, but there was only a white-coated man with cold hands and a warm voice nearby, offering comfort. She felt her mouth open to scream, and the man turned quickly towards her, a syringe gleaming in his fist.

This time she slipped into the Oblivion without even rippling its surface. She crowded her mind into a tight ball that plummeted like a stone. Then she unfolded and floated back up carefully as the peace grew within her like a bubble. Was she drifting through infinity, or wedged between seamless seconds? Maybe she was just a speck without dimension. Who could tell, and who cared?

When that glimmer of light appeared again, she cringed. Waves of fear lapped at the widening slit. Fear of the pain of being hauled out and revived. Fear of the predatory anguish of trying to trap elusive memories, the slow, hard, vicious and futile rehabilitation, the guilt that choked her when she thought of the people she loved. Dim faces peered at her, fingers clutched at her. She recoiled, moving away from the responsibility, desperately snatching at nothingness.

It was time to leave her body to others. They would feed and wash that heavy inert mass, with no more abnormal needs of its own to create trouble. She shrugged the last few tattered and sordid thoughts from the splendid nakedness of her mind. The light above her shrank to a glittering atom and disappeared.

><

Destination: Us

M.G.

I've never done a good job of answering the question, and I never will. I stumble over it awkwardly, inarticulate and almost inaudible, feeling ridiculous. How do I explain our decision to leave the country we were born into, the one that will always be home no matter what? How do I justify moving permanently to a land neither of us has even visited?

'*To live together,*' I say; '*To have a life together,*' she says; and the inadequacies of those answers leave me saddened.

I can never find the right words to tell the women who know us for what we are why living here is not possible, when in actuality it is. I can't find the words because I don't know them. All I know is that I've felt them, *we've* felt them and lived with them till it came to a point when we couldn't any longer. Maybe those words include parents, aunts, sisters and brothers. Maybe they include upbringing, religion, society, friends and strangers. But I think, no, I *know* that the most critical word in there is '*us*'.

It was because *we* couldn't live together in this city, or for that matter, this country. It was not because it couldn't be done or hasn't been done or isn't being done. It was because *we* couldn't have done it.

To be fair to ourselves, we didn't know, or know of, any two women living together here in this city or any place in our country. We didn't shut out the knowledge nor did we go after it, we simply hadn't come across it. So we lived in our own world—and it wasn't a small or narrow one, mind you, at least I don't think so. And by the time I met my first lesbian, by chance, at work, a happenstance I will always be grateful for, we had taken more than our first few steps towards getting out. We had cleared our medicals (separately of course, we couldn't apply as a couple!) and had been through our immigration interviews.

I sometimes wonder, briefly, whether our decision would have been any different had I made contact with the community any sooner. I couldn't believe my ears when I first learnt that there were six couples living together in Bombay. Six couples! Here, somewhere in this city of millions, there were SIX! The awareness amazed me. I looked around, stunned, and examined my city in a new light . . . and I wondered if—but never for long.

We were still more comfortable paying substantial monies to the man who said we met the requirements and promised us quick and legal access to the country that would be the easiest to get into. A man whose loud and sometimes unpolished ways irritate me to the point where I lose sight of his basic good nature and forget the vital role he plays in the 'move'.

We paid up, not because we thought of setting up home together, or buying a car together, or opening a bank account together or building a family together. We paid because we hungered just to *be* together. To go to sleep at night together and wake up in the morning together. For the days I'll read a book in bed and look down and see and feel her lying asleep beside me. For the times she'll hear me clattering about in the kitchen trying to put something together for dinner while she watches something on TV that doesn't interest me in the least.

And strangely enough, just from that, I guess we both know the rest will follow. That it will be the start of a new life together, *our* new life together.

Words, Yours and Mine

Mani and Palash

When your words
come and meet
my words
an image
is imprinted
impossible
to separate
a complete picture
the ink
binds together
in its silent chain
the whole story

It is not easy to capture moments that we have lived with such intensity. And yet there are some memories, *our* memories, that are still unexpressed, waiting to be clothed in words and scattered upon the page.

This is no story created from our imagination. The moments we write about, the two of us have been through together. It is difficult to isolate the times of joy from the sorrow, from the loneliness that would descend on us when we were away from each other.

When did we meet? How did we meet? All of it comes up in memory as a picture that I can see through closed eyes. It was a part of the fresh enthusiasm of going to college. The hues of the salwar kurtas that had replaced the white school uniform threatened to colour the bare canvas of the mind. I still remember clearly the first time I set foot on the college staircase. A Mistri stood in my way, absorbed in some electrical repair work. I slid carefully past, reached my seat and sat down, and then realized that the Mistri was a classmate. I had to laugh at myself, but I was a bit embarrassed as well when I came to know that she was the genius of our class. I could not share this incident with anybody then, but today I think back and know that on that day my life, my happiness came up right beside me and then stayed hidden for the whole of the next year.

By the second year in college I had grown very close to her. Each time I went home I would ask myself what it was that kept drawing this face and this person to me again and again, from amongst the many that were there. But I did not attempt an answer to these questions even in my thoughts. Gradually life became the flow between two hearts.

Every day witnessed the rush and hurry to reach college and the search for corners where we could spend long hours alone. We would sit together, near one another. Our eyes searched for something in the other's gaze. Silent songs echoed in our ears. Our tongues were mute, but with each breath we implored the other to stay a while longer.

If for any reason we could not meet on a particular day, we were overcome by a strange and threatening fear that some disaster had struck. We ached for each other the way the two banks of a river yearn to meet. But there were so many restrictions at home. Who could have understood our agony? If we managed to get out of the house, rebukes and remarks followed: 'What is this friendship?' 'What need is there to meet so often?'

College friends had their own share of fun at our expense. We saw their suppressed laughter and heard their comments but we bore it all. Some questions hurt but we could do nothing except smoulder within, so the suspicions gathered strength.

As time passed, our attachment to each other grew and so also grew our distance from the rest of the world—the social and family canvas which neither needed any colour nor wanted any reshaping or moulding. And thus passed each day with its share of misery and pleasure, sunshine and shadow, as we braided new emotions into happy memories.

Our life continued at its own pace until it was paralyzed from all sides by its own powerlessness. Our studies were coming to an end. It seemed that our time with each other would also come to an end. Our lives began to seem like a river's drifting, widening banks. Then when our families began to suggest marriage, we were left completely shaken.

It seemed to us that everything was over. The red bridal garments that would adorn our bodies looked like a golden future to our families, but to us it was as though they were buying us our shrouds. And this immense pain of being separated, possibly forever. Who could we speak to, what could we do, where could we go? Nothing was apparent. There seemed to be only two alternatives. Either we could end our lives or we could move far away from all these obstacles and create a new life for ourselves. 'A new life for ourselves, together'—envisioning this strengthened our resolve.

But an insurmountable wall seemed to loom between ourselves and 'our life', and we decided to silence our beating hearts. We had come too close to each other to retreat. Agitated in mind, we even started out to lay our bodies on the railway tracks. But a friend persuaded our defeated minds and souls to return, a friend from whom we had not hidden our dilemma.

We were trudging through an endless desert with no shade or tree in sight, the sun pounding our heads, the soles of our feet burning. But we glimpsed a ray of hope. From a newspaper we got an address and decided to give it a last try. Wrote a letter, got the reply immediately. Some of the suffocating tension was released when we confided in two male friends who were experiencing similar pain.

It felt very good to share our life and its confusions with someone who understood. Even now their advice echoes in my ears: 'First, you must leave behind all ideas of ending your existence.' Our friendship developed, and with it, our self-confidence. Slowly but with certainty we were advancing towards a new life.

And then one day we made up our minds. We had to make a dangerous choice, no matter what might befall us. Whether we met death on the way or were forced to confront our deepest fears, we knew we could not continue to lead such a stifling existence. We expected and believed that to gain something we would have to sacrifice everything else. What is to happen has to happen, and we knew that it would be for the best. We left, taking with us our dreams of a small, shared world and the greatest treasure we had, that of courage.

Time affirmed our decision. A still mind, closed eyes—and all of a sudden the quiet breeze whispered in my ears, pleading with me to forget those claustrophobic memories. After all, what had that life given me? Yards of heaving sobs and fistfuls of tears. Is that all? No, no. The repression and opposition had also given me the endurance and the strength to fight. How could someone spend a lifetime broken within? And why should she?

My mind continued wandering through the lanes of my past. I was jolted out of my reverie when the speeding wheels began to grind to a halt. The shouts of coolies . . . We too would have to get down after a few stops to enter a city completely unfamiliar to both of us. The train started once more. We were not afraid, but we were anxious—was there even a path ahead?

Moving forward now, staring out of the window at the trees and fields left behind, at the houses speeding by. At the sight of them, once more we were reminded of the home in our dreams of the future, our own house. The hope shining on both our faces and the soft smiles reflected back—we took a breath of relief.

The thought exhilarated us. I placed my head on her shoulder and surrendered everything for the day that was to come. The train halting at stations, crowds climbing in and out, the faces of strangers and our eyes searching them, terrified that some familiar voice might summon from behind. Drag me back to the same prison I had left.

What strange circumstances. On the one hand an unknown future but lifelong togetherness, and on the other hand, the memories of days spent with our families. The speeding train was carrying us to an absolutely alien city. We had left everything behind—our homes, our people, and a life led according to the wishes of others. After a prolonged struggle, after agonized introspection, we had set our feet upon the threshold of our chosen destination.

At one point we had felt so helpless we had wanted to embrace death. We had been about to place ourselves in front of a running train. Yes, it does seem foolish today. But at that time, such an act seemed the only path open to us.

An unnamed bond was born between us without our even knowing it. Today we have a roof over our heads, we have enough to live on, and we have each other's trust and love. We have 'our life' and everything else as well. That is enough.

Life seemed so remote
everything in chaos
no one of my own
to lend me a shoulder for this grief
in the fiery heat
my tears were drying
I do not know when
from her distant terrace
she called out to me
and the caravan of life
began to move
slowly . . . slowly . . . slowly . . .

(translated from Hindi by Chayanika)

A Promise of Forever

Scriblerus

It feels lovely and lost to be alone in this moment.

My hand travels in an unfamiliar way on the paper. It is more used to caressing you than writing to you. So listen! And I know you will be listening, your ears pricked up and waiting for word just as mine always are. But I am not going to call you up yet. I'll keep writing.

My pen is quivering while I wonder how best to write. I need a thinking cap, silken, embroidered with best-quality titanium thread to keep out the world.

Remember when we made that hare-brained plan to get married at the Arya Samaj mandir? I regret that we never tried it. I have always wanted to go through the kanyadaan—except *I'd* be the one giving me away, with another kanya to receive me and offer herself up in that 'sweet surrender'. But if I can't be married to you in the temple of our gods, I will marry you in the sight of our sisters.

That's what this is all about.

Did I understand you wrong all along? Don't you want this too? Because I still believe the 'no matter what' we said to each other, and isn't that just like 'till death do us part'? I want it formalized, that's all! No more men, no more . . . watching out for the Red Flag every month. No more women, either. Ever.

Even though I'm afraid to be clinging, I'm too full of love to hold back any more. So . . . will you truly be with me forever?

From everything that I am to you. Your Teddy Bear who squeaks, 'I luf you. Take me wif you' in baby talk. Your Pope Joan who will never shift the moving toyshop of her heart. Your drinking buddy from the days of pal mode, 'How now, brown cow?'

For everything you are for me. My other half: 'How can half love double?' My Suckling Piglet: 'Why so pale and wan, fond lover?' and 'Love is such a mystery! I want! I want!' My beloved stray dog: 'You're the only one who's touched my heart and mind . . . so, two out of three is OK!'

I remember our first fight and how quickly it was over. 'I can't hold you if you don't want to be held . . . on to.' You tacked that on at the last minute, corrected yourself lamely, and I laughed through the tears because I couldn't help it. You are such a stickler for grammar.

When I whispered to you that I wanted you most, more than anyone else, you growled, 'That's tautology!' *before* you let me kiss you. Rat!

You're still my baby, you're still mine, and I still want to make you happy, whatever it takes.

I want you to marry me.

Declamation

Sagitta

I will plunge down, plummeting deep,
fathoms and fathoms below
and tell them, all those scaly shapes
that wind and weave through trailing weeds:
See—this is she!
Whisper it into glistening
curls of shell ears;
murmur through coral corridors;
brush past the drifting, prey-seeking
fringed fingers of anemones;
sink deeper yet to where the
bivalves lurk in rainbow mud
red and yellow, blue and green
oozes with fantastic names,
and into the crevices 'twixt
those fast shut halves
the sea's voice shall carry my words.

I will penetrate dark forest
and shout above bright macaw cry

and the chittering fig stealers;
louder than the booming cough
of tawny, striped majesty;
shriller than frou-frou of green leaves
and scampering of tiny legs
that creep and crawl—
clearer than these, all these;
See—this is she!

Soaring into the star-pricked night
I'll tell the seven Pleiades
and hoary old Aquarius
and Gemini the star-twins:
This is she—this is the one!
And every star shall stand stock-still
and, for the space of a heartbeat,
cease to twinkle.
So shall I see that they
have heard and know.

Guided by a Nameless Force

Mina A.

I was the youngest of several children. My mother had multiple
sclerosis and she died when I was sixteen; she had been
bedridden since I was five. I don't recall her ever picking me
up, caressing me, expressing maternal love. I was brought up

by servants and my strict father, while my four sisters were in boarding school. I remember my mother's ten years of agony: screaming in pain, suffering from bedsores, praying for death. My father was a rich businessman. He took my mother to expensive clinics abroad, but no treatment worked. All my life I was very close to him; he said to me once, 'I am your mother and your father', and I replied spontaneously, 'I am your daughter and your son.' He was a domineering and forceful man, but he thought he was acting in our best interests. He had high expectations and I tried to live up to them. He was able to instil confidence and authority in me. Some of that came from financial privilege.

My first sexual relationship took place in college when I was seventeen. I was drawn to two older girls who were physically well developed. I found their maternal aspect very comforting. I used to drink beer and carry on one night with one lover, the next night with the other—both girls were in a constant state of jealousy. I didn't know the term 'lesbian' in those days. I assumed the attraction was a natural phenomenon, and followed my instincts. One of these girlfriends had been sexually abused by her father from childhood onwards, and had undergone two abortions. She was generally very reserved, but she opened up to me. I analyzed it later for myself—it occurred to me that she was looking for a child and I was looking for a mother, therefore we were able to fulfil mutual needs.

My father was very conservative. We were five sisters; not one was allowed to meet boys or go out. We grew up with the idea that we would be married off as soon as we were eighteen years old—marriages arranged and organized by my father. The circumstances of my own wedding were somewhat drastic—a letter written by a boyfriend was intercepted by my sister and shown to my father. He was furious. He beat me and locked me up, regardless of my broken tooth, bleeding nose, black eye . . . I begged him to let me graduate at least. He refused to listen. I was engaged within a week, married within a month. I was a complete rebel so the idea was hateful, to say the least. I refused to get dressed up for the engagement. Finally I wore a plain pink salwar kameez and grudgingly allowed my sister to push earrings into my ears. A stranger slid a ring onto my finger. I was obliged to be committed to this man! It was meaningless. I hadn't spoken a word to him, or he to me. And I was supposed to have sex with him! I didn't know anything about sex with men. I was very curious. But our lack of interest in each other was so obvious; in all our engagement photographs he is looking in one direction, I'm looking in the other . . .

My fiancé took me for a drive in his car. That's where we had our first conversation. He said, 'My sister's marriage broke up last year. She was a lesbian. Her lover went with the doli, refused to let the husband get into bed with my sister. She ran away with her. They disappeared. Neither the family nor the police knew where they were. They hid in the house of some friend who was also a lesbian, but we didn't know that for a long time. My father had a heart attack because of this tamasha. I don't want to increase his tensions or his burdens. I was forced into this engagement. I don't want to marry you.' I replied, 'Well, I don't want to marry you either.' Then he unzipped his trousers, put something wet and flabby in my hand. I felt sick and disgusted. I wanted to vomit. I immediately made him drive me home. I kept wondering, is this going to be my future?

On the evening before my marriage my two good friends, the ones I was having simultaneous affairs with, came to spend the night with me in my room. Somehow I managed to satisfy each, without the other knowing—it was no small feat! The next day I went through the marriage ritual. For our honeymoon we went to Kashmir. I was determined to exhaust him, so I kept insisting we go trekking, riding, climbing all day long. Then I pretended I had my period. My hymen was intact until one and a half months after the marriage, which lasted about eight months. Then we separated and had it annulled. Until then, I somehow endured the physical aspect; I would lie on my back with my hands under my head and I would say, okay, do what you want, but don't come near my face, don't try to kiss me . . .

My husband was a playboy, rich and spoiled. I accommodated him so that I could escape into the company of his jet-set friends. I got into the habit of drinking and smoking. When he spent time away from me with these companions, I was very relieved. But internally I was suffering, I knew the marriage was doomed to fail. I used to cut myself with a blade. That was an early symptom of my later self-destructiveness. After the marriage was annulled I went back to college. My new girlfriend and I carved our initials into each other's arms and had them engraved in a gold band. Later I donated the ring to Vaishno Devi. In college I continued drinking, smoking, even gambling. I was quite the hero—all the girls were in love with me. But I was faithful to my lover—she was a teacher there, a little older than me. She was quite conservative; once she found a book on gays among my things, and she was shocked. She wouldn't ever let me go down on her, or experiment sexually . . . I had a brief fling with another woman, and my girlfriend threw a hysterical fit, locked herself into her room and refused to come out. The whole college gathered to watch and offer helpful suggestions while I tried to break the door down after banging on it and begging her to open it, pleading, promising and cajoling. Finally she relented, after hours of high drama. That incident made me realize that one should be careful with other people's emotions.

· After college I went to the US on a year's scholarship. I smoked my first hash there and that's also where I received some detailed sexual education. 'You're a quick learner,' remarked a woman who picked me up one night. She took me home, gave me a smoke, and then was amazed that I was too inhibited to take my clothes off in the presence of a stranger! But that was only the initial phase. I was the talk of the town, the hit of the bar . . . I received offers galore. My friends typed out my papers, fed me and pampered me. I spent the entire year in gay company. When I came back to India I went through severe culture shock, but I was no longer ashamed of using the word 'lesbian' . . .

I joined the civil service. My father was so proud when I passed the entrance exam. I enjoyed the training immensely, I could easily walk six miles, do yoga, play tennis and badminton, and ride—even to this day you have to pass a riding test to qualify as an officer! It's a disaster for most people. The entire town would line the street to witness the humiliation. I smoked hash and drank as much as the men, and I'd still be sober. My male colleagues would say, 'You've made a pass at everyone in the women's block.' I laughed, I didn't care that I was the chief subject of gossip in the academy. No one could fault me on my work, which was outstanding. The male officers would say, 'Why can't you tell your friends to be more like you? They are all so hung up.' I'd answer, 'If they were all like me, you'd really regret it.' And the women officers would say, 'We wish we could be more like you,' and I'd answer, 'If you were like me, the men wouldn't come near you and you wouldn't want that!'

I was assigned to the Jammu and Kashmir cadre and posted in that region. The conditions were tough. The political situation was extremely tense and we were openly accused of being spies and traitors. The locals would address us as 'you Indians', with anger and contempt—our work was always being obstructed. Often we were given no work at all, which was a problem for officers like me who enjoyed being active. I was not surprised at the high incidence of alcoholism and drug addiction in the cadre. I myself got to the point where I could smoke hash around the clock—it cost me Rs 5 per week. My servant obtained it from somewhere and kept it in a special drawer in my dressing table. On a working day I would smoke about fifteen joints, on a holiday about thirty. I could work better, drive better, I was stimulated, energetic. Sexually I got so aroused, I could keep going night and day. All I wanted to do when I was high was to get into bed with somebody. And Kashmir was a wonderful place for seduction: all you had to do was drive five miles from Srinagar to find lakes, forests, mountains, rivers—it was so incredibly beautiful.

Despite these external problems and my need for drugs, my career was going well. I was a very good officer, I worked all the time. I was in a passionate relationship with a very good-looking Sikh woman. The irony was that her mother was half in love with me. She kept giving me long meaningful looks, while my incorrigible father kept making passes at my lover; he would say, jokingly, 'What are you doing with my daughter, come with me and I'll give you a crore right away!' And I would laugh and tell her, 'You should accept, you would at least be comfortably off!' Then things became complicated. My girlfriend had promised to come to Kashmir with me, but she made the mistake of telling her mother about our relationship. She had two hefty gun-toting brothers; one had actually killed somebody, but had been exonerated somehow. The brothers came to know about us from their mother. One night at about 1 a.m. when I was dropping my lover home, these men showed up, pulled the door off my car and hauled their sister out. She fought them and lay down under the car, behind the tyre, while the girlfriend of one of the brothers was going hysterical by the roadside. They yelled to me, 'Drive off now!' I said, 'How can I drive off with her underneath my car?' They threatened, 'If you step out, we'll break your legs!' They dragged their sister out and the girlfriend pushed her into the house. I picked up the door and drove off. I had to spend the next day getting it fixed . . . the whole situation was ugly and absurd, as sudden violence always is. Then my worst fears came true—my lover got married. Her father took off his turban and put it at her feet. He said, 'You're my only daughter, I have to marry you off, there is no choice.' Imagine your father in front of you, weeping and pleading . . . She agreed, for the sake of the family honour.

I was still posted in Kashmir when I met my ex-husband again, at Srinagar airport. I had lost my father that year. My ex-husband, who had remarried, came to offer his condolences. He said, 'I don't bear a grudge against you for leaving me, but I regret that you didn't give me a real chance to be your father's son-in-law.' On hearing this, I softened. We began talking. I said I had left him because I was involved with a woman. He said, 'I assumed you were involved with another man.' I said, 'I'm a lesbian.' He asked, 'Haven't you had sex with a man since our marriage?' I answered, 'Sex with you was awful. After that, why should I go near a man?' He said, 'Give me a chance, you don't know how good it can be.' At first I was adamant in my refusal. But he chased me for months. Wouldn't leave my house, my office. He bribed my servants to let him in. He brought champagne, flowers, begged, ranted . . . He went a little mad in his obsession. He threw out all his wife's photographs and replaced them with mine, in fancy frames, all over his house. He invited people to massive parties so that everyone would see my photos on the walls. Finally I succumbed. I enjoyed it as long as he let me do what I wanted in bed, and dominate. And if he didn't satisfy me, I really let him have it. But I laid down one clear condition. I said, 'When my girlfriends come you'll have to leave, I don't want you hanging around.' He agreed.

My equilibrium started getting shaky. My brother called in a psychiatrist. I was diagnosed as borderline manic-depressive, and was put on lithium. But I soon developed toxicity to the medication. My thyroid and kidneys began malfunctioning. I became really ill. Finally the doctor took me off the medicine. But even in that awful state I did whatever I wanted—some evenings I would drink a whole bottle of wine, even though I knew it would react with the medications. I'd drink till I threw up and passed out, but I couldn't stop myself. When I was manic, I was hyperactive, energetic, gregarious, wilful; when I was depressed, I was the opposite. These mood swings were very self-destructive. I tried to make sense of what was happening to me, the course my life was taking, but I couldn't get a grip on myself.

I got involved in a turbulent relationship for some years, with a married woman. She had two children, her husband was a businessman. She was a clever manipulator but such a charmer, and gorgeous, voluptuous, everything one could wish for in a woman. She lived in another country and I had to make extended trips to spend time with her, but I was so in love I did all of that, at the risk of angering my superiors and jeopardizing my career. I was holding a high-level administrative position, and I wasn't supposed to take off and disappear whenever I felt like it. This lover possessed the kind of sexual magic that allowed her to satisfy her husband, and satisfy me, in the same night, in the same house . . . Later on there were threats and abuses from him, and harsh reprimands and formal warnings from my bosses regarding my unexplained absences. My lover broke off with me, and after a while took up with a close friend—that hurt me terribly, even more than her saying, 'You are boring now' because I had stopped drinking and smoking and being wild. My career took a nosedive. I was not given a posting. I sat at home for seven months; my peon would bring my paycheck to me. I was very frustrated, and emotionally I was a wreck.

Finally a posting did come through—to Ajmer. A

suffocating provincial town. No one to talk to, no gays anywhere that I could see. After the Kashmiri wazwans I found the Rajasthani vegetarian food awful. And I was accustomed to working in English in Kashmir; here, all the work had to be done in Hindi. I couldn't even tell who was the appellant and who was the defendant. I used to fall asleep on the bench, listening to the lawyers droning on and on in Hindi, case after case, day after day . . . I slid further and further into deep depression. I couldn't bring myself to eat. I lived on Limca and Pan Bahar. The one thing I enjoyed was to sit at Chishti's dargah in the evenings and listen to qawwalis. I never asked God for anything, except my ex-lover's happiness . . . After a while I started to fall ill. I was poisoned by the medicine, and my feet were so swollen I couldn't walk. I came to Delhi for treatment, stayed for some months. I tried yoga and meditation and found that they brought me some measure of peace.

But without work, and neglecting myself totally, not eating, not being able to take antidepressants for medical reasons, my emotional condition began to get worse. I kept praying to God to take my life. Then I began to find myself losing control, having tantrums, becoming irrational. I locked myself in my house, yelling, banging the doors, beating on the windows. The servants fled. My family finally realized the seriousness of the situation and the hell I was going through. Twice I tried to commit suicide by slashing my wrists with imported kitchen knives, very sharp. There was blood all over the bed. I had to have twenty-one stitches. Using a dupatta I tried to hang myself from the fan but I failed—either the ceiling was too low or the bed too high. I passed out, and the next day my sister had to break down the door. Once I swallowed a year's supply of sleeping tablets but I didn't become unconscious, I just threw up all over the room. My niece and nephew found me. In an effort to bring me under control, the family had me hospitalized and I was given electric shock therapy, three times, when my fits of violence and fits of despair became dangerous. At one point I was hallucinating, yet I had enough control to drive myself to the hospital and get admitted. They strap you to the bed and give you anaesthesia before administering the shock. I thought I was simply being sedated. I had no idea of what had been done to me till I saw the hospital bill when it came to the house later. I was horrified, and furious with my brother for allowing it, and with everyone else for consenting to it; but it couldn't be reversed, I had to accept the fact that it had happened.

Electric shocks make you lose your memory for a while. After a month or six weeks things start coming back, slowly ... I lived in my brother's house after the treatment. I was like a zombie. Worse, I was put on an experimental new medication that affected my capacity to speak, to move, even to react. I just sat, paralyzed, immobilized. I couldn't recognize anyone. My sister kept her two kids away from me. I couldn't understand why, though I vaguely felt deprived because I am very fond of my nieces and nephews. My sister would put a rolled-up chapati in my hand in an effort to get me to eat, and I would stare at it for two hours. I nearly drove her round the bend. The doctor told the family, 'This is your collective responsibility. Make sure she does not live alone.' Earlier my family had defined my sexuality as an 'illness'. When they came to know I was seeing my ex-husband again, they proclaimed hopefully, 'Now you are cured.' But when I had my breakdowns, they began to understand that gayness was an intrinsic part of my nature, and 'illness' was certainly connected to it, in my case, but was a separate phenomenon rooted in other factors.

It is a very tough project, trying to overcome this level of pain and depression. For months I sat in an empty house, holding imaginary conversations in my head. If I am not capable of an enduring relationship—I don't relate to men, and women have let me down terribly—whom should I turn to?

This question tormented me, as did my memories. But being with my family, being medically monitored, following a routine of yoga and meditation, prayer and natural healing, as well as a regular diet, has helped to bring stability into my life. I want to convert the negative energy of my past into something positive. I spent three years in the safe environs of an ashram, and am now involved in a lot of volunteer work. As part of the process of transcendence, I try to treat everyone equally. Spiritualism has helped me in a way that logical analysis has not. Rational approaches invariably tend to compartmentalize my problems and they keep returning to obsess me. I'm trying to develop a major project for street children in which I will invest my own money and which I will personally administer as social work. I don't want to take orders from anybody. I simply am who I am and I don't pretend to be anything else. Some force is guiding and protecting me, and more than once has saved me from killing myself. I can only say to this divine will, just lead and I will follow.

(*as told to V.S.*)

Glossary

doli – formal departure of the bride with the groom's party after the
    marriage ceremony
dupatta – long scarf
tamasha – upheaval
wazwan – traditional feast

Home

Leaving

A.G.

We strain against each other,
She, trying to thrust me out
Me, stubbornly resisting.
I want to stay with you . . . please.

I don't know the world outside
I can't face it on my own
I'm not yet ready
ready to be born.

Mm, Mm . . . Dhuk, dhuk . . .
Muffled sounds filter through
to relieve the monotony
of her frantic screams and keening.

She is wiser
and bigger and stronger than me —
it's a losing battle —

I'm out!

No wonder I feel like crying.

❦

Memory Feed

Firoza

My grandmother spreads a piece of newspaper on the dining room table. I am sitting across from her with my books. This is my permanent study corner. Often, around ten o'clock or so, grandmother and I find ourselves at the table, she at some task while I am studying. Today she is making her tooth-powder—salt, peppermint oil, clove oil and some kind of chalk powder are sitting in a neat row. Carefully, she pours a few drops of the clove oil onto the powder.

'Why did you give up a man like Rustom? He didn't smoke, drink, gamble. What got into your head?'

I am taken aback. Can it be that she suspects something between you and me?

'Oh, he was a nice man, but he was boring,' I mumble as I bend my head into my books.

'Is that any reason to give up a good man?'

I am twenty-three years old. Right now, only you are in my mind, our daily lunchtime discussions about literature. You and I are both budding poets, inspired to write by our beautiful and brilliant teacher Elena—I have discovered an excitement to life . . . the intellectual horizons that lay hidden before. I think of you now and wonder what I can possibly confess.

'Be serious, think for a minute.'

My gentle, kindly grandmother is really being pushy.

The baby smiles in her sleep. Swish swish the swing goes back and forth. I feel as attached to this child as though she were mine.

Twenty-three years ago we were sleeping on a cane mat on the floor of your aunt's living room in Parel. Just a few months earlier we first experienced the ecstasy of our bodies touching closely, lying side by side, but now the intensity, the hunger was growing.

The baby has your dimples, the shape of your lips. I look at her to check her breathing—again she lifts one corner of her mouth and smiles.

In 1974 we thought we were the only lesbians in the whole of Bombay.

We spent every day together. I'd wait for you in that right-hand corner of the library in our college, the one near the English carrell. We would read together, eat lunch together.

For me, there was an urgency to our daily meetings, as though my life depended on seeing you.

My family never gave a second thought to the fact that I was spending more and more time with you—after all, we were studying together.

Baby opens her eyes, her nap time is over. I want to see some more smiles. My eyes make contact with hers momentarily. Such vulnerability, such precious trust in those big, dark eyes. I feel so much affection rise up in me, but I won't pick her up yet.

I am the aunty, 'masi', for this baby with her shining eyes and her charming toothless smiles. She recognizes me now and calms down easily.

Ironically, we are back to the intimacy we had once shared for fourteen years. While you sit on the bed and pump your milk into plastic bottles, I lie beside you and we chortle over family anecdotes.

> *Sometimes baby Shireen lies between us. Often we spend*
> *all day taking turns with her, feeding, cleaning and calming*
> *her. Should I dare to unravel the complex layers of such ease,*
> *now that you are straight and I am still a lesbian?*

When I was twenty-three and you were twenty-two, we were
scared even to utter the word lesbian. To whom could we say
it? India in 1974 was totally consumed with the dynamics of
social change. We were too concerned with discussions about
Janata Party politics versus Congress politics. As women from
middle-class families, we were sheltered and protected. And
of course our major focus was how we could get a chance to
study in America.

> *The chime is activated by pulling the cat's tongue. 'It's a*
> *Small World' plays, and Baby is distracted.*

In 1988 we traveled around South India, all the way to where
three oceans meet. One evening in Kanyakumari I told you that
if you had a baby, I would stay home and look after it. I was
always one for a domestic life. That was when you dropped
the bombshell. You said: 'Deep down inside I am fairly
conventional. I think I want to marry and then have a child.'
   Stunned, I thought to myself: 'What are we doing locked
in passionate embraces at night, traveling like a couple in India,
if this is your underlying wish?' I was devastated, but I mostly
live in the state of illusion that psychologists term 'denial', so
within a few days I had erased your brutal statement from my
mind. The wonder of discovering rural towns in India took
over. I swaddled myself in a cocoon of contentment, much like
my after-lunch naps on the buses in which we traveled from
Madras to India's southern tip. I am practised in allowing
myself to quickly feel stable in the present, satisfied with little
doses of happiness, believing that the moment will magically
evolve into a bright future. I forgot the few statements you

would make, every now and then, about the changing shape of your desire. After all, we had got back together after your one-year relationship with Julius in Vermont. I thought that our bond was solid as a rock, that it would withstand all storms, that you would seek shelter in my arms no matter which man caught your fancy—*that* would only be a temporary flirtation.

> *Baby's shrill cry penetrates my meandering journey into the past. I must hold her and comfort her. This child is my memory feed.*

When Paul comes home at night, I know I must leave right away. He is the kind of man who is unassuming and quiet and he is very good to me, but when he enters the house, I feel our charmed world is disrupted. Perhaps I am still clinging to the hope of a family—you, me and the baby—a fugitive fantasy which your husband destroys when he arrives to claim his lawful wife and child, without speaking a word.

❧

Mama

Inaiyat Moosa

When I was very small, I had to stand on my toes or pull myself up into a chair to look into women's faces. But that was hard, ya? So I got used to sitting on their laps with my ear to their chests and hearing their voices through their bodies. When they laughed, my body would shake along with them. When they said something quickly or moved suddenly, I would raise my face to get their attention back. Then they'd pat me on the head and pull me back to them.

Then I grew up and women pulled me onto their chests by the collar of my shirt, into their waiting arms. They pulled me deep inside them and I went in as far as they could take me. I tried to get inside women's bodies to hear that sound again. Of a woman's voice coming to me not from her mouth but from her chest to my ear. And when I found I couldn't get that far in, I went down on my knees and tried to do it head first, but their voices were still loud and clear and from far outside me. I urged them, with my mouth between their legs, urged them to give me what I wanted, pleaded with them to show me the voices I knew. But they couldn't understand and heaved me off. They were good women.

When I pass by you with my ears up waiting to hear my name, I am praying once again for that same voice. I want to hear it through your chest, with your arms tight around me, shutting off all other sound.

Every time the urge fills me, I stop myself from writing your name. And that's what hurts. That it is forbidden, that it is unthinkable and unspeakable, yet I think and I speak. I am so afraid that one day someone will come to know about us and you will be hurt for life. I must stop right now, I know that. I must not be selfish any more. If I love you, I have to prove it by letting go.

And I will learn to respect you and your life—though I wish very much that it could have been different, I must wish just as much for this to end. It will be my gift to you. Since we cannot have each other for that purest of loves—mother and child.

The roads we follow can never meet. It would make you bleed to run from the road that is your life and catch hold of me as if I were your own, your blood son, your blood daughter.

I am worth millions in my world and nothing in yours. Yours, the world I left behind. To even want to see me smile will be death for you and death for me.

We could never recover from the purest form of love, you and I.

❦

One and One Is Three

Radhika

I never felt 'different' when I was small, even though I was a tomboy and most of my friends were boys. It was when I went to a Catholic boarding school for girls that I began to realize that I could have crushes on other girls, and eventually I fell in love with one. It was mutual—we were thirteen or fourteen—and that's when I realized I was gay. I didn't even know what it meant then. Though I did know it wasn't the done thing, and that it had to be hidden—we could have been expelled if we had been found out. But the sharing of beds was very secret, done at odd hours of the night. It was frightening as well as exciting, because the nun on our floor was a holy terror. My girlfriend and I were together till I was sixteen. It ended because we each moved to a different city after we left school. I've met her on a number of occasions after that, but I've never had the courage to refer to what had happened between us. She did the traditional thing—the straight number—and had an unhappy marriage, like mine.

After school, I fell in love with my best friend's brother—and that was mutual, too. He was older than me—at seventeen, it was a hell of a romance. After I was married I managed to suppress being gay for a few years. And the sad thing was, I was never able to discuss it with my husband. If I had been able to, things might have been different for us. Then when I finally did tell him—while we were still married—I was so relieved. I told him I felt guilty that because I was gay, our marriage wasn't working out. He was a bit of a bastard about it . . . you get it off your chest but later on it gets thrown back at you.

Of course, I had realized much earlier that this was not the way I was meant to be, living with a man, but I did want to have kids and that seemed to be the only way to do it. But he couldn't produce kids! So there were even deeper pressures on our marriage than just my being gay.

The other thing that used to irritate me about marriage was the double standard. There's one set of rules for men and one set of rules for women. He was far more free to screw around, but every time I said to myself, 'Hey, I want some of that too,' it was not available to me. There was a period of a whole year during which my husband was not around. Only then did I have my first affair. And I wasn't carrying on with women, I was seeking out men.

By then the marriage was already breaking up. So he left and I didn't divorce him for almost six years after the separation.

That was when I knew that what I wanted was to have an affair with another woman. But I couldn't find one, and I had been depressed for so long, it terrified me even to think about intimacy. Finally, it happened—I had affairs with women, one after the other, all of them unsatisfactory. As if I was searching too hard for something when I didn't even know what I was looking for.

Then I fell in love. She was also single and very maternal and much like a wife. I think that's what I wanted at that point. We decided to adopt a baby. I had made up my mind anyway that I wanted to have a child, but I had never thought about adopting. But I didn't want to go through natural childbirth by myself either. The men that I had spoken to about it already had kids, and they all said, 'Don't trick me into anything.' And I didn't think marriage was worth it a second time around. She pressured me, for her own needs as much as anything else. She wanted to have a kid too but she didn't have such a well-paying job, or the kind of prospects that adoption agencies insist upon. You have to give an undertaking that the kid will always be looked after financially. But she did give me wholehearted support. I didn't know very much about bringing up kids since I was an only child, but she knew. I learnt very fast over the first few months. I wouldn't have had any idea what to do without her.

We didn't enter into any verbal agreement or contract with respect to the kid since our life together was going well. She didn't ask for assurances from me, so when we did break up it was quite a blow to her. She said, 'I want my half of the kid.' I said, 'On what basis can you have him? Legally, I am the mother.' So she did the next best thing—she went around telling the world that I was a lesbian. She was such a quiet, unassuming person that I never guessed she had this streak of viciousness. But anyway, I realized that she was quite serious about the kid, and that all she really wanted to do was to spend a little time with him. Now we've organized it so that she has weekly visitation rights.

He's grown up to be a very smart kid—he's gone from one school to another without help from anyone. The nursery school he goes to now is the same one I went to. It was started by two women who were living together—are still living together, after so many years. Nobody says they are dykes. So two women *can* actually live with each other in our society without people assuming that they are gay.

But my son is soon going to see that his mother doesn't have a man around, and then he will also begin to notice that there are other women. I've figured out that honesty is generally the best policy. Now if you ever meet my son, he's going to ask you why you look like a boy. At five and a half, he doesn't know about sex, but he knows the difference between boys and girls—boys have short hair! I have to ask myself how I will handle his questions. Part of bringing him into my life involves being responsible for educating him about all these things from a very young age. I'll have to teach him not to grow up homophobic.

My life is much more complicated, now that I have my son. Even if I tell society to fuck off, the crap is going to come back at me through that little door. I'd like to meet other lesbians who've brought up kids. You never know what to expect, how to do it. It might even mean giving up my sexuality for his sake—not having another lesbian affair.

That's why I think courage is such a prerequisite for this game. Of course you question whether you're doing the right thing, how you're going to explain it to people who matter to you, what their reactions are going to be. But I've got my own home, my own life. I have no brothers and sisters, so I don't know who'll take care of my kid if something happens to me. But I'm not pessimistic. I want to tell you that you can be lesbian, you can be independent, you can have babies and families and extended families, and not be ostracized.

I'm at peace with myself now. Earlier, I was going in many different directions. Recently I lost a lover because of her fear of public opinion—she didn't want it to be known that she was a lesbian. She gave me lots of reasons why two women can't ever live together: there's no security, no legal status to the relationship. 'What will happen if you throw me out or we break up; how do we start dividing? I am not saying that it will happen, but reassure me.'

How can you reassure someone about what the future might bring?

From my experience, I would like to suggest some rules and regulations that might save other couples similar heartache. Think about making a contract to cover the logistics of moving in together, the apartment, the kids. Come to an understanding about what you will share, what you wish to keep, what you are willing to give up if you separate. And write out an informal memorandum to that effect.

I'm constantly told by other people how difficult, how impossible, it is to sustain a lesbian relationship in the society we live in. But what is the alternative? Will you say, 'Okay, I don't want to be a lesbian anymore,' and get married and lead a straight life?

(*as told to L.A.E.*)

❦

Wifey

A.G.

As he leaves
for another day's work
I close the door
and shut me in.
A perfect wife

— grace under pressure
content in her confines
(as is evident from the laugh lines
— little fissures on her face).

Arranged marriage
a meeting of minds
(with compatible bank balances).
So neatly wrapped up
in the perfect nuptial knot,
there is no escape.

No place
for even a hint of disgrace.
Doomed like Anarkali,
fated like Danae
in my bridal bower
of engagement-ring diamonds.
A masonic work of art!

The wedding band plays phantom tunes
on and on, around my finger.
Its vein to my heart . . .
Is it my own life that I hear
throbbing?

Like mother, like mother,
like mother, like . . .
No question of dislike.
Unlike daughter . . .
Like Mother whom Daddy set free.

Leave home, to work.
Carrying his name,

his smell, his child.
Secure on the leash
of his old-boys' network.

I grow tired of his face,
our bodies, a woman's place.

I am shushed and hushed and calmed.
I see red—no—a vermilion gash
stretches across my head.
I can't breathe, I can't think.
I straddle the fence of indecision,
cowardly, swaying on the brink.
He snores. On my side of the bed.

❧❧

Mouth to Mouth

Archana Pattanaik

I am a housewife with two children. I have no way to travel
outside Orissa—unlike all of you in Bombay, Delhi, Calcutta,
my time and position in life are not so free. I have my own
work; I have my family. So what can I do for the lesbian cause?

This is what I know: how to maintain your body naturally,
how to make eastern food from Orissa, how to sew dresses for
female children, roof gardening.

This is what I can share: I will write all about erotic
cookery, specially for women who love women.

To sweeten women's juices and make them flow:

Take one glass of cow's milk, very fresh. Cook it in an aluminium pan, cool it and add some ground cashew nuts. Keep the full glass aside for two to three hours. Both women should drink it. Take it every week, not only before lovemaking.

To give women a good mood and to refresh the private parts:

Take small sardine fish, one inch in size, about 1 kg. Wash carefully and clean. Mix with a little turmeric, a little salt, and 200g of mustard oil.

Get a piece of manja (the middle part of the banana tree, a white solid roll, one foot long), and cut into very small pieces.

Now you take eight and eight banana leaves, and divide up the materials in between the leaves and bind into packets with twine. You put the packets into red-hot coals, and after one hour, take out and eat. This is a perfect food for women who enjoy women.

Make it in your garden and play there also.

For a moist womanly mouth during the enjoyment of kissing:

Roast a handful of sesame seeds for about five minutes, and grind. Mix with crushed cardamom, black pepper and cinnamon. Add some sweet jaggery and make into small balls.

(*partly in Oriya; translated by O.P.*)

❀

Coming Home after Tuition

Balarama Bai

She wore sad shoes the colour of ripe figs.
The wind was a whistling schoolboy
picking up and dropping trash,
running along the street
on his way home.

We had walked this way before
hand in hand
side by side.

Today she turned her back
to my bedroom door,
my eyes on level
with greasy belly button,
winking open and closed
as her stomach heaved thrills
under sari gauze.

Cheap Aunty, exchanging one rose
for the sweetly overlapped petals
between my thighs.
As she gobbled me
I saw my hands
grip thorns and force
her rose to blooming.
My frightful fingers
twisting it out of bud.

She touched me—
Then, when my bony chest dreamed of breasts.
Here, where I carry the memory of dreams.

You cannot twitch nipples
which are still asleep
under the skin, cannot
pluck full breasts
from a childish body.
It took her hours to notice,
before she laughed
and went away.

Left me heavy
with the grief of anger,
the anger of guilt,
the guilt
of a pleasure-seed planted.
Years before her dried pig-shit
flaked away.

❦

A Memory

Maya Sharma

Was it at a wedding one summer
Or was it winter?
Which one of the seasons

Or what the occasion exactly was
Is hard to tell now.
At home in the family
I remember a waking,
Under the dead weight of a faceless hand
Pushing, pressing, petting, preying
Down upon the centre of my being.
I remember, but of course I remember . . . member
A rash of memory breaking out
Against a voice inside me, denying me
Telling him I want to p . . .
And then just like this
It comes back, the squatting
Searing wait of a forced pee.
Anything something anything
To get away and reach my mother
Lost—simply dropping to sleep.

Drops of memory
Congealed on cement floor
Have no name, face or place
But a history like everyday.
Riding the back of a breath
It comes,
Seeping suddenly without warning
A strange familiar suffocation
Of sightless eyes tracing finger marks
In the colour of the light.
Refracting sensations all the way
Through the folded dress of childhood.
Layer by layer
Day by day
Guilt like a crease within a crease.
Difficult to tell apart

The fault of the woman from the earth.
That family gathering
Could have been a funeral.

(*with thanks to the Writing Retreat at Norcroft, Minnesota*)

❦

The Letter

Kanchana Natarajan

The bell rings, and my son immediately rushes to the door.

'Amma! Oi Amma! a letter for you . . . a registered post for you,' shrieks the surprised boy.

'For me?' I swallow hard and walk blindly in the direction of the door. It is not easy to believe that the postman has brought a letter for me—addressed only to me. Once in a while a wedding invitation does arrive by post. It is meant for the husband, but since convention demands that it be addressed to the couple, a cursory 'Shrimati', followed by his full name, Varadarajan, is embossed on the envelope.

Who can this person be, who gives me so much importance?

I sign the postman's receipt pad. I go hastily into the kitchen and dry my wet hands in the fold of my sari before I inspect the sender's name . . . one A. K. Amba from far-off Delhi! 'Who is this?' I mutter to myself, and tear open the envelope to find a brief, neat handwritten letter.

As I read it, I have to squat on the floor to allow my surging feelings to calm down. After fifteen years . . . or fifteen hundred years . . . I am hearing from Apeeta . . . my Apeeta. I can still taste the sweetness of that name in my mouth, Apeeta whom I loved so much . . . To erase her from my memory, they drugged and hospitalized me for two long years . . . How strange! Despite all those electric shocks they could not blot her out from my mind!

How many times have I re-read the letter? Apeeta has promised me a new life.

Holding the letter tight, I weep inconsolably in my mind, something that I have learnt to do well. How could I have spent these fifteen long years living like a wooden doll? All the tightly corked emotions well up. But this is not the time to succumb. I need to act. A reply will have to be sent immediately or I may miss the chance of meeting Apeeta again. I hide the letter near the hip knot of my petticoat hoping that my son will forget to mention the arrival of a registered letter to his father. He just might overlook it, finding it irrelevant in his scheme of things.

I pull out some of the money that is kept in the little tin box near the Ganesa on the kitchen altar. I mutter a small prayer to Him to ward off the obstacles that may stand between Apeeta and me this time, and hasten in the direction of the post office. Halfway there, I realise that I am walking without chappals—the tar on the road has melted and is sticking to my feet. All I know at this point is that I have to send a telegram to Apeeta expressing my willingness to start life afresh with her in Delhi. I dash back home with the same speed. The post office is perhaps half a kilometre from the house, and I can see my son standing at the doorway blocking my entry. I look at him, and wonder why he has to be so much like his father.

'Where did you run to like a mad woman, leaving the house wide open?' he demands. I do not reply. I push past him. I have more worthwhile things to do now than answer him.

'Have you gone deaf or crazy? Let Appa come and I will tell him about this!' my son shouts as he follows me suspiciously around the house.

Still impassioned by the letter, next to the hidden surface of my skin under the folds of my sari, I tell him with an air of indifference: 'Listen, I care neither for your Appa nor for you . . . you and your Appa are the malevolent Saturns in my life. Stop screaming like this.'

I see shock on his face. In all these years, he has never heard his mother raise her voice. Anybody could spit in her face and she would remain silent. Today, he has been rudely shaken.

Since I am going to move away from this wretched household, I decide I can afford to say what I truly feel.

I am triumphant even at the thought that I will be deceiving them, and that it is my turn to take revenge. I know I have a sinister smile on my face. I walk into the kitchen and open the windows to allow the light and air in. I lie down with my head on the raised threshold. This has always been my place of rest, from after lunch until coffee time.

'Give me food! I have to go out!' the boy yells again.

'The food is ready, go, feed yourself! I am tired of cooking and serving you and your Appa, do you understand?'

His face is red with rage. 'I am going to telephone Appa! You have gone mad again. You ought to be taken back to the hospital!'

I jump up as though stung by a wasp. The mental hospital again! The torture of those excruciating shocks . . . and these threats from this boy who can not know what it is to receive such treatment week after week for two long years.

'I must not spoil my chances,' I warn myself. 'Am I not clever enough to get what I have been desiring all my life? Let me again become the wooden doll.'

I immediately change my tone. 'Son, you see . . . I have this very bad headache. Please leave me alone. I had only gone to the chemist to get some Anacin tablets. You don't have to tell your Appa about this . . . ' I pretend to plead with him.

At once he feels victorious. I hear the loud bang of the door. He will not go hungry—this is a good pretext for him to eat outside. 'Well, it's his father's money . . . let him squander it,' I muse aloud.

The house falls silent save for the sparrows' chirping. I need my kitchen door-sill, to lie down and be with myself, to feast on my suspended excitement and to think of my past . . . of those days with Apeeta.

Some seventeen years back when I was still young and fresh, my hair neither grey nor short, I met Apeeta in a small dingy room.

The house was huge, with eight tenants, all of whom were Brahmins—the owner would make no compromise about that. Each family had one room and a very spacious kitchen, which also served as a dining room. In the centre of the house was a circular cemented well. Men bathed in the open courtyard near the well, the women in the small makeshift bathroom that did not have a door. They would hang a sari as a curtain whenever they were inside. Some of the younger women either bathed before sunrise or after the men had left for their offices. There was a huge stone in one corner of the courtyard, used for grinding rice and lentils for idli or dosai. Women congregated in the courtyard for washing and grinding, and for animated discussions on forthcoming marriages, vratams, festivals and the annual sraddha ceremonies.

How could I ever forget that small room meant for the menstruating women of the house? It was situated at the very entrance, so that they would not go further in and pollute the entire household. This room had a small wooden door and a worthless zero-watt bulb. The bleeding women occupied this dark, airless room for three nights and days, and had to circumambulate the big house and go by the cowshed to use a small, never-washed toilet. The tiny room always had an occupant—sometimes two or even more. The women all kept track of each other's periods meticulously.

Unexpectedly one hot afternoon, Apeeta walked into the room with a look of uncertainty. The prospect of having someone to talk to during those three days made me welcome her. She had recently moved into the house with her husband and a seven-year-old daughter, causing quite a stir amongst the women. The first time I saw her I stood transfixed, delighting in her dark, soft, silken skin. Her eyes were expressive and her large forehead indicated astuteness. When she walked I could hardly take my eyes off her seductive gait. A long, neat plait of hair would sway and swing as she walked, touching her waist. She had a string of malli flowers tucked into her hair, and her brightly-coloured sari enhanced her glow.

This was her first visit to the room.

I raised my eyes to say something but felt silenced by her earthy presence. 'Is she the dark goddess Uma?' I wondered to myself, staring at her. She did have the name of the goddess—Apeetakuchaamba. I had heard her husband call her Apeeta.

Early in the evening, while we were still engaged in the conventional exchanges about children, husbands and other such matters, Apeeta's little daughter came hopping near the room, bringing with her a neat bundle containing the things her mother required for those three days—old rags, a few tattered magazines and a small brass box that held betel leaves, lime and cracked betel nuts. Apeeta instructed the girl about the food that had to be prepared for the night. So the child was already trained to do a bit of cooking! My ever-demanding son was the same age as Apeeta's daughter, but with so much pampering from the father and the grand-aunt, he was already a good-for-nothing boy. *Maybe I should try and have another child . . . this time preferably a girl . . . I will teach her music and groom her to be a grand singer like M.S. Subbulakshmi.*

Quickly I shrugged off my fantasy and resumed my conversation with Apeeta. Having nothing in particular to talk about, I asked her how she coped with three days of isolation.

Immediately she said, 'Actually, I feel relieved. I don't mind being out at all. I need a change from that kitchen and the house. Let him know what it is to sweat and worry with salt and tamarind day after day.'

What an answer. I had heard other women grumble about the hardships their husbands faced when they were out. Some even considered it a real curse to be sitting out like this during their periods!

Apeeta looked directly into my eyes and whispered: 'Also, you see, he cannot chase me or trouble me during these days.'

'Who?'

'My husband, of course.'

How can a wife say this! Indeed, a good wife should not even think in this manner. Does she not know that?

But I was also puzzled. Ever since Apeeta had moved into the room next to ours, I had been watching her from my kitchen window while cooking and performing other chores at various hours of the day. I had thought that she served her husband most sincerely. When he arrived from work in the evenings, she welcomed him with hot filter coffee frothing in the big silver tumbler which, I presumed, she must have received from her mother as part of her dowry. After sunset she would light the lamp near the framed calendar pictures of gods and goddesses while her daughter would settle down with her homework.

The husband would sit in an easy chair with the morning

newspaper and Apeeta would lean against the pillar staring into space. At this, I knew that it was time for me to shut the kitchen window and go into the big room to wait for my husband's return from work.

'Why are you quiet? Did I say something absurd?' Apeeta asked falteringly.

'Oh no ... not that ... I just thought that you were happy with your family . . . I mean your husband and all that,' I blurted out.

She remained silent for a while, gazing at me a bit uncertainly. Each time she said something, she would pause to look into my face and note its changing expressions.

'Have you ever been to a circus?'

I was amused at her question. 'Yes ... but only as a child.'

'Do you remember the animals, doomed to their cages for the rest of their lives? Imagine losing the freedom to roam in the forest, and hunt and sleep at will, to the greedy men who trap them and push them into those small cages for human profit and pleasure!'

'Listen ... what do you mean by all this?' I quickly asked.

'I feel trapped in just that way . . . and . . . I pretend everything is fine because I can see that nothing can be changed.'

She said this as though struck by great tragedy. Listening to her was as exciting as biting into a green chili, sliced and seasoned, in curd rice ... with the thrill that comes from letting hot saliva flow freely into the mouth. Afflicted by the sting, swearing never to bite into a chili again ... but after a while craving it once more.

'We cannot say such things against our husbands. What would we be without them? They go out, toil and earn for us and for our children. Sitting at home and eating their hard-earned money, we cannot say such things.'

I was repeating everything that my husband had drilled

into me. According to him, as my god and saviour he alone could put some sense in my 'log-like brains'. But for him, I would have been a patta maram—a bare and barren tree like that one across from the house.

He would hit me occasionally to reduce the corpulence that causes stubbornness and sloth. 'How can a man tolerate disobedience?' he often growled, adding that a disobedient wife would never be forgiven by the gods. By hitting me he was only helping me to earn some merit for the lives to come.

But why should he beat me up? I am not a mule or a ploughing bull. However, does he not lovingly whisper into my ears, 'the hands that beateth alone embraceth', in the silence of the night when he wants to feel the warmth of my breasts and body? Am I angry with him? I cannot be. He is my Purusan.

But it had long been my secret wish to beat him up just once with the big bamboo stick with which I draped his washed garments onto the clothesline tied along the length of the kitchen ceiling.

I realised that I was cherishing improper thoughts. I would have to be stern with Apeeta, her company was slyly affecting me. As someone older than her, maybe I should even counsel her. And what if other women who were walking in and out of the house overheard her inappropriate remarks?

But in my heart of hearts I could only marvel at her words about the circus animals. Maybe she had been to a good school. Even while I was chiding her, I knew that I was attentive and alive to all that she chose to say. Had I not felt the same way?

Instinctively I took hold of her palm and whispered in a low tone, 'Apeeta, that is fine, but speak softly. I am worried that others might hear you talk and spread wrong tales to your husband.'

I saw tears well up in her large eyes. Was she crying? Had she had a fight with her husband that morning?

Do I console her or ignore her? She will calm down on her own.

I should let her be.

After a while I told her, 'You are tired, lie down and sleep for a while. This is how life is for a woman. What can be done now!'

Apeeta reminded me of a drowning man seeking help and refuge in the waters.

Shall I dry her hot tears with the edge of my sari?

A mysterious passion raised its hood within me, like a black cobra that I had once seen in the fields of my natal village. It had never stirred for anyone, much less another woman. I felt a great compulsion to calm her by caressing her silky skin. I knew then that I had to clear my mind.

I felt slightly relieved to see Apeeta preparing to lie down to take a nap. She must have chewed betel leaves after her morning food; her lips looked red. In the corner of the room there was a dirty pillow with a plastic cover, used by all the occupants. I took the smelly pillow, covered it with a piece of cloth and gave it to Apeeta. She lay quietly with her eyes closed. I tried to browse through an old magazine but my eyes kept drifting towards Apeeta, so close to me. The room was sultry and she was sweating. I tried to fan her with the magazine, slowly and carefully so that the rustling of the paper would not disturb her. Her skin shone like black satin in the dim light. The strange urge just to touch her arms, and the little soft portion of her ankles that was visible, became intense.

I was brought back to the world of men and other matters with a big jolt as I heard the husbands of the house returning from work, talking to one another. As usual they were discussing something in loud unconcerned voices. I did not bother to listen, it never interested me. I was only worried that Apeeta's sleep would be disturbed.

It was now totally dark. I got up to switch on the zero-watt bulb to repel the sinister-looking scorpions that would occasionally come out during these hours. Of course, one was never sure whether the bulb benefited the women or the scorpions. Men of that big household, however, thought that such a good-for-nothing bulb was enough, as none of us was preparing for an IAS examination! I resumed fanning Apeeta. She was fast asleep.

'Amma, Amma, food for you!' announced Apeeta's little daughter. She was carrying an old aluminium plate which contained rice and some salt. She pushed the plate in the direction of her mother with precision, and poured watery buttermilk on the rice from high up, careful all the while not to touch the plate.

Apeeta was in deep slumber, but in a minute she had regained her normal self. She pulled the plate closer and started gulping the food in great haste. She must have been very hungry to have eaten that insipid food with so much relish.

By the time my meal came I was famished and ate all that I was given in one go. I knew it was quite late, for the entire household was silent and settled. The small shop across the road pulled down its shutters with a bang. Apeeta was once again ready to sleep, even though she looked rested enough. In any case, there was nothing else to do.

Being so close to her in that room once more aroused and intensified the peculiar blaze leaping in my heart. I had been a regular visitor to this room for quite a few years, and yet this was the first time I had found myself swayed by such feeling . . . wanting to caress a woman. I had touched women before without giving it a second thought. But I yearned to discover Apeeta's body, just as my husband had wanted to discover mine in the early enthusiasm of marriage. I looked at her the way heroes looked at heroines in the film talkies that I had avidly watched.

How would her skin feel? Maybe like the satin cloth that the saibu brings for sale during festival days. What would she think if I were to touch her brown and full lips with my index finger?

Am I deceiving the man who tied the tali around my neck, making me his possession for this life? The husband should not be wronged, truly he is the living god. Moreover, husbands are almost omniscient and they know how to extract secrets from their wives.

Fear gripped me as I begin to worry about my husband finding out about these strange passionate feelings. Was I losing my chastity? I tried to seize each thought. The older women of this large household, constantly preoccupied with deciding and declaring what was or was not the correct attitude and behaviour of a chaste woman, had never even whispered about the possibility of a woman feeling this way for another woman.

I inhaled the fragrance of the malli fading in Apeeta's hair. It was completely dark now, in keeping with the landlord's instructions that no lights should be on after ten at night. I slowly picked up the courage to lie down next to her. Glass bangles jingled as she tossed and turned. I slowly and timidly entwined my arm around her slender. waist and whispered, 'You are indeed beautiful!' I saw her eyes open wide, those sparkling eyes sharply lined with kohl.

'What did you say?' she muttered as though in a stupor.

'Oh . . . nothing,' I replied, my hands sliding uncertainly across her back.

I wondered why she did not resist my breath so close to her face . . .

I was awakened in the early hours of the morning by the milkman's call and the sound of the bells tied around the necks of the cows. Apeeta lay next to me. I embraced her once more before I got up. I touched the tali around my neck and felt secure. With some bashfulness I recalled how we had exchanged our talis in the still and dark moments of the night.

A night as passionate as the two that followed.

Thoughts of Apeeta lingered like the wonderful aroma of the morning coffee I was preparing in the kitchen. I was thinking of her all the while that I was engaged in household chores.

Apeeta started coming often to my house, and would sit for a long time talking about various things and entertaining me with stories of the neighbourhood. She helped me with the grinding, and sometimes even with sweeping the floor. We sat together and designed new kolams and recipes for the kitchen. She became a part of my life. The old aunt did not like us being together, but tolerated it. This did not bother me much.

Those two years were spent in great joy. We were always meeting one another on some pretext or the other. The kitchen was a safe place—men would not enter it unless they were hungry, and the grand-aunt always sat in the front room reading her Ramayana. Apeeta would come to help me with my work as soon as her husband had left for office and her daughter for school. By this, she contrived a way for us to be together. We would go out in the evenings to the nearby temple, where we sat by the tank holding hands and staring at the pond. The minutes passed, and it would be time to part, to go to our own houses, light lamps near the altar and wait for the men to come home. Each day we suffered silent anguish as we anticipated their arrival.

Gradually the attention of the other women began to shift in our direction. They could not understand what was happening. They asked me, puzzled, 'Why is Apeeta always in your house?' I replied casually, 'She is trying to learn some embroidery patterns and stitching.'

The women of the house also tried to talk to Apeeta's child to find out what her mother and I were doing, always in the kitchen. She would answer, 'Why don't you ask Amma!' and run off. The women approached the grand-aunt with the same question. 'What do I know?' she snarled. 'Does this even look like a house? People walking in and out all the time whenever they feel like! All the money is eaten by these people. Is this a guest house? Who pays heed to me, a helpless old woman?'

Both Apeeta and I ignored everything till we realized that the news had reached the ears of the two men concerned. We ensured that we were back in our houses when the husbands returned from work; we served them coffee in the evening, dinner at night and fresh food in the morning in the manner of dutiful wives. However, my husband could never understand why I did not let him come near me. We all lived in one room, so he could not force me to satisfy his lust. That filled him with anger, but he did not connect my resistance with Apeeta's constant company. Like the other curious tenants, he must have thought, 'After all, what can two women do?'

Months passed thus, and then one morning Apeeta arrived, distraught, after her chores. Her eyes were red, as if she had not slept the entire night. I took her to a corner of the kitchen and asked her what was wrong. She wept then, her tears flowing in streams.

'How long is this hell going to continue!' she whispered fiercely. 'I want to leave everything and be only with you. I can't play this double game. Let us do something!' I held her as she sobbed. 'Last night he just fell on me like an animal. I tried to get free, but I could not.' I noticed that her lips were cut, her flawless shoulders bruised. 'I cannot live there any more; can I come and live with you?' she begged.

My heart was pounding. How much I wanted her to be with me night and day! But how would I manage it? Why couldn't we two be together and leave those two men to manage their own lives?

My house was small, but I thought I could accommodate her. The father of my son could sleep in the open verandah where all the older men slept on summer nights. This could be an immediate temporary arrangement. But what about the other women? Would they realize what was happening? Had they not already detected what was in our eyes when we gazed at each other? Had they not seen our tears, heard our passionate whispers as we waited for our men to come home in the evening?

I agreed to Apeeta's moving into my house. I did not ask what she had told her husband. She would go to her house to cook and finish her chores, and would come away when her husband left for work. I felt the tension building daily, but I also felt that as long as she was with me I could meet all challenges. My son hated the sight of her; he sulked and malingered. His father came and went grimly, on the verge of exploding with rage. The old aunt went around grumbling viciously about the peace of the house being destroyed. Apeeta's child sensed all the hostility, but she played in the compound as if she did not have a care in the world. Somehow we continued to live this way, aware that we were offering the other households a feast of material to gossip about for years to come.

After a week, the curious women of the clan had started to murmur that I was practising black magic and had bewitched Apeeta completely, compelling her to come to me and finish all my chores. 'Only black magic can make a woman forget her house and her husband!' The agitated tongues hissed like snakes. When they spat the accusations in my face, I laughed. I was not even tempted to dispute their idiocy. But perhaps I should not have underestimated the power of collective malice.

One day I whispered to Apeeta—we could only whisper, because of the ears itching for further evidence of our 'crime'—that perhaps she should reconsider her decision and go back to her house, otherwise both of us might break down under the strain. We were a hair's breadth from collapse.

Apeeta cried, 'No! I will not got back there at night to sleep!'

I did not have the heart to insist.

As I had expected, Apeeta's parents were summoned once the frenzied arguments with her husband had gone beyond what he considered normal limits. The old couple arrived early one morning. Apeeta became very flustered, but I held her hands and told her not to worry. 'Just pretend that everything is all right for as long as your mother and father are here.'

She went into her own house. The rest of the household did not know that her parents had been specially called to convince her to return to her husband. He wanted the issue, whatever his concept of it was, to be settled through her parents' mediation, instead of through daily harangues with his wife, or a public scene that would violate his rigid sense of masculine privilege and pride. I wondered how he had phrased his wife's 'problem' in the letter to her parents.

Hours ticked by. I finished my evening chores. I could not bear the emptiness, I did not know what to do with myself. The wait was unendurable. I could not eat. The grand-aunt still hobbled around muttering, but she was clearly relieved that Apeeta was not there. I sat down to eat, but got up without having swallowed a morsel. I went to the well as if to draw water. Apeeta's door was closed. What was happening within? I knew she would not deny the accusations, if they were made.

I went inside, picked up a magazine, but could not concentrate on a single word. What were her parents asking her? What answers was she giving them? Would the old couple notice the change in the tali? It had been designed for her by her mother, who would surely spot the difference. Perhaps Apeeta had covered it with her sari.

She had only been gone for a few hours, but I just could

not cope with the separation. Could we not have gone away together—somewhere far away—and lived like a normal married couple? We could have found some work, what would have prevented us from doing this? Boys and girls eloped—why was it a crime for two women to do the same? As long as we were together, who could possibly harm us?

The hours dragged on and my torment intensified. I wanted to cry but I did not allow myself tears, because I looked on them as a sign of weakness. I was sitting in the dark kitchen, alone, when Apeeta's little daughter suddenly ran in, stumbling over utensils as she gasped out that her mother was crying bitterly, and that her father and grandparents were all shouting at her. I took the child in my arms, soothing her.

'When you go back,' I said, 'tell your mother that she should not worry, I am always with her.'

That whole evening and night there was no further sign of Apeeta or the child. I did not light the lamp in the corner where God was worshipped, till the grand-aunt viciously reminded me to do so. Then I got up slowly and began finishing my chores. My whole being cried out for the sight of my lover. She was just a few steps from where I stood. But the whole world stood in between.

Moving from room to empty room, I felt my anger grow. It was time for the husband to come. Why did he have to come at all?

I had still not oiled or combed my hair, or even removed yesterday's withered flowers. Apeeta and I used to comb each other's long thick hair and braid our glossy plaits with fragrant malli and bright kanakambaram each afternoon. At three o'clock the flower woman would come with a huge basket and we bought flowers from her together, as a ritual. We sat and strung thick garlands to adorn the picture of the Goddess, to pin in Apeeta's little girl's hair, and to decorate our own. Today the flower woman was surprised to find me alone. She asked for Apeeta, knowing that she could not resist flowers. I told her to return the next day. I did not feel like undoing my plait and dragging a comb through my hair. And I did not want to pull out the flowers Apeeta had woven into it the previous day. I combed the front of my scalp with a few dead strokes.

The father of my son arrived. He looked inside the kitchen, surprised. 'So you are alone today?' he asked venomously. I longed to slap his sneering face. But how could I? Only men were allowed to be violent.

Biting back my rage, I silently brought him some coffee and went into the house.

The whole of the next day passed, and there was no sign of Apeeta. It was intolerable. I had been drinking a lot of coffee and was feeling nauseous. In the evening the grand-aunt described Apeeta's parents' visit to the father of my son, with spiteful relish. He sipped his coffee, adding, 'I hope they, at least, are able to put some sense into her head. What kind of stupid irresponsible woman is she, neglecting her husband and child!' I took his empty cup away, wishing savagely that I could vomit on his face. But I remained silent.

The following afternoon I drank a bowl of buttermilk with a few grains of rice in it. At about four o'clock Apeeta's little girl came to the kitchen and blurted out, 'Amma will meet you in the temple near the tank at five o'clock,' before scampering away.

I held my breath, feeling as if my heart would burst. Oh God, at last I would be able to see her! My body burned as if I had a high fever. I could not contain myself. I went from room to room, to the well and back, in and out of the kitchen like someone who had lost her way. I washed my face, combed my hair and put on a fresh sari. After half an hour I told the grand-aunt I had to go out, and did not wait for her permission. I knew the child would inform Apeeta that I had already left.

The throb of my pounding heart filled my ears.

Is this what is called love, waiting interminably for the desired one to arrive? The sweetness of conspiracy, the thrill that comes from a secret meeting?

I did not even go inside the temple—I sat on the steps of the pond and waited. Within a few minutes I saw Apeeta walking towards me with a small basket of offerings in her hand. I could not control myself. I rushed forward and embraced her. In silence we stood there, unable to break away, unaware of how many minutes passed. Our yearning dissolved time and space. We were everywhere and nowhere, within our bodies and outside of them. The heavy footsteps of a man passing nearby hauled us back into the world. We sat down on the steps, our skins touching. We were quiet for a long time. I held her hand. Her softness, her sparsha, which I had so missed . . . I gripped her wrist as if she was about to run away. Slowly I looked into her haggard, exhausted face and reddened eyes. She lifted my hand to her trembling lips and kissed it.

Suddenly I felt very hungry. I went to the counter and bought two packets of special prasadams. We devoured them like starving people. Then Apeeta began to talk. She described her husband's complaints, her parents' angry advice and the innumerable threats. All through the assault, she had fixed her mind on the image of me and had not allowed a single word to get into her head, scheming instead how to meet me. Her parents were leaving the next morning. Till then she would remain obediently inside her house; after they had gone she would move back in with me. I nodded, weak with relief. We sat quietly until night fell, holding hands. She left before I did, promising to return to me the next morning.

I felt light and relaxed. The whole world had suddenly come alive. I glanced into the temple, enjoying the sight of the lamps, the deities, the flowers, the offerings. I rushed back home, thinking over and over, only one more night of separation to endure! At night I cooked while humming an old film song as if I had no cares. My husband returned. I never talked to him, for there was nothing to talk about. How had we ever lived as a couple all these years? His comments were always petty, sarcastic, grudging, poisoned, heavy with prejudice. Only the grand-aunt was able to satisfy his ego, with her whining and groveling and flattery. I was sure my son's arrogance and rigidity were inherited from his father. He observed me in a fresh sari, hair combed and plaited with flowers, and called me to where he was seated. I pretended not to hear. I began washing utensils and sweeping the kitchen. He was nothing to me, only the father of the child I had conceived.

The next morning Apeeta's parents departed. Her husband and daughter left too, and at once she came to see me. I was elated and ran to meet her, despite the darts of hate that were shooting from the old aunt's eyes. In the kitchen, Apeeta told me that her husband had threatened to shift from our locality by taking a transfer from his office. But at that moment she was ecstatic, because we were face to face once more. Her mother and father were convinced that I had cast a spell on their daughter, and they were going to hire an astrologer to perform some rituals to counter my black magic. I laughed in sheer relief. The gossiping tongues had actually created a screen and an alibi for us! The best policy would be for us to play along and let the absurdity proliferate.

Apeeta remained with me till dusk fell, then went back to her house. Her husband arrived. There was a sharp exchange of words, which escalated into heated abuse. For the first time I heard the man scream and rant—normally he avoided raising his voice to such a pitch because he was concerned about his reputation. I heard him shriek my name and drown me in a torrent of vitriolic epithets. All the other households were absolutely silent, the women craning their necks so that they would not miss a single juicy detail. Not a dog barked, not a child whimpered. Apeeta's husband did not want her to sleep in my house. This was also my husband's wish, he raved. My husband had told him not to send his wife to my house in the future, ever.

The neighbours' interest in the quarrel increased over the next few days. They would go from doorstep to doorstep, passing on what they had heard. All their sympathy lay with Apeeta's husband. A helpless man, needing their full support. They cast apprehensive glances at me whenever they encountered me in the courtyard. I began to feel suffocated. I had to do something, but what? Apeeta ignored the gossip and scathing remarks and stayed by my side as usual, going about her chores as if nothing unusual had happened. I realized that we would have to remain calm and not provoke anyone as far as possible, because the threat of being separated was a real one. 'If we move out of the city, our problems will be solved,' her husband said grimly.

The women got busy plotting ways to exorcise Apeeta and disengage her from the evil power of my supposed black magic. They talked loudly about various shrines where priests could perform rituals that would negate my demonic influence and release Apeeta from my clutches. In the midst of our passionate moments, we laughed about this. How hard their devious, myopic, jealous brains worked! And how violently their shuttered minds resisted even the faintest suggestion of a sexual tinge to our intimate friendship!

One afternoon when Apeeta was with me, her daughter came running to us in a panic, saying that her father had come home from work and had sent for his wife. This was unusual, for the man never returned to the house in the middle of the day. Apeeta looked anxiously at me. I felt instinctively, as she did, that something was very wrong. She embraced me suddenly, whispering words of love in my ears. I refused to consider that something untoward might happen. How was I, how was she, to know what fate had willed.

I started my chores mechanically, struggling with the fear that slowly filled my veins like blood. Apeeta's daughter entered the kitchen suddenly, panting and crying aloud, 'We are leaving this house, Father says that we are transferred! In the early morning we are going to catch the train. My grandparents are coming in the evening to take Amma and me to our new place! Amma is crying and fighting. Come home, Amma wants you to come!'

Even before the child had finished her sentence, I was rushing over to Apeeta's house, into the room full of angry voices. Apeeta pushed through the thronging relatives and stood at my side, declaring that she would not leave me and go anywhere. The husband reached across and grabbed her arm.

'You had better go and pack your things,' he yelled. 'Don't make a fuss, you will repent, I am warning you!'

Bruises erupted on her tender skin as she fought him. She clung to me, pleading. I felt her desperate weight, her pulsing fear. I wanted to seize her and drag her from the house, but I could not move. I stood there, holding her, dazed. The husband lunged forward, slapped Apeeta's face and thrust me outside with a furious shove, bolting the door from the inside. I lay in the courtyard, half conscious. When I opened my eyes I saw that I was surrounded by women and old men who thought that I had just received what I deserved. I struggled to my feet and forced my way through the accusing circle. I entered my kitchen feeling as if I was dead.

Then I screamed. 'No! Apeeta cannot be leaving me like this!' There was a fire in my stomach; my head felt as if it had been pushed inside a furnace. My whole body was ablaze. I shrieked again and again. The frightened grand-aunt tried to approach me, then retreated as my cries grew wilder. Hoping Apeeta could hear me, I ran out again and banged on her door, but it remained closed. I beat on the wood till my fists bled and my bones ached. I tore the flowers from my plait and let my hair pour down my back, the scream that clawed free from my throat looping the courtyard in a spiral of shame and need.

The tenacious old woman somehow hauled me to the kitchen and locked me inside. Alone, for hours I shouted my voice ragged, as though my bellowing could shatter the walls. Weeping, cursing, I hurled the cooking utensils, snatching them from the orderly shelves and throwing them with all the force of my arms. I do not know how long my frenzy lasted. Only one thought raced through my brain—Apeeta, Apeeta, Apeeta, my beloved Apeeta was being taken away from me.

At night a doctor was called. I was given some injections, I vaguely remember. I was heavily sedated. I did not regain consciousness till the next evening. For a few minutes I lay stunned, wrapped in a swirling nausea. Then memories hit me like a hail of rocks. Immediately I started shrieking. 'Apeeta! Where is Apeeta!' I lurched through the courtyard to her door and was confronted with a huge padlock, glinting like an evil eye in the sun. A neighbour told me that Apeeta had left with her family that very morning. She had been injected with tranquilizers and carried out of the house.

I was unable to accept what I was hearing. I howled hysterically and grabbed the objects nearest at hand, flinging them at people. The sight of my self-righteous husband, gloating at my misery, aggravated my fury. I recall slamming a big tin of talcum against his head. Blood poured from the gash and powder dribbled onto his nose. I clapped my hands and laughed. The grand-aunt tried to soothe me, but I drove her away with foul invective. Nothing could console me. For a week I alternately ranted, or collapsed when I was sedated. The moment I got up I would fly into an uncontrollable rage. Whenever my husband came near me, I clenched my teeth to prevent myself from sinking them into his repulsive flesh.

One morning a strange van drove up. Two doctors grabbed me, swathed me in chains and took me somewhere. Later I came to know that it was a mental hospital.

I knew that I was not mad. My supposed lunacy was pure, uncontaminated anger. My frustration built and built, and was expended in futile tantrums. The moment I woke each day, I would begin screaming for Apeeta and spitting curses and a flood of profanities against my husband. The sedation continued. Days and nights flowed together like a filthy sluggish river, interspersed with the icy jab of needles. When I was not raving, I lay like a corpse. I could barely stand or walk. I wept till I thought I had no tears left, yet the next day I scalded my cheeks with more.

One day I realized that my husband had stopped coming to visit me. A huge space dilated around me, like a pool of water into which I dropped like a stone. The doctors and nurses did not bother to ask me anything. They had accepted my husband's version of the story. I did not know how many months, perhaps years were passing thus. I did not know how long I was doomed to live shackled in that vile place. The one fact that I accepted, with ferocious calm, was that I would have to start manifesting 'normal' behaviour if I was ever to be released. If I stopped shouting and weeping, the doctors would be convinced that they had successfully 'cured' me; they would summon my husband to take me 'home'.

He arrived, stood by the bed, smiling down at me. I balled my fists to stop myself from hurling the pillow at his face. I tortured my lips into a grimace, bared unwilling teeth. I drooped behind him as he signed the discharge papers. I followed him into the taxi, sat rigid as wood as he talked and talked about our son and the now-senile grand-aunt and the new house he had purchased in a decent locality. The sun was blinding. His voice grated like a rusty iron implement. I uttered not a word. My stay in the mental hospital had resulted in one ghastly blessing—it had brutally taught me how to detach myself completely. He asked me questions, but I felt as if he was addressing the taxi driver. I leaned my head against the seat and pretended to rest. The taxi went down different streets, stopping at a big house very far from the place I had lived in with Apeeta. I moved my limbs like a doll, following him inside.

The house was new, huge. The boy had grown up. I learned, with numb terror, that I had been locked away for two years. I did not talk to my son, nor did he feel the need to be with me. Occasionally he addressed me as 'Amma' when he needed coffee or food. Mechanically I put my hand to all the household chores. I never took Apeeta's name in the presence of the family, and they pretended to have forgotten the incident totally.

But at night, alone, I would repeat her name like a mantra, remembering.

Now, after fifteen years I receive this letter from Apeeta urging me to join her in distant North India. I cannot control my joy, nor can I do anything to express it. The letter is short; I ache as I read how she started a new life with her daughter. Apeeta earns her living as a teacher in a school. She lives in a small flat. She will meet me on Friday at the temple pond where we used to sit; she will take me with her, directly to Delhi.

So many years away from her, yet a few lines are enough. I will not hesitate to leave my house, my family, everything, to go and live with her. My hands reach for the tali, her tali, around my neck. What does she look like now? I remember her long glossy hair, her swaying hips, her dark and sensuous skin

. . . I hide the letter and plan my strategy for the next five days. How shall I behave? No one must suspect anything. I must conceal my excitement, my feverish jubilation.

I look at myself in the bedroom mirror. Is this how she will see me, so much older, with a lot of grey hair and dark smudges under my eyes? Till this moment, I have not thought once about my appearance. I have simply worn the first garment that came to hand, I have not plaited flowers in my hair, I have not celebrated Deepavali or Navratri . . . since the day Apeeta was taken away from me. My family thinks these lapses are a habit that came about during my stay in the mental hospital. I have disguised my longing for my beloved under a facade of general coldness. In the beginning my husband berated me for being a 'wooden doll', but it did not really matter to him as long as I was there to manage his domestic life.

He could not guess the intensity with which I have nurtured the desire to take revenge on this family.

I will leave this house. They will never have the smallest idea where I might have gone. I will disappear. This Friday I will pretend I am going to the temple and I will never return. They can search and search, lodge a report with the police, do whatever they want—I will not come back.

Thoughts crowd my brain like bees as I plan for Friday's departure. I decide what clothes I will wear, what I will take. I ask my husband for all my jewellery, saying that I wish to wear it now. He is delighted at the idea that I have approached him to ask for something. For once he does not taunt me. Unsuspectingly, he retrieves the ornaments from the bank locker. I wear them, with a silk sari, for the next two days. Inwardly I shudder as his gaze follows me around the room.

By Friday, I am almost beside myself with excitement, but I somehow manage to suppress it. Apeeta, Apeeta, my mind chants like an ecstatic devotee. My husband notices that I am radiant with joy, but he does not ask me anything. I have told him that I will be visiting the temple after dusk, to listen to a pravachanam. 'Praise God, the wooden doll is coming to life,' he remarks, with his sickening gloat. I control my fury, thinking that this is the last day I will have to see his face.

At four in the evening I leave the house key with my neighbour and walk to the temple. My heart beats like the wing of a frightened bird. I reach the pond that I have not seen for fifteen years. Apeeta, my Apeeta, is sitting on the steps, looking in my direction. She leaps up with the same swift graceful movements that I remember. She utters not a word, doesn't even embrace me, just seizes my arm and pulls me with her, hailing a taxi at the gate. She tells the driver to take us to Central Station. We get into a first-class coupé and shut the door.

As soon as the train starts moving I take her into my arms. We weep and weep, as if our tears are part of an ocean of infinite bliss and infinite sorrow. For half an hour neither of us can speak, then I wipe her wet cheeks with my pallu.

'I knew you would come,' she says in a choked but determined voice. 'I have worked hard all these fifteen years so that I could be with you.'

But the years of separation seem to have collapsed in this moment of rapture. Standing in the empty compartment, we hold each other up, almost losing our balance as the train shrieks and pitches forward, hurling us into the tunnel of night.

Glossary

kolam – decorative pattern made with rice powder outside the entrance to a house
Purusan – husband
saibu – Muslim vendor
sparsha – touch
tali – gold ornaments strung on thread, worn by a married woman

She Is Her Children's Mother

Rea

The day I left Su was, like our months together, hard to situate in nouns, verbs, adjectives. I watched her mutely, anxious to address the dumb wonder in her eyes, but all I knew was foetal relief.

'Did you not find shelter enough in the space between two of my heartbeats?' she half-quoted, half-sighed.

'I did not want shelter, but sunlight,' I said, trickling a tear of pure absurdity.

She thought we could flog into existence a world that would contain us; I knew better. When we made love, my own skin could hardly hold me, and the foolishness of our distinct bodies and the tangle of disparate limbs were a cause of unceasing distress, since flesh was the only place where our lives met.

When she called out my name, it was an act of unkindness, forcing me to be me when I would rather have focused on the illusion of being us. She would surrender her body to me with unthinking thoroughness, while I agonized over the meaning of our mingling.

Especially when I did not know, I could not know—in giving herself to me, was she taking herself away from those pink morsels, her children?

And with what right?

How to explain who I am—Your Mother's Lover—to such unseasoned infants? Impossible. So there was a lack of definition to the kisses I left on their cheeks, and hugs were firm but vague. I was pleased that their arms clung tighter, pressed closer—innocent but somehow aware of the inadequacy of our trying to connect.

'Know that I am unknowable, dear ones,' I would whisper in silence.

In Su's family photo album, all are so desperately earnest in their desire to be understood, pretending openness. Do all photographs hide secrets? I look, bemused, at stills of Su, and at details which escape other eyes. I have too much private knowledge of befores, afters and the meaning of a shawl thrown around her bare love-bitten neck in spite of the June heat.

My knowledge strips her. She invites my gaze but threatens blindness. I could not play Peeping Tom to your Lady Godiva forever, I want to explain.

Much easier to return to what was. The Mother's Friend stopping by of an evening after her work is done, for tea and talk of books and writing.

'Rea, oh darling Rea,' said Su to me one night, 'in *your* sight, I love you and we are one, so what does anything else matter?' Her voice, sorrowful and sweet, refused to acknowledge the possibility of an answer to her question. I felt my silence drop a curtain between us, but she was deaf to it and continued to smile with gentle yearning. 'Dearest,' I said finally, mocking myself.

Not all of my reveries are bleak and futile. I remember the refrains of sex, her constant declarations of love. She could declare with frisky assurance, the words bouncing out like kittens. 'I love you! I love you!' she would mew and purr. I carry with me the most delightful thoughts of back then, but we had designed a definition of Us with different components in mind, Su and I. Her contributions, I cannot forget, were fit to dwell in doll's houses and a diminutive aesthetic; my ungainly ones were less easy to accommodate and kept spilling outside domestic lines and evoking dismay: trying to tiptoe over the threshold in search of public approval on ill-formed leg buds, painfully flap-flapping too-small wings.

Su and I rubbed shoulders in the close quarters of space that was purely mental and much contrariness was ignited by the friction.

Still—I made her live, she said, and nor did I contradict her. Meditatively I would reach for her white breast that shed heartbeats as abundantly as a tree unleaving in autumn, and which I collected one by one in my marveling palm.

But one day the weight of uncertainty overwhelmed my desire, which turned pale in the light of our darkness.

'Gay is, after all, in the beholder's eye,' I said, meaningful to the last, watchful over the brisk rise and fall of her bosom as we parted ways.

❦

Closeted in a Triangle

Sunayna

In a country where an IAS officer murders his pregnant wife for carrying a female foetus, where female newborns are thrown into wells with their parents singing 'send your brother to us', life can be hell for women—lesbian or not.

Right from infancy, it is drilled into our minds that we have come to this world to serve men. Our lives, hopes, desires and ambitions will all be guided by men, first as fathers, then husbands and finally sons.

We are thoroughly trained to become model wives and mothers. We are given dolls and kitchen utensils to play with, much before we are able to think properly about ourselves. Our grandmas tell fairy tales, where the princess held captive by a demon is always rescued by a handsome prince on horseback. We learn that it's a man who will give us love, security and companionship. No one tells us that we can also get all these, and perhaps more, from a woman.

In school we are taught home science and needlework. In the house we learn about hygienic cooking, cleaning and removing stains from clothes. Soon we realize our dressing up has only one purpose—to make us attractive to the male gaze.

The day comes when mother comes rushing and announces gleefully that a suitable boy has been found—someone unparalleled in looks, family background, wealth and education. And if he is not grabbed immediately . . . We find ourselves getting ready for marriage, whether we want to or not. Right from our childhood, we know we will get married one day. We have seen our parents investing money in government-approved units for their daughter's marriage and their son's higher education.

Whether it's the school syllabus or Hindi film songs, we are indoctrinated thoroughly with the concept of man-woman procreative relationships. The thought of any 'alternative' never crosses our minds. Thus, with anticipation we visualize the first night with our husbands. But when that time comes, we realize there's something wrong somewhere. The first physical contact turns out to be unforgettable in a negative way. Some husbands find our reaction an affront to their manhood. So they prove their point with force. Marriage becomes a nightmare. But who cares about our bodies? Or our emotions?

Some of us may be less unfortunate in that we have husbands who are considerate and understand that we have a problem. We are taken to psychiatrists who are either ill-informed or prejudiced against homosexuality. They can't help us and it's back to square one. We convince ourselves that one more time could make things right. One more time and then yet another . . .

We never get a chance to discover an essential part of our identity. Frustrated and lonely, little do we realize that a woman lover would have made existence meaningful. The worst sufferers amongst us are those who realize their lesbian identity after marriage. That, in fact, is the story of my life.

I got married without knowing my real desires, or that I might want a female partner some day. I could never pinpoint the reasons for my lack of interest in 'heterosexual activities', until it was too late. Following my doctor's advice I continued trying, and six months later realized two things. One, that this brand of sex was not for me; and second, that I was pregnant.

The sheer drudgery of living through a sexless marriage would have driven me mad but for my daughter's presence in my life. She made me forget my sorrows.

Seven years have dragged by. I am convinced that I will never feel complete till I meet a woman I love who will help me feel free and happy with myself. Then I will walk with my head held high, devoid of guilt.

What does the future hold for me and all the women in my position? We can walk out of our marriages and start living on our own. But would society sanction such a move? Most of us are not financially independent. Even those of us who are would probably lose our jobs if we were to declare that we are lesbians, that we have divorced our husbands and left our families for a female lover. Won't our children be rebuked and laughed at because their mother 'ran away with another woman'?

Thus, forced to lead our double lives, we Indian married lesbians continue with our marriages. Because we are *so* invisible, we are ignored in whatever media coverage there is of gay people and gay issues. We are at the centre of a triangle, our children, our husbands and our lovers at the three vertices. But do we really have a choice?

❦

Tired of the Broom

Supriya

From the beginning I have always felt that there is nothing called 'right' and 'wrong'. What God has given us to do in life, we will do. Until two years ago I used to work in other people's houses, sweeping and cleaning, and when they left money in my way, I would always take it, very happily. I never felt that this was theft, just that they kept on giving and I kept on taking.

Seventeen-eighteen years ago, I was married off to a man in Bombay. He had a wife already, but she was just not having children—who can understand one's fate? So she herself told him, get another wife and I will not speak one word against her. Whatever *she* felt, *I* was not happy with the idea. But my mother said, 'You are sixteen and even the dogs in the village are staring at your body. Your marriage will take place right away, otherwise I know what will take place instead!'

My father did not feel good about me marrying a married man. 'What will Supriya do with the other wife, take her on her head and dance around?' he kept shouting. What did he know about what I could do with her . . . But he could not afford to give me all the gold and drama that the younger men wanted from him, so I married this drunken fool. Even right now, you will find him sitting in the corner of the room killing flies for a living, his face swollen up like a fat tomcat with drinking and still more drinking.

For two months after we were married, we were staying in his village and Husband wanted to do nothing but make mischief with me, all day, he did not leave me in peace for a minute. Is it any surprise that I was pregnant when we left? He was very happy because now he knew that he was a man.

My friendship with Lakshmi, the first wife, began slowly. In the beginning she did not say much to me. When I first came with Husband to live in the chawl, she was standing outside, and with her were some three-four other women. She looked at me and said, 'Whose wedding are you coming from, dressed up like *this* and like *that*?' And I started to cry. She said, 'Just sit there and cry, don't feel shy. It does not cost any money to cry and if it keeps you happy, that is first class.'

My two sons were born one after the other, and from the first day Lakshmi took care of them. All I had to do was nurse them with my milk. And if Husband was troubling me, she would nurse *him* with booze and send him to sleep. When she sang for the baby, she was also singing to me because she said I was like her daughter. The tears would come to my eyes—my own mother had never been so loving to me. Husband did not understand why we were so close, but he would try to start fights between us by putting ideas in my ear. He said, 'Who are you, and who is she—you and your two sons, and she without any children. You should beware of her jealousy.' I just kept quiet, but if Lakshmi heard him she would shout that he was as full of evil thoughts as a meddlesome mother-in-law. He was not bold enough to talk back to her.

Lakshmi was taking care of the children, so I had to start working, washing clothes and washing dishes all day long. Husband's job as bank security guard was not worth asking about, a thousand times he was thrown out for being a drunk.

Whatever anyone says, a woman's life is full of hardship, working until you drop dead and for people who care nothing about you, whether husband or strangers. On my mother's soul, I had no right to think about my life in those days. Work and get kicks in return, that is a woman's life.

I could no longer call myself a woman when this thing started between me and Lakshmi, but she never let me feel any pain because of it. To this day, not a word of abuse has come to my ears from these women in the chawl. The sons have never said anything, either. Probably they do not know, because we never do anything until they are asleep. She is more like their mother than I am, but they call her 'Kaki'—like all the children of Husband's brother do—what other name is there?

How this thing started, I can't remember. One time she said, smiling and laughing, 'In my next life, I want to come back as the rice grains that you are cleaning. You hold them in your lap, and shake them so gently, up and down, up and down...' Husband was going to whores, so I told Lakshmi I was afraid that if he touched me, I would get diseases. The two of us would sleep together next to the children, and he would come back late stinking of booze. One or two times he put a hand on my shoulder but Lakshmi shooed him away. Now he does not do anything to anyone, whores, wives—he has no thought in his head except for booze. He lies there crying, 'Pandurang, Pandurang!' or 'God, give me an easy death!' I sometimes feel very sorry for him.

But back then, it was a different story. If the drink had really put some courage in him, he would try saying, 'Every night she is with you, now for one night you give her to me.' Lakshmi was not afraid of him, she would say, 'Buy a new wife from the dry goods merchant. Look, why just one? He will give you three for eight annas. Go, run there now before he closes.' One time he shouted, 'Be careful, my head is heating up.' She just laughed, did not even get up from the mat, and told him,

'Then go outside and cool it down, or I'll put the pan of water on it to make tea.'

I have no worries now about my life. By doing something some way or the other, we make enough money to live. Husband cannot do anything for the house, he has no strength left in his body. But the demons in him have also flown away. The two boys are smart and always come first in school, and an organization gives them money for books, pens, everything—there is no problem about that. Most important is, they are both good boys and always show Lakshmi and me the respect that is due to a mother.

(as told to, and translated from Marathi by, U.S.G.)

❀❀

And the Lamp Kept Burning

Shama

I am a Muslim woman, married for the past nine years. My husband works in the Gulf, and we hardly meet twice a year. I look after his family here, in Bombay—we have two stubborn and mischievous sons, whom I cannot control! I admit that my sexual encounters with my husband are satisfying, and that is the main reason for our getting on well. But when I am alone without him, my mind is always disturbed. I need company, someone to talk to, someone to make love to.

After a few months of our marriage, God knows how, but all of a sudden I developed a terrible crush on the actress Dimple Kapadia. I was desperate to see her, so I wrote a letter to her, and soon realized my dream of meeting her when she invited me to one of her film shoots. And so from then on, I discovered the courage to look around at all the beautiful girls. The easiest ones to find, to refresh my eyes with their pretty faces and lovely figures, were the sexy models on TV . . .

My hubby has a man's typically introverted nature and is completely ignorant about the fun side of life . . . though undoubtedly he is a dutiful husband and father. But as I am very enthusiastic, adventurous and romantic by nature, I acquired a passion for the same sex, because all women share a love for good times and enjoyment.

The other reason, maybe, that my desire for girls surfaced, is my devotion to the way of nature and religion—that is, the theory of one man for one woman. So I did not let my mind fix on any of the males around me, or think of developing relations with them, as I have always believed that sleeping with men outside marriage is adultery and a sinful disease.

I have been through a tough time these past eight years. Although I had many good friends, I could not confide in any of them about my turmoil. I even fell in love with one of them, but she stopped talking to me when I told her how I felt about her. Sometimes I think I have confused true friendship and lesbianism.

By chance, twice I got involved with women, but unfortunately, neither of these relationships could last—my partners had no similar desires, but allowed me to touch them because they wanted to make me happy. For example, some time after my husband had left for the Gulf, I had relations with my sister-in-law. But she felt that what we were doing was wrong, and said that she came to my bed only because she was sorry for my lonely state.

In this middle decade of my life—well, I am thirty-one now—all of a sudden it struck me to place an ad in the penpal section of a local magazine, asking for female friends. To my good fortune, a woman by the name of Raagesha replied, and to my surprise, she said that she was a lesbian like me.

I was very happy that she had contacted me, but I started wondering why her voice on the phone sounded just like a man's. I was really curious to meet this mysterious being, so I paid a surprise visit to the postal address to which I had sent my letters. A man opened the door, but insisted that he was not Raagesha, and so I left. To this day I do not know the truth about him or her.

But from my conversations with Raagesha over the phone, I learned that there are clubs for lesbians in several major cities of India, and I was dictated telephone numbers for some members of the group in Bombay. At the get-togethers of the organization I met many girls, but I was constantly on the lookout for a married woman like me—I had always believed that only another married woman could sympathize with my concern for my family and my household. So I asked one of my new friends to find me a partner. Because I made my arranged marriage with my husband work fairly well, I knew I could develop a successful relationship with a woman too.

It seemed that my luck had changed—I soon met a woman who was about the same age, and she had a son. When we met and talked, I thought, 'She is my life partner.' But my assumption that love with a married woman would be easy turned out to be completely wrong. She was not my destiny: she did not want me to get emotionally involved with her, and started to withdraw when the affair became serious. Her mother-in-law was shocked that a Muslim woman kept calling at their house, and since my lover was very attached to her husband and in-laws, we had to stop meeting each other.

Now that I am on my own again I have set resolutions for myself and my partner-to-be. I always want to be faithful to her, to walk hand in hand with her through life and thus develop a healthy, trusting love. Some lesbians have more than one partner, I know, but I am a traditional Indian woman with traditional Indian values, and I want my lover to be the same.

I want to be with her until I die.

Though I admit that on my part it's going to be quite a dangerous step, as no one in my house suspects. They all trust my moves. I am aware that I am betraying my family. But I cannot face the idea of leading a lonely life.

Update: one year later . . .

Today, with pride I can tell you that I have met the partner of my dreams. We are both seriously in love with each other. It did not turn out the way I had thought—she is not a married woman, she is single and working, but she is in every way understanding of all my difficulties.

We do not want our families to know about our relationship. We have set our sights on the future, and hope that we can live together one day. But for this dream to come true, I will have to leave my husband and his home. I am waiting to seize every opportunity to invent quarrels with him and make his life with me a misery, so that he might divorce me. I do not let him touch me any more, and tell him that I do not want sex from him. If that doesn't work, I shall have to find another way to live separately, with my partner and my children. We are looking forward to that day.

❦

With Respect to Marriage

Molly/Manju

The maternity ward of Winchu Hill hospital has a waiting room which is a warm colour, like cream khadi cotton, a very welcoming room indeed, but since it is about half-past eleven on a rainy Sunday night, it is almost empty. Sunday night is not a very common time of the week for infants to be born, as all humans have in their nerves from the very beginning a dislike for Monday morning.

The only person you are able to see inside the room is a slender young man with big innocent eyes and nervous hands. He is sitting there, clutching seriously at the knees of his white churidar, hair falling into his eyes. There is a shuffling at the door, and a bony ward boy enters, holding a metal tray on which a metal tiffin gleams.

'Doctor Madam shent food,' he says, and the man cannot help but realize that the boy's breath smells strongly of methylated spirit.

'Why?'

He is quite startled by the show of such concern for himself, he is not the one having the baby.

'Prospective fathers all the time forget food,' mumbles Ward Boy, as if he is reciting a lesson taught to him in school.

Prospective Father relaxes his fists. Sweat has dissolved the starch in the churidar and has left sticky grey creases in the shape of hands.

'Yes, I must eat something,' he says loudly to no one. Ward Boy has shuffled away, having deposited the tiffin and a thermos full of hot tea.

The man's twitching, agitated hands examine the container, and find pickle at the top. No, none of that unfortunately, because it is unbecoming to a father-to-be. Sad, really, because he is very fond of pickle, especially mango, but no more hot, spicy things for quite a number of years. He takes a piece of dhokla, but no chutney with it, and chews thirty-three times until it is soft as baby food. He swallows it with a gulp, immediately suppressing a burp.

He is about to become a father! He is determined to be as

firmly gentle with the new child as he has been taught by his mother, and there will be absolutely no rage from him, because he will avoid pickle and all masala, which are the only big hindrances to good temper, as his mother repeats often.

Doctor Madam is his sister-in-law. How glad he is that she is inside the delivery room with her little sister, his wife! The doctor is such a reliable woman, with her slim, athletic form, and her short curly hair and her strong-boned hands. Her eyes have a calm strength which compels him to trust her completely, and to bow to her judgement as a friend.

It was three years ago that she had written him the letter. He thought afterwards that it resembled her, white and stiff-looking, bent a little to to fit into the letter-box. He found it there that Monday when he returned from work at the family business of textile retail.

My dear Tushar,

I hope all is well with you. I write with respect to marriage. No, I do not refer to a marriage with me! That is frankly impossible as you are a man and that is not suitable to me, as gossip must have long since informed you.

It is my sister Shirley who is seeking a nice boy. I write to you because the neighbourhood sings your praises constantly. Our acquaintance with each other also reinforced my opinion.

It does not matter to us, the fact that you are not Catholic. We hope you feel the same. There must be no talk of conversion on either side. I am firm in believing that humans must lead their lives in the ways that God has intended for them, in all respects.

Shirley will come with me for the purpose of meeting you at your residence. May I suggest Saturday in the afternoon?

> *Do not trouble yourself with entertaining us in any special*
> *manner, Tushar! Simply a few pakoras to eat, to keep us*
> *busy when there is an awkward moment!*

> *Your friend, Irene*

On that fateful Saturday Tushar prepared for the guests himself, as the bai was on leave. Sharbat; pakoras, bhajiyas, kaju and pista mithai, also some vegetarian sausages. Nervously, he hoped it was not too much or too little.

'Maybe marriage will save me from a lonely life,' he thought with anguish as he wiped the dusty glasses and plates.

'Arre! Now what is all this! And for what!' exclaimed Mummy, bouncing into the room. That was the way she walked all the time, like a happy little girl going to school.

'Irene and her sister are coming today,' Tushar said, embarrassed. 'I have never met Shirley before, so Irene wanted us to meet each other. I think Shirley was most of the time away in boarding school and then until this May she was working in Delhi.'

'Sweet boy you are to take so much trouble,' said Mummy, who was not at all stupid. 'But why worry, beta? I know you will be settling with a nice girl very soon without all this silly nonsense, you are a good boy and it is not important that you are not handsome or smart.'

She was walking around, looking for her glasses, which after a few minutes she found in the pocket of her salwar kameez. (Mummy was always making the tailor sew pockets in all her clothes, even her sari blouse where the pocket was located between her breasts). She took some dark chocolate from the pocket of the kameez, made of bright pink silk from the family's own shop.

'I am really wishing I could stay because you will be feeling shy, I know,' she said, 'but I am going to meet Jayshri

Masi for chit-chat and time-pass. I have been telling her since long time that I will come. You will be a good boy, no?'

She popped some chocolate into his mouth and skipped out of the room before he could reply.

But when Mummy came back after three hours and saw Tushar, Shirley and Irene ignoring the food, she knew right away that it was all settled. Shirley, a tall and very lovely girl with dark brown hair falling to her slim waist, smiled hopefully. Mummy gave her a big hug and a jasmine-scented kiss. Then she gazed thoughtfully at Irene, who was looking very smart in a navy blue suit and a striped silk tie, and shook her head.

'Now I cannot be flirting with you anymore,' Mummy sighed almost unhappily. 'You are the sister of my new daughter and so now you will be seeming like a daughter to me.'

What a wedding! It was certainly enough to put to shame all other newly-married couples in the neighbourhood. One fat Catholic priest and one equally fat Hindu pujari were present to do the needful. Angry and jealous, they did not glance at the couple even once. Even if two women or two men had been standing in front of them, the priests would not have noticed and would have joined them together in holy matrimony. Their voices simply got louder and louder, and by the end of the ceremonies when they said 'Om Shanti' and 'I pronounce you husband and wife', they were trying to out-shout each other.

Then the guests sat down to a hearty lunch which had cost Tushar and Shirley Rs 100 per thali. Pure veg Gujju food was served to the groom's family and non-veg Goan food to the bride's family, so everyone was smiling radiantly.

I can't believe I am actually getting married to the woman I love, Tushar was thinking, lost in a heavy daze of joy as he looked at the beautiful bride, the shimmering pleated fan of her sari pallu spreading onto his lap. She had chosen him from dozens of ardent suitors. He shredded a thepla, unable to swallow a morsel.

Shirley tossed back her hair. The delicious fragrance of her perfume enveloped him, and he glowed until he was sure the light of his bliss must be bright enough for all to see. Oh Shirley, Shirley, he cried out silently. She was not only beautiful, but fine and noble—how children would run to her when she walked along a street! Her wit made him feel so proud of her, and he loved how everyone would always bend in her direction like sunflowers seeking brilliance.

Now she was pointing out some members of her 'crazy Anglo-Indian family', quietly whispering sly stories about them. This grand-aunt was a hypochondriac and told even passing strangers that she had dislocated her whole stomach, and that paranoid old lout was afraid the government was going to arrest him some day for opposing India's becoming independent of good old Britain in '47. Tushar was torn into two pieces by his desire, not knowing if he should listen to her or look at her.

Shirley continued to gossip gently about the pageant of guests, many wearing silk dresses and saris from Tushar's family shop, given as gifts to the family of the bride. Irene, in an embroidered sherwani, pure white with small silver beads, smiled at them. She was escorting a woman as dazzling as a peacock in purple and green, gold jewellery with meenakari work, and gold stilettos. 'Don't you think she is a Sindhi?' said Shirley wickedly.

Tushar loved each moment of his wedding day. Everyone saw him as the short, happy shadow of his new wife, and she was completely at ease as the centre of attraction. But when all the singing and dancing and feasting was finally over and they were alone in their room, he froze.

He wanted to kiss Shirley and stroke her lovely brown

skin, hold her close and nestle into the curve of her warm waist like a puppy. But he was sure that reaching out for her would seem crude. So he sat on the edge of the bed and looked down silently at his feet, in his usual posture of defeat.

Gracefully balanced on a three-legged stool and combing the thick brown hair which fell around her in loops and curls, Shirley was watching him in the gilt-framed mirror, smiling to herself. She put her comb down and, turning around to face him, stretched out her hands like a woman who knew what she wanted. Tushar staggered to his feet and fell into her arms.

It was quiet suddenly, there was no longer the incessant humming of the neighbour's radio, and the ragged cats had stopped fighting each other in the street. The open window let in a cool breeze. Tushar held on tightly to Shirley's shoulders. Embarrassed and confused, he imagined her earlier lovers grinding their hips into her dainty body. He felt sick.

'Just do it, man, do what comes naturally,' had been the advice of his cousin Shekhar, drunk on too much strong Goan feni at the evening reception.

And so he did. Suddenly they were kissing. All the blood and heat in their bodies had rushed to their lips, burning, swollen. He sucked her breasts with the sweet instinct of a baby, moaning as her long fingers squeezed his nipples. His mouth was passionately kissing her warm mound. Her head moved from side to side and her hips quivered in pleasure. And then it flashed through Tushar's mind that she was the food which he had been longing for the whole of that day, he wanted to be filled by her, to feel her inside him.

So their life together began. At nine, Tushar left for work, and Shirley, after waving goodbye, would sit down to work on the book she was writing about Anglo-Indian women. In the evening they would have dinner, Tushar would listen to his wife talking about her discovery of yet another member of her community who had started a charity for children and had an affair with a maharaja. He handed her the shiny silk scraps she asked him to bring from the shop, and she would stitch them into the beginnings of a quilt, quickly and methodically.

And at night when the plaintive buzz of mosquitoes was thickening into a drone, they would be cuddling up together in bed. They would whisper contentedly, giggle like lovers who were also friends. Tushar stroked Shirley's hair, his left hand sliding between her legs. He pressed it into her body. His fingers lay together like five little babies in a safe womb. His smooth gold wedding ring grew warm inside her.

Two years passed that way. Then one day Shirley had to go for afternoon tea to a neighbour's house. She was close to finishing her book, and was not very pleased at having to leave it for a meaningless gossip session with Sangita, who had been married for just six months. It was five o'clock on a hot summer afternoon, and Shirley was feeling in the mood for fresh nimbu-pani, not sickly sweet Gujju chai which would be sitting on her tongue for hours with its aluminium aftertaste.

Wearing a sleeveless top and a skirt, she stamped down the stairs and was soon crossing the street to Sangita's building. Not even a slight breeze stirred the air. She was irritated to feel sweat on her face and neck.

Mummy and Sangita's upstairs neighbour Jeanie had also come for tea. So had Irene. Mummy hugged Shirley as though she was seeing her after months.

'I know you have been writing, writing, writing!' she said, eyes twinkling. 'I have some chocolate for you. One piece?'

Shirley took it, her mood lightening a little. She was prepared even to drink the sticky milky chai syrup Sangita was giving her.

'Your poor sister is also tired,' said Sangita, stroking Irene's shoulder.

'I delivered four babies last night,' sighed Irene. 'Frankly,

I do not think one of them weighed less than five kilos. I felt sorry for the mothers. Babies, indeed! Elephants, rather.'

'How cute!' exclaimed Sangita.

'Wait until you have one, then talk,' said Jeanie, twisting up her mouth.

'They are really not so cute,' Mummy said seriously. 'My Tushar was a frog, and even now, he is like a frog only! His children I am sure would pop out looking like frogs, even though you are beautiful, Shirley. So I am glad you are not having any.'

'You must tell me what kind of prevention you are using,' said Jeanie, who had four children. 'Pill, sponge, this, that and the other, I still get pregnant.'

'I'm not using any birth control,' said Shirley stiffly.

'Tell that to the priest,' Jeanie said, sniffing with pure disbelief.

'I *want* children,' said Shirley.

Jeanie raised her eyebrows, turned to Sangita and furtively whispered, 'I suppose the truth is that Tushar can't father children, such a frail man! Poor Shirl!'

But Irene, who was standing behind Sangita admiring the way the sunlight touched every curling strand on her head and made her hair look like a plaited rainbow of a hundred different tints of black, had overheard. She looked with hidden concern at her sister, whose face showed strangely mixed feelings of embarrassment, longing and irritation. She quickly said goodbye to the women in the room and gave Sangita a swift thank-you kiss.

When she walked into Tushar's shop, he was bent over the big yellow ledgers in his cabin with its glass door. He looked up and saw her weaving through his workers with their tape measures and rolls of cloth, and he dropped his pen. What on earth could be wrong? Had something happened to Shirley? Irene patted his outstretched hand. And in the end she found that it was actually very easy to talk to him.

When he understood what she was saying, he sat down in his chair again and hid his face in his hands.

'Dear Tushar,' Irene said softly. 'I do assure you, I understand and sympathize completely with your distaste.'

Tushar was looking up now and nodding slowly, his eyes full of trust.

So that night when the couple said goodnight to Mummy, went into the bedroom and shut the door, Tushar tenderly rolled Shirley onto her back, pulled himself on top of her, placed his member between her legs and pushed it carefully inside her. Shirley's eyes grew big with surprise, but automatically she tilted her body to accept him in the way he was offering himself. Like a creaky and awkward machine, Tushar began to move in and out, up and down, his eyelids clenched shut. Shirley stopped trying to understand, put her arms around his back and held him as he started to gasp and moan. When she felt him surrender his seed, her body received it like a priceless gift. She knew what it had cost him.

In the waiting room of Winchu Hill hospital, the clock's tick seems very loud. The man looks up and sees that it is almost four o'clock, lays aside the tiffin and stands up. The rubber soles of his shoes squeak loudly on the big white tiles as he walks up and down, wringing his hands. The ward boy, who is trying hard to sleep on the other sofa, mumbles and turns onto his side, flinging his arm over his ears.

Quick footsteps. Tushar turns sharply. Pale with fatigue, her skin stretched and shiny as plastic, Irene comes through the swinging door that leads to the maternity ward, dragging off her surgical mask with one hand. She smiles lovingly at her brother-in-law.

'Congratulations, my dear Tushar. You are the proud father of a beautiful baby lesbian.'

Tushar gazes at her open-mouthed, then looks through the glass. A nurse is holding up a dimpled bundle with Irene's calm lips, Shirley's delicate cheekbones, his own shy eyes. He feels his face light up with a joy that comes bursting out of his very soul.

❧

On Creased Earth

Revathi

Glass bangles trill sweet in my ears when her long fingers ease them off her wrists, one at a time. The gold necklace reflecting chinks of sun lies heavily on her throat. She makes love like an actress on a stage, all past and future emptied from her smooth-browed mind before she steps into the bed bare of pillows and sheets. She flows over the bed, the air itself moves to make space for her, its currents embracing her. She gives me life, fingers fluttering on my skin, palms wide in splendid symmetry. She gives me breath, lips filling my dense bones with lightness. She gives me hope. Her moth-hands, poised on the arching brown branch of either arm, open their wings and drift onto my tired breast.

The beauty of her lovemaking is such that even I, her own beloved, I am left stunned and overcome, as if I am a simple witness to a spiritual rite which suddenly demands the use of my limbs. My body is claimed by a many-armed goddess. I am taken into her, a part of her being. She is with me, swallowing me up as her dance of life consumes her. She has poured her entirety into our loving, and now after it is over she is only a shadow in the middle of all the other shadows in the house, dim and pale. Lying against me with her face pressed into my shoulder, she pulls my arm over her. She will lie sheltered like this for hours.

Or she would have, but her daughters' voices chasing birds in the wet garden disturb her. She lifts up her head, not startled but just drawn by the sounds. She is no less a lover, but the sleeping mother has arisen. In an unbroken silence she ties back her hair, only sighing softly, completely naked. She begins to dress herself, smiling into me.

Her stirrings and grindings are meticulous, her hands work a rough magic when she absorbs herself in making food. She holds out an idli palpitating with steam on the blade of a blunt knife. I bite into it and she releases herself into my mouth and I am lost in layer upon layer of her slow labours. I am forbidden to touch anything in her kitchen, I am also forbidden to help her with her chores. So I merely watch as she stands in the middle of a damp fall of clean clothes hanging in the shade, or as she goes in light-footed pursuit of dust shaken from its rest. She lives within the wholeness of the moment. Only the task that occupies her hands is real.

My sweet love, not rich but wealthy with her inheritance of a thousand rebirths. The glow of suns long since burned dead, the liquid resonance of dark underground water, move within her. Her eyes carry the sureness of ancient discovery, buried and seldom revealed. Meeting her is escape from life itself, it is a punctuation in hasty time.

Sitting on the hard ground to eat afternoon food, I am made to feel a part of them all, mother and daughters. They spin strong webs of loving energy in which I am happy to be caught. It is not always like this. Sometimes I slink from one corner to another corner like an intruding man, a threat from the outside. At such times, they fulfil each other and exclude me without saying even a harsh word.

But now, the vivid strength of her grows in my heart, brings quiet happiness. I gather the objects of my other life. Car keys, they are my escape from her beauty, which is too perfect, which I cannot possess. I dress in the other clothes and she frees me without question.

'Speak, will you,' I say, struggling with her language.

She blinks twice, and from her the sign is so excessive that it is a yielding of her soul.

She comes out into the heat of the sun, back bowed, eyes squinting and shy as she hugs me. Framed in the door's shade, she struggles like an evening moth into the glare of day.

꼭꼭

Foreplay

Amita

The cab took the last turn towards her house. The road widened to a large clearing next to her building. Asmita peered through the glass to catch a glimpse of her big bedroom window and her heart stood still for a moment. Then a stabbing pain, and finally a dull and deadening numbness. The second floor window was open and the ceiling fan stood still in the oppressive heat. Naseem was not there as promised. Maybe she had come, waited, fumed and left! Perhaps for good.

Asmita went through the motions of paying the cabby, getting the change, climbing two storeys and unlocking the door. She flinched, thinking of the emptiness of the weekend ahead, perhaps of the entire life ahead.

She had planned and eagerly awaited this weekend, when

she could be alone with Naseem. They were to have the entire house to themselves. Asmita's teenage daughters would be spending the festival days with their grandparents. Intimacy, romance, lovemaking was becoming more and more difficult in the small flat.

Asmita and Naseem with their demanding jobs and family responsibilities—Asmita's growing daughters and Naseem's ageing mother—had very little time for each other. Besides, they were very particular about their privacy and felt inhibited by the presence of the two growing girls only a few feet away, despite the wall and the closed door. During all these years of the relationship, the children had regularly spent weekends at Asmita's mother's. Then the time was theirs, the small apartment was theirs to relax in, to snuggle and kiss in, to bathe together in, and in which to luxuriate in each other's bodies. It was also the time to settle scores, clear misunderstandings, set new norms of behaviour and exchange sweet nothings. They could take their time and choose their place. No need to confine intimacy to the semi-darkness of their hundred-square-foot bedroom. The privilege of making love on the narrow divan in the living room clinging to each other for dear life, or sprawled on the floor, or giggling in front of the TV in the children's room. Of touching each other standing in the shower, the water caressing their bodies as they caressed each other. Of having a friendly or not-so-friendly argument at the lunch table. The weekend was something they longed for. It was worth enduring the demands of their respective jobs, the separation from time to time, the bitter awareness of the illicitness of their connection.

That was the most painful thing—the injustice of it! Asmita remembered with shame and anger the way she had designed their conjugal bed. They had just become involved, and they were tired of sleeping separately, she on her mattress on the bedroom floor and Naseem on the living room divan. Coming together to make love and then parting to sleep on their own. Asmita was scared and shy of flaunting a double bed, since she was a single mother and Naseem officially only a flat-mate (paying guest, as some people insisted). So finally she decided on a bed four feet wide which was just fine to make love in and sleep cuddled. But since they could not lie on it without touching, when they fought Naseem always grabbed her sleeping bag and marched off to the living room.

Not that it solved the problem entirely. They were scared of a friend or a relative ringing the bell late at night and discovering the sleeping arrangement. Once, while lying entwined on The Bed, they were startled by strings of tiny light bulbs being lowered in front of their window, accompanied by approaching voices. It was the neighbours illuminating the building for some festival. The architecture of the building would not permit anybody to look in through their window, yet they were frightened. And similarly there was the time when they had gone to Gorai island for the weekend—voices outside their door had made them nervous and had spoiled a lazy afternoon of lovemaking.

Today it was all Asmita's mistake. She got bullied into going to work for two hours. Then, she was blackmailed into joining her family for the festive lunch. The latter task was like rubbing salt into Naseem's wound, since she had gained an exemption from visiting her old mother for the entire weekend.

Asmita didn't mind the work. It was her responsibility and her joy too. She methodically and single-mindedly bulldozed through it, clearing it in less time than expected. But the family lunch was excruciatingly slow, awkward and painful. Her parents, her brother, his wife and children, her sister, her husband and their children. Only her own soul-mate was not present. Naseem had no locus standi in the family. This awareness was a throbbing pain throughout the meal. Asmita knew that her relationship was much more intense and meaningful and romantic than anyone else's in her family! Yet she and Naseem could not be together around her relatives.

She became increasingly silent and indifferent, as if she was in a restaurant watching a strange family at the next table.

She had frittered away four hours of their precious weekend and had come home to an empty bed and an immobile fan. She did not switch it on that sweltering afternoon. She wanted the cruel heat to punish her. This was her life.

She wondered where Naseem was, recalling their last fight, the anger and the bitterness in Naseem's voice, her tears of frustration.

Why do two people who have been in love with each other for twelve years still find leading their day-to-day life together so difficult?

Asmita lowered herself onto the The Bed. Dry sobs of despair shook her body. She pulled a large pillow over her face, shutting out the world. Ages later, the storm subsided. She turned and let out a big sigh. What was that whirring noise? Damn! The girls must have left their fan on.

Though she herself was more prone to such lapses than her children, Asmita stood up with self-righteous disapproval and pushed open the door between the two rooms. And there she was! There on the floor, the object of her love and lust, the cause of her ecstasies and rage, lay fast asleep, sprawled naked on a chatai directly under the droning blades. Lying on her back, arms stretched above her head, a knee drawn up, the other leg limp. Desire flashed through Asmita's body like a bolt of lightning. Those small pointed breasts still maddened her. The fine pale hair in the armpits made her want to swoon. She stared at the inky black thicket between the legs, hiding the spring of passion. A gush of wetness started to trickle along Asmita's own thighs.

She almost pushed the door further open, to scoop the woman into her arms and do all kinds of unimaginable things to her. But she stopped. Naseems's clothes were lying around her in a peculiar, almost mystical configuration. The grimy blue jeans splayed in a wide fork, the seam at the fly repaired with black thread that looked like soft, curly pubic hair peeping out through the frayed cloth. The soft white shirt crumpled as if she had tried to wring out the last drop of sweat. The bra gone limp without the firm yet soft mound, and the tiny panty. How does such a little garment even fit over the big bum? Asmita stifled a mischievous giggle. Despite her sexual ardour, she dared not enter the magic circle of discarded clothes. She took in her lover's beauty and shut the door gently. She lay down and shut her eyes.

The foreplay had begun.

Worlds

How Does It Feel to Be a 'Problem'?

V.S.

How does it feel to be a secret?

How does it feel to be invisible?

How does it feel to be unutterable?

How does it feel to be forbidden to be?

How does it feel to be called a joke, a threat, a mistake, a freak?

How does it feel to keep your deepest feelings bitten back into the root of your tongue?

How does it feel to choke on your own truth?

How does it feel to be a living, breathing fact that can't be denied?

How does it feel to be a thinking subject already positioned, interpreted, judged, spoken for, mutilated, overriden, overruled, constructed as absent, silent, mute?

How does it feel to be persistently ridiculed, mischaracterized, distorted, erased, ignored?

How does it feel to have your credibility, validity and legitimacy constantly interrogated?

How does it feel to live with the daily risk of accidental or deliberate disclosure of your sexual self?

How does it feel to ruthlessly juggle illusions, subterfuges, defences, excuses, conspiracies, lies, masks, disguises, ironic personae?

How does it feel to loathe your body as 'wrong', as a living cage of ceaseless torment?

How does it feel to deny, deflect, suppress, elude, evade the demands of your sexual preferences, and relentlessly fight the uncompromising energy of their assertion?

How does it feel to endure insulting scrutiny and be mocked

as a phobic object?

How does it feel to have your emotions, desires and erotic rituals described as deviant, filthy, perverted, abnormal, inferior, criminal, taboo, grotesque, sinful, worthless?

How does it feel to have eager doctors waiting to stun you back to 'normalcy' with pills, syringes, electrodes?

How does it feel to be told that the best you can do in life is to mirror those who are unlike you?

How does it feel to be told that you are diseased?

How does it feel to be called sexually 'addicted', 'afflicted', 'converted'?

How does it feel to engage with the barbaric stupidity and malice of 'How do you do it?' and 'Which one of you is the man?'

How does it feel to search for gay cultural models and be repeatedly submerged in a crashing tide of heterosexual images?

How does it feel to be missing from the dictionary?

How does it feel to grope for historical evidence of your own reality, and plummet into an unscripted void?

How does it feel to be a nightmare from which your bludgeoned parents cannot wake?

How does it feel to be a transgressive phenomenon?

How does it feel to violate safe categories?

How does it feel to exist between the lines?

How does it feel to live in fear?

And yes, how does it feel to go to sleep at night in a heterosexual household and wake up each morning thanking God that you are gay?

❀

Silence and Invisibility

Giti Thadani

Ignorance. When something is ignored, it will gradually lose any vitality it once had, first becoming invisible and then finally disappearing altogether. If memory is not passed on in some coherent way, that which is not remembered no longer exists, and it can then be said that it never existed. This is what is happening to the histories of lesbian sexualities.

In India, the phenomenon of lesbian invisibility is linked to the myth of tolerance which makes two contradictory statements: firstly, that lesbians do not exist, and secondly, that there is no discrimination against them. This was similar to the nineteenth-century Victorian debates around the earlier British law against unnatural sexuality, which has been incorporated into the Indian Penal Code. Section 377 explicitly linked criminal sexuality ('unnatural offences'; 'carnal intercourse against the order of nature') with male agency, and hence did not have to criminalize lesbian sexuality, though the provision remains within the law.

The raison d'être behind this logic was that the implicit tutelage of women's sexuality under heteropatriarchy was not as complete as it appeared to be. In other words, rendering lesbian sexuality explicit was tantamount to acknowledging it and thereby going against the other punitive strategy of silence and invisibility. One is reminded of the Nazi regime's strategy of monitoring lesbian sexuality by providing for other laws which punished women who opted out of heterosexual roles, defining them as 'asocial'. Thus a distinction was made between explicit and implicit punishment of male

149

homosexuality and lesbian sexuality respectively. This difference was then further encoded through coloured badges: male homosexuals were marked with a pink triangle, whereas lesbians, prostitutes and other categories of 'asocial' women were forced to wear a black triangle.

A similar logic of implicit and explicit tutelage governs the legal and cultural status of homosexuality in India. The unspoken discourse of rendering invisible results in the creation of categories of sexual behaviour and sexual identity. This intersects with the myth of tolerance where homosexual behaviour between women can be ignored if it is not seen or articulated in any form. In other words, it cannot be validated as an autonomous identity or enter into indigenous historical or cultural canons. By inference, therefore, the self-identified Indian lesbian is viewed as inherently Western, and is subject to frequent criticism on this account. This same reasoning lends itself to the claim that there is no criminalization of lesbians. The earlier British law is spoken of simply as 'the sodomy law'.

However, some instances of 'criminal' lesbianism have been reported in the media. The following case appeared in the magazine *India Today*, April 15, 1990. Tarulata changed her sex to marry her girlfriend, Lila Chavda. Muljibhai Chavda, Lila's father, went to the Gujarat High Court, saying that since this was a lesbian relationship, the marriage should be annulled. Penal action was called for under Section 377. The writ petition contended that 'Tarunkumar (Tarulata) possesses neither the male organ nor any natural mechanism of cohabitation, sexual intercourse and procreation of children. Adoption of any unnatural mechanism does not create malehood and as such Tarunkumar is not a male.' The petition was accepted by the court. No further information about the case is available.

Instead of the colonial nature of the law being questioned, it is used as a technique of coercion and repression, linking it to the indigenous ideology of normal sexuality = procreation.

The term 'sexuality against the order of nature' lends itself to very dubious interpretations. It is not only the act of 'phallic penetration' which propels this law, but the establishment of 'correct gender codes' grounded in an earlier brahminic and caste ideology. Thus, abnormal sexuality = abnormal gender = death: 'That woman having a male form and that man having a female form are possessed by Nirrti.' (Sacrificial Texts, 1000-500 BC).

The internalization of this ideology is clearly manifested in the court's attitude to Tarunkumar. Gender crossover is not enough to establish malehood. Non-reproductive sexuality is enough to constitute abnormality. Tarulata can never be a 'normal' man and hence is considered to be incapable of 'normal' (= procreative) sex, the only legitimate, sanctioned and approved kind.

Another case reported in the Hindi newspaper *Sandhya Times* of September 11, 1995, narrates the following: 'Manisha weds Madhu by putting blood on her head. Not bothering about society or legality, two twenty-two year old women from Muzaffarpur, Manisha Kaushal and Madhu Arora, took vows to become lifelong companions.' The report goes on to say that Madhu's parents tried to get her married to a man, whereupon the lovers fled to another city. There they attempted to make a living by selling leather slippers on the pavement. The people who had rented them lodgings subsequently objected to their relationship, and the couple were eventually arrested by the police. Madhu is reported to have said that if the world tried to separate them, they would leave the world. And if they had committed a crime, then they were willing to go to prison. At least there they would be together and not be bothered by society.

Besides reflecting familial and societal violence towards lesbians, this story also clearly testifies to the criminalization of lesbian identity. Section 377 makes it possible for families to go to the police and avail themselves of this coercive law in order to bring women back into their 'fold'.

Activists have reported cases where the threat of Section 377 is used to break up lesbian relationships. This is very difficult to document due to the intense fear of public humiliation, ostracism and exile.

The stigma of being a 'criminal' as well as a specific social deviant constitutes a double form of victimization. Homophobic assault is seldom publicly reported, though there have been known cases of lesbian battering, rape by male family members, and even murder. The major psychosocial implication of Section 377 is that the lesbian, in being categorized as criminal and abnormal, has no recourse to any kind of justice to counter the multiple violences meted out to her.

❀

The Bi-line

Gauri

I think one has to be slightly mad to be in the ad-world, especially as a copywriter. And being bisexual in this business puts you in the category of completely mad. So I'm mad. So sue me.

I started work in advertising quite late in my life, so I haven't been in this field for very long. I'm not out as a bisexual at work, but they know. How? Hey, if your girlfriend is the only one you talk to on the phone every day, if you go to work on Monday with all these love-bites around your neck and when they ask you how you spent your weekend, you mention your girlfriend's name, if she is the only one you call from the office and the only one you go out of town with, they'd have to be really dumb not to realize what's going on. Right?

What really amazes me is how it's tolerated. Nobody behaves strangely, nobody shuns me, it's taken as just another way of life, but a thing of curiosity. I'm sure they're all dying to ask me questions about myself, about my girlfriend, but since I haven't said anything concrete, they've all restrained themselves. I love it when I'm in control of the situation.

When I look back on how easily it's been accepted, I ask myself, 'So why am I still closeted?' 'It's safer that way,' comes back the answer. How is it safer, you ask? Well, if A tells B, 'Gauri is gay,' the other will say (I hope), 'Has she told you so?' And A will have to say 'No', so then B says, 'Well, how do you know?' So there is that doubt, that hope, that people aren't really sure. I guess I live in an unreal world.

Also, if I come out at work, there's the possibility that my parents might find out in a roundabout way. That scares me. Am I doing anything about it, like telling them on my own? No! Do I feel like I could come out to them in the near future? No! Talking to my parents about being gay would be like climbing Mount Everest in the nude, and standing on the summit with my chest out, fighting the wind. Phew! I'm out of breath just thinking about it.

I come across more and more gays and bi's in the advertising world, all closeted, and I tell myself, 'You're doing the right thing.'

But I still think I'm making a difference at the office—I go around flirting with the women and shouting to the men: 'I hate you male chauvinist pigs!' But seriously though—if I find a statement that one of my senior copywriters has made that's pro-male, I point it out, or include the fairer sex when we've been conveniently left out of a campaign.

I do my bit, but I wasn't born to change the world. I leave that to my girlfriend. She's good at these things. As for me, I'll take life one day at a time.

❀

Burning in Bollywood

Charity

'Check the stocks of raw stock!' I shouted experimentally, my voice rattling around inside the abandoned sets as though it was a small sharp pebble in a wooden box. The line did not sound right at all. I cleared my throat, *kkhrr*, just as villains do before spitting paan on the street, and tried again. 'No, no, Milan, you will most positively have to better that take. *Please* understand that your mother has committed suicide and you need to look at *least* a little sad.'

'Deepa?'

Billy, back already from the shoot in Powai. My skin crawling with venom, I whirled around, meaning to face him dramatically, but I had forgotten the polished waxy floor, and my body kept revolving around like a ballet dancer on leather-soled chappals so that I made one full gyration before returning to the starting point. A one-woman revolution, that's what I was. As I made my clumsy pirouette, I had caught one dizzy glimpse of my tired, dirty man. He was still getting his eyes used to the darkness. Now I stayed with my own eyes on the wall, stubbornly.

'Deepa, I thought you were going to wait in my dressing

room,' he complained. There was a wet sound, something slippery and slithery, and I wished I could vomit. I knew from the squelch that he was wiping sweat off his face and flicking the drops onto the ground.

I was as rudely silent as I had been vibrantly loud two minutes before. He came up beside me and looked at me from the corner of one eye while tying his shoelace.

'Dippy . . . '

We were in a bedroom set, with copper chips cuddled into the blue paint on the walls so that everything would glitter like fire when light broke up the false dark. Do you remember that scene in *Rakhi Behen*? Of course you do, it was unforgettable. Extending through the window, a single silver beam, parting the sumptuous breast of the night and setting alight a thousand supernovas in her dark heart. Me in my balcony seat and a thousand tapori types in the stalls felt the air drain from our lungs when a sleepy Shilpika opened up her kajal-smudged eyes. The empty universe was redeemed; we knew there was a full moon because she was smiling at it.

I pouted at no one, at nothing and walked past Billy to study the wall, pretending to be busy with it. A star came off in my hand and cut my finger under the long, pearly nail. I looked at it as if it didn't belong to me.

'By the way, Abbu was saying you'd make a beautiful heroine, and he knows of some really good roles going right now.'

'You and your agent can fuck off. Every pretty girl with nothing better to do tries out acting. But you promised you were going to talk to Avi about me watching him directing you in *Dil Pasand* and maybe I could help somehow, somewhere, but of course you haven't said anything to him . . . '

My voice faded away, because I wasn't sure what I was asking for, really.

'Baba, we'll go to the Film Institute next month before I

have to give my dates for *Bandook Putra* and you can see what directing is really—'

'Asshole. I don't want to see the Film Institute, I don't want to read books on the Art of Direction, all I want is something to *do*, damn it.'

None of my lines were sounding quite right today. I felt like a puppet manipulated by a bad ventriloquist.

At my outburst, Billy winced and shrugged, and I was starting to think that he had gone away when I heard his voice behind me.

'Hey.' The long front part of the Dev Anand wig he'd jammed onto his head was hanging crookedly over his eyes like a badly designed curtain. With one stylish, mincing palm he swept the hair to one side, giving me that squinty smile to match. 'Kuch kaho, na.'

I smiled at him and let him kiss me, and we walked out together hand in hand, meeting the sunlight.

Afterwards I cried hopelessly, alone at home lying in my own bed after Billy had gone back to his flat. My head was spinning at frightening speed, full of pictures of make-believe policemen in rented uniforms, holding onto tin handcuffs which snapped like the jaws of dogs. Tawdry fakirs had entire coils of the Indian rope trick, and sent them rolling threateningly in my direction. Knotting itself in loops and nooses, the rope moved mysteriously, slipped itself over my depression and tightened bit by bit. I could do nothing. The less I could move, the less I felt that I wanted to escape. Struggling, my natural reaction, suddenly felt unnecessary, and I fell asleep like a child sinking into the snow with the knowledge that by the morning, she will be frozen dead.

The next day I didn't go with Billy for his shooting.

But Billy's sister and my sister-in-law-to-be, Vinita, invited herself for lunch. She had such strong onion breath that afternoon.

'What sort of person has onions for breakfast?' I shouted at her.

She just rolled her eyes and ignored me.

Maybe because of her bad breath, I couldn't enjoy her filmi gossip that day, and I prayed for her to shut up quickly and let me be alone.

This one's 'bad health' was actually an addiction to real Russian vodka and that one's attempt at suicide ended in poison vomited out in a green flood over a Bandra balcony; one man with one wife and two secret love affairs and one woman with half-a-dozen bastard pregnancies aborted; here a fading actor who still raged expensively at the dying of the light, and there a new-born long-lashed child star Baby Guddi-Lilli-Munni. Since the day Bollywood began, how much has the basic story changed? But still we listen. And who doesn't, secretly, want to be a part of it? Even control a part of it . . . somehow.

As soon as my baby hands were uncurled enough to hold some *Filmdaze Moviemagic Starbright* magazine and turn its shiny pages, I was madly in love with the tinsel industry. My eyes first learned to focus by looking at bright pictures of women with beauty spots on their upper lip, nose, chin, cheek, looking up at me from their silky sprawling Kama Sutra poses. Mouths like ripe fruit cut open, eyes as big and full of promises as the freshly-painted hoardings on the side of the road. They were all one hundred per cent certain that they had been destined for this one costume, role, movie, and I looked at them and believed it.

Because my mother was afraid of the germs in cinema halls, as a child I never saw many real Hindi movies. And since she had banned TV from the house, thinking that it would make me grow up into an introverted person with no friends, I never saw much on video either. I must have been ten at least when I first saw a hip-swinging heroine; she had a suave pilot boyfriend and lots of money. The movie, of course, was *Aakash*.

'Are there any more rotis?'

'Should I ask the cook to make some more? Where is that bastard, never around when I need him. He didn't even tell me he was going out.'

'Oh, I should get back to work, so no worries.'

Vinita is a style designer or image stylist. What is it called, exactly—it means turning some person from a vulgar trashy piece in leather miniskirts to a loving mamma in chiffon saris and big red bindi and back again, but just for the eye of the camera.

'Bye bye, baby girl. I'll see you soon.'

For just ten seconds we stopped pretending. We kissed each other, as carefully as though both of us were afraid of something breaking. But what was there left to break. Five years ago, she still hadn't married my cousin and I hadn't yet become her brother's girl—maybe both of us still had a hangover from that old high.

I didn't notice onions on her breath, though. Or maybe I just couldn't come up with any snide comments to make about mint mouth spray.

Reena stared meekly at the ground while her pink-eyed mother covered her in kilo after kilo of spiky gold jewellery.

'You will come to love him, yes . . . ' she sobbed.

'Mera dil itna bada nahin hai,' Gazing blankly at her stunningly gorgeous self in the mirror, Reena spoke without passion. 'There is room inside me only to protect the honour of our family.'

'Cut!' happily clucked the director. 'Time for the saat pheras, get to the shaadi ka mandap.'

Reena got up like a martyred saint. From nowhere, dozens of Ramus and Chhotus appeared and started running around crazily with bottles of mineral water and reels of orange cable.

Reena's eyes were watching the ground again as she followed Billy's dragging footsteps around the sacred fire. The man she was giving herself to in holy matrimony had been destined for her sister. Of the twelve original plots which are the solid roots of the family tree of Hindi cinema, this is the most shamelessly virile. It has fathered more children and grandchildren and great-grandchildren than Abraham himself.

Angrily I slapped at a mosquito, but when I looked at my hands to scrape off the bloodstain, I saw that the thing which was smashed on my palms was actually a free-floating cinder. I had seen the film's superstitious chief controller wander up to the fire with a whole tub of ghee to feed it with, and now the flames were full of energy, with sparks and black ashes jumping from them like little insects.

'What would we do if no one had invented marriage?'

Avi, the director, had come to sit next to me while we all cooled our heels, waiting for Reena to refresh her make-up.

'I tell you,' he chuckled, 'in this industry, we are so dependent on mother-in-laws, dowry, karva chauth, good Hindu wedding ritual with loud shehnai playing.'

'Someday the audience will get tired of it,' I said. 'Then what?'

'Ah, *then*,' he said, shaking his head. 'Gay logon ka hai kal ka zamana.'

I had nothing to say to that. It did not matter, because Avi had started talking to someone else. Maybe the screenplay writer.

'Find a sizzling climax, yaar,' Avi was complaining. 'With one good fight. You people are always giving us a khazana of bad plots.'

'It's not the plot, it's Billy! This is not an action-action movie; you had signed Johnny Khan in the first place, remember, and he would have—'

'Shut up, yaar, Billy's girl is right here.'

I grinned at them stupidly as they craned their heads to stare into my face.

'Sweetie, you're coming to the party, no?' the director dismissed me with his drawling voice. 'Hasn't Billy told you? Tonight at my place. Which is, La Champagna, C-Block, eighth floor, flat 15. Come any time after eleven.' He went back to his other conversation. 'Hinky? What does Hinky know? What has he produced except Tamil skin flicks?'

Since Billy had not in fact mentioned the party to me, I took a taxi and went there on my own at some time after midnight. A servant opened the door and let me in. Avi's flat was only quarter-lit, and maybe half-filled with people who were doing the usual party things. I was wearing a blouse with sleeves to the wrist and a skirt to my ankles, so I looked like a piece of the backdrop and no one even noticed me. I wandered around the flat, since I could not see Billy in that group of people. When I opened the door of one bedroom, I was not surprised to find him there, fondling the shoulders of his make-up artist Shruti as they stood side by side in front of the tall window, looking over the sea. Since they had their backs turned to me, I walked in quietly and found a small chair to sit in, hidden in the dense shadow of a bookshelf. Anyway, I was sure that Billy and the lady were both too drunk to notice me.

'Chupke, chupke . . . ' he sang.

The scene unrolled like something from a really cheap porn movie. I felt that I knew each step of that stale act so well, I could predict it before it happened. He leaned forward to kiss her, then his hands came up to her chest. Vigorously he squeezed her breasts a few times, like the roadside juicewalla trying to press a threadbare living out of a pair of sweet limes, then he peeled away her short tight top, pulling it off over her head with both of them giggling. I don't know what was so funny, it was a joke so old, I myself was beyond boredom.

Silently I sat, waiting patiently for each inevitable move to take place: 'Now give them a quick suck', I thought, and on cue his mouth descended on each nipple like the bee that can only sting once. Fumbling, his fingers hurried to undo her snug skirt and tug it down. I put a black mark against his name for taking longer than he should have. His trousers were unzipped and hitched down to the knee, and then up! onto the bed with the two of them. The plunging and grunting started at once, and was over also, with a quickness that was exemplary. He rolled off, breathing hard and chest heaving, while Shruti mumbled her praises of his performance. Though, it is certain, he could not have done it without the full support of her complete passivity. After all, tali do haath se bajti hai, let's be fair. They started shuffling for clothes.

Before the lights went up, I walked out.

Waiting for the lift downstairs, I found Reena in a purple pantsuit. Her eyes, glazed as usual, looked me over closely.

'You look strange,' she said. 'I don't want to go to the party, I want to take a walk. Do you?'

Like glass bubbles in the grass, little fountains lit from underneath decorated the garden of La Champagna. So the water and the lights played on, night after night, even at one o'clock when there was no one to see them? Posed on the lawn like ghosts, we met big white plaster models of Rodin statues, thinking and kissing away between the tall Ashoka trees.

'I don't want to be a ghar ki lakshmi, I feel sure I will get bored by it,' I said. 'Even if it is a position to be proud of.'

'Being a wife is the same thing as being an actress,' Reena said wisely. 'Even as a starring heroine, I really don't have much power, and my characters never have any power at all.'

'But are we saying that because your career is headed downhill, and my boyfriend is fucking a painted face-painter?'

'If we are, so what. Is it not true that all revelation has to come from somewhere?'

How do you want this story to end? Me getting together

with Reena? 'Nahin karna tha pyar, lekin . . .' A plum role which I should snap up, in your opinion.

Reena and I unsealed the wine which she had brought for Avi by pushing the cork down into the bottle, using the blunt end of the kajal pencil from her handbag. We slowly got drunk, lying on our backs with the stubble of cut grass scratching our skin through our clothes, and eyed the moon overhead, while the loyal old watchman of La Champagna distrustfully watched us.

Glossary

Gay logon ka hai kal ka zamana – The future belongs to gay people
ghar ki lakshmi – new bride entering the home of her in-laws
Kuch kaho, na – Say something, won't you
Mera dil itna bada nahin hai – My heart is not that big
Nahin karna tha pyar, lekin . . . – I didn't want to fall in love, but . . .
Tali do haath se bajti hai – It takes two hands to clap
tapori – loafer

❁

A Lesbian Crime Reporter Takes a Day Off

Kokum

Socialite Scoundrel 'Nimi' Recaptured in Bar Drama
In a perfectly planned operation yesterday, a beautiful young woman on the wanted list of every single man in Bombay, was picked up from a bar on Marine Drive.

It was around 10 p.m. on Wednesday, February 14, that

Lady Inspector Sushila Deshpande of Malabar Hill Police Station, who happened to be off duty, received a tip-off from a well-known socialite that the woman, Nameeta Bhelpurwala, alias Nimi, would be coming to the Plush Pussy bar, along with male friend Ima Gé.

According to well-placed sources requesting anonymity, Inspector Deshpande's determination to nab Nimi was of long standing. Nimi had been held in Inspector Deshpande's custody four years previously, but when the latter had subjected her to rigorous interrogation about her connection with notorious female gangleader Jasminabai, Nimi had absconded, and had proved since to be untraceable.

Lady Inspector Deshpande lost no time in calling Constable Sunil Raote, detailing to him to distract Gé while she herself took on Nimi. The two officers then dispatched themselves in plain clothes to the bar.

By 11 p.m., Inspector Deshpande and Constable Raote were inside the bar, and within a few minutes two people who matched the description of the suspects entered. Inspector Deshpande winked significantly, which was the signal agreed on by the two officers to close in.

Unfortunately, Nimi intercepted the signal and interpreted it as a move preliminary to a pick-up. Recognizing Inspector Deshpande immediately and fearing a trap to detain her under Section 377 of the Indian Penal Code (unnatural sexual acts), she tried to leave the bar quickly and without incident.

However, Gé, who had had a previous encounter with Constable Raote while operating under the alias Dolly Dupatta, was once more in the strong arms of the law. Since he was having a heated exchange with Constable Raote in a darkened portion of the bar, he was unable to abet Nimi's attempt to escape.

Nimi had no choice but to surrender, and Inspector

Deshpande promptly swooped on her. During interrogation at Inspector Deshpande's residence, Nimi broke ·down and admitted that her love had not been diminished over the years she had been absconding. Thereupon Inspector Deshpande vowed to provide Nimi with police protection for the rest of her life.

❀

The Score

Preeti

It *is* a fact that women at work play the 'female card' to defuse tension between the sexes. Not by fluttering their eyelashes, obviously; the levels of disguise are very subtle—refined flirting, acting helpless, and so on. But I've seen women resort to this kind of manipulation over and over in offices where there's a certain amount of hostility from men—because men are threatened by strong women.

In every workplace, men can always spot a woman who doesn't play the game of the sexes. And that's when the trouble starts, because they don't know the rules of any other game, and are completely at sea when trying to deal with someone who doesn't pretend that she's kowtowing to them, trying to impress them or hook them. It wasn't that I was unwilling to do all this, exactly, I didn't even know how. I didn't react to male colleagues as men, but as fellow human beings, and they had no clue what to do with me.

I had a strange experience at one of the advertising

agencies where I was working. A friend of mine who's gay himself, and also knows about me, came and told me that the previous night all the guys had got together—the famous 'male club' syndrome. So, inevitably, the talk veered around to the topic of women in the office, and they started discussing their levels of sex-appeal, taking them one by one. So for a while it was 'Oh, Denise, my, Denise, isn't she sexy,' but then they started on the ridiculous business of giving women scores, which has been happening all over the world ever since that film *Ten* with Bo Derek. According to my friend, they were going about this game in the usual raucous kind of way, 'this woman's a seven, and that woman's a four', but when they came to me, apparently there was silence. And then they all said, 'You know, the funny thing is, she's so desexed.' There was general consensus on that, and when they tried to imagine what I would be like in bed, they just couldn't come up with any image of me at all. So they dismissed me as someone who was completely frigid. When I heard this, my first response was to burst out laughing. My friend had thought I was going to be very upset. But, as I explained to him, 'If women were to sit around giving men scores, you'd also get a zero because they don't get any sexual signals from you.'

Though the men in that office thought I was desexed, the women began to realize that I was gay, either from something that I had said or from something in my attitude. Obviously word got around, especially because I had not bothered to deny it. I was very idealistic, I thought, in this day and age what difference does it make, especially to these people who're not from conservative, orthodox families? I couldn't have been more wrong. They had accepted this gay guy, but when they came to know about me, the backlash that I faced was terrible. When people started becoming aware of it—*is she gay, we're not sure but maybe, is she, isn't she*—suddenly I found people reacting to the most innocent physical gesture from me. If I was going down in the lift and I just put my arm around somebody's shoulder, I'd find him cringing. Not once was my gesture even tinged with sexual feeling, but they would recoil from me, or they would literally detach me as though I had tentacles.

I know even gay guys go through this—there's always been at least one at every place I've worked at—but while there's teasing, there's ribbing, even some level of witch-hunting, at the end of the day they're part of the male pack, and the men will rally around them.

But the women at the office were not at all supportive of me. I started feeling this antagonism even from them. For example, I had a female colleague who knew a lot less about the business than I did, but because of my particular faith in women I used to step back and give her a lot of space to discover things for herself, never enforcing my point of view. Still, she was always engaged in a game of one-upmanship with me.

What's more, as soon as she realized that she could take advantage of me, the situation deteriorated to the point where I was taking shit all the time for things she had slipped up on. I finally had to talk about it to my immediate bosses. And with my own eyes I saw her play the 'female card'. One of the bosses started off arguing with her because he knew she was in the wrong, but then she began to sweet-talk him, and baby-talk him, and the next thing was, he was physically moving towards her, as if drawn by a magnet. You could almost see the pull, she was using her sexuality so strongly. And then, of course, I was the villain of the piece.

I didn't stand a chance on the grounds of pure fairness or justice, free of gender. The quality of the work was really suffering—she didn't know very much, but everyone was conceding everything to her, 'Yeah, yeah, do it the way you want to,' standing there with their tongues hanging out. Finally

I decided I had to get to the top man, the managing director. I went off for a drink with him, and I said, 'I want to talk to you, do you know what's happening with this woman?' He turned around and said to me, 'Look, I know why you're so hostile to her, she's told me how you feel about her and so I don't want to hear a thing.' She had prepared her defences so beautifully: 'Do you know so-and-so is gay? She wants me and because I don't give in to her, there are all these problems taking place between us. She's frustrated and she'll come and tell you things, but this is what it's really about.'

That's when I realized, it's all very well to say, 'What the hell, I don't care if they know I'm gay', but it can easily be used as a weapon against you. Just because you're gay, and encouraging of women around you, other women might not be as positive. Women operating in a man's world play by the same rules as the men do. Unless the woman you're dealing with is evolved, you're facing exactly the same kind of shit that you would with a man.

Later on, I joined another organization. The people there were very middle-class; many of them had recently come to Bombay from Haryana or Madhya Pradesh. They didn't have the veneer of sophistication of Bombay's modern society, yet they were much more open to my being gay than my colleagues from the place I had just left. They didn't question it, they didn't put any labels on me, they simply accepted me for what I was. And the women were very comfortable with me—after all, I wasn't threatening in any way. They would come up from behind and hug me, or hold my hand and ask me if I was upset.

It's sad that in urban society we've lost that particular simplicity which you find if you go outside the major metropolises in India. When I was a child, we sometimes lived in small towns when Dad was transferred from place to place—he was in the army—and there I used to find such naturalness in the bonding between women. The word saheli literally means saheli there—close women friends, bosom pals, and there is no sexual interpretation of it. If two women hug each other, or a woman is lying in another woman's lap, or goes to sleep with her head on the other's shoulder, no one thinks anything of it, it's taken for granted that women are emotional and touch each other and express themselves with great tenderness. That is what we've lost. Importing concepts like lesbian, gay, sex, sexuality has actually been detrimental to women's relationships.

For example, at the very beginning of my career, in one of the first workplaces I was in, my immediate boss was a woman, much older than me. She would come into my room and nuzzle me and say, 'What are you doing?' I would tell her, 'I'm working on the job you assigned me—you've given me a deadline!' and she would say, 'No, no, come and sit with me and chat.' And then she'd talk to me about all sorts of things which were strictly non-professional, including her emotions and emotional life. She started calling me over to the terrace flat where she stayed with her sister. She was very caring, and since I was vulnerable and extremely lonely, I started developing feelings for her. I happened to tell one of my friends, a gay woman, and it's my bad luck that one day she came to my office and said, 'Where's that boss, I've been wanting to see her ever since you told me you've got the hots for her.' I told her to shut up, for god's sake. This friend went over to the wall, which was part glass, separating my boss's cabin from mine, and she kept peering through it and saying, 'Where is she? Where is she? I'm dying to see her, show her to me.'

The other person in that room kept working quietly, but she must have been listening, because from that day onwards, my boss turned so hostile to me that it became impossible to sit in the same room with her. Before that she used to praise all my work, but afterwards, no matter what I did, she would turn it down and throw it out of the window, saying, 'You're not even pulling your weight in this place, you're not doing your job, this is absolute trash.' It was her way of dealing with the words my friend had used to describe our relationship. I knew what was happening, and I knew my days were numbered in that agency.

My sexuality has continued to affect my career—when I moved to another organization, the news traveled with me. At the next place there was this guy I'd already worked with before, and we were good friends. One day he came into my cabin and he said very seriously, 'I want to talk to you, but I don't know where to start, I'm so upset. I just heard something about you, and in fact I fought with the person who told me, on your behalf.' I sensed what was coming, and he went on, 'I met somebody from that last agency where you were working, who said, "You know, so-and-so is gay." And I said, "Impossible, impossible, she's completely a man's woman." But this person was absolutely sure, and insisted, "Don't you know, the reason she's left so many organizations and changed so many jobs was because she was always found out and had to move on."'

My colleague went on, 'I argued so much for you, I tried so hard, but then I met somebody else the other day who said the same thing. Why are they saying all this? You're not gay!' I looked him straight in the eye and said, 'But I am, I'm sorry but it's true.' He said, 'Impossible, you're not butch.' I said, 'But I don't have to be! You're not very macho for that matter, I could have imagined that you were quite gay. No, I know you're not, but frankly from looking at you no one would imagined that. There's a tremendous amount of woman in you and that's why no woman thinks anything of it if you pull her onto your lap or put your arm around her neck.' He was so stunned, he said, 'I can't take this, please tell me it's not true.'

Three months later, he was still coming into my cabin and saying, 'Tell me you're not gay, you're so natural with me, you're so free with me!' That wretched stereotype that women who are gay are not comfortable with men . . . that was what first opened my eyes to the fact that it's the men who can't cope.

The news about me also got around at the last place I was at. This youngster who was a trainee under me, who used to be quite scared of me, suddenly starting thinking he could rattle me by hinting that he knew. Once he came up to me in this simpering way, holding a model's photograph, and he said, 'How d'you like this? Quite nice, isn't she?' I put him in his place, but a week later, someone else picked up the ball. So I'd be sitting there in the room with these guys, with everybody baiting me, and I'd have to pretend I didn't understand—there was no point telling them to shut up, because then they would just get a bigger kick out of it. One guy would say something about a woman: 'I don't think she's got a good figure, what do you think? I tell you what, let's ask a *woman* what she thinks, maybe she'll have a better idea.' And another guy would add on: 'Yeah, what to do, did you know there are some women who *like* women, and maybe even more than me! Maybe there's a woman in this room who's getting worked up right now . . .'

Once I did some work in which the whole slant was very sensual—that's only natural when you're talking to a woman consumer about lingerie! But because *I* had done it, there were a lot of snide and smutty comments passed around: 'Have you ever wondered how come all her campaigns are about women's bodies . . . ?'

Being gay is one of the biggest possible handicaps in the workplace. I became paranoid about anyone knowing, but at the same time you can't hide what you are.

The last incident in this sorry saga happened three months ago. I was trying for a job, and called up a guy I had got to know about ten years ago. He's the head of an agency, the CEO. He was a great friend, but I was not blind to the fact that he was trying to get me into bed—he used to ring me up, and his idea of offering me a job was to say, 'Would you like to love me or would you like to work for me?' The job never came to anything despite months of wining and dining, all apparently with the object of discussing my joining his agency. He said to me, 'What is it, I want to know, are you one of us?' I said, 'What do you mean?' He said, 'No, just tell me, are you different from the rest of us?' I deliberately acted dumb. He said, 'You know, some people are different, that AC/DC thing, so are you one of those AC types?' I was so disgusted, but it got worse, he said, 'Is that why you aren't interested? I mean, I've been so sweet to you, and I've taken you out to dinner so many times.'

This man used to say, 'You want to go on a business trip to Madras? I'd really love to spend time with you, you're so intelligent, so good at your work.' And now the same guy was trying to explain to me that I wasn't fit to work in his organization. It was an absolute volte face. Now whenever I speak to him there's always a snide remark passed: 'I called up at home and your mother said you were at *this* number. How come you're always at this place? What do you do there?' One day I had to tell him, it's none of your business.

Being gay at work is a no-win situation. You can't fight the system. You've just got to leave with as much dignity as you can. Even the next place I go to, my past is going to catch up with me. I will know the exact moment when someone's found out, because I've seen it happen time and time again: as soon as a woman resists the accepted world with its boundaries, and ignores the rules of the game that men and women play . . . she's out.

(*as told to A.S.*)

✹

Some Funny Business

Rashmi

Nobody who works in my office suspects that I am anything but a heterosexual. If you happen to be in a job like mine—business or finance—you will immediately understand why I am so hush-hush. All the people at my workplace are single young men in suits and they would make my life a complete hell if they knew. Now it's easy, because they flirt with me, I make hot and wild statements about their cock size, everyone is happy. Sometimes a man will come up and ask for a date, I'll say 'Sure, when you can get it up!' And that is literally that. The End.

In a business like this, you can't think of going crying to the boss every time a man passes a sexual remark. Money is really just another word for sex. You just have to keep on proving to them all that your balls are the biggest ones around.

So I am only true to my nature when I go to the ladies' room. Because I am the only female executive, the whole bathroom is only for me. The amount of time I spend in that place, all the boys think that my bladder is extremely weak. So I go in, and the first thing I do is look into my own eyes in the mirror to see the 'real' me. Then I wash all the 'buddy' jokes away from my mouth—with Listerine! I'm like Superman who goes into a public phone booth to become ordinary Clark Kent. I go into the bathroom and I am a mild lover of women again, for a minute.

I told my girlfriend all this, and she didn't say anything, but the next day she showed up with a present. One dozen panties, and on each she had painted the 'L' word. She laughed and laughed when she saw my face. She had made them so that whenever I went to the toilet and pulled up my skirt to pee, I would have to remember that I was not one of the boys. It would be staring me right in the face!

But the first time when I wore one of the 'lesbian panties' I was as nervous walking around as if I wasn't wearing any panties at all. I kept my knees tightly together at all times when I sat down, despite there being no chance of anyone seeing the writing on my crotch just like that. I was really afraid of falling sick and fainting, because then if someone loosened my clothes, everyone would know I was not what I pretended to be. I can hear them now—hey guys, she's not a ball-busting aggressive bitch! She's a soft little lesbian!

On Non-Resident Angels

Ruth Vanita

To entertain an angel is harder
Than it sounds, is indeed a dangerous
Enterprise. Think twice when your stranger glows.
Angels have a disconcerting way
Of stealing hearts, and flying away.

To One Who Went Away

K.K.

July 25

Dearest G.,

Thinking about you has made me smile these past few weeks. When you read this on the plane to Dubai, I want you to know that my life has been that much happier because of you. No matter what the future might hold for me and you, I am happy to have spent this piece of my life with you: you are the first woman I have met who doesn't act like being a lesbian is something she has to endure—you revel in it.

And when I am with you, I revel in my lesbianism too. I don't feel that you love me in spite of my woman's body. No, I feel you love me because of it. I am so proud I want to tell the world, but of course I can't!

I am looking forward to reading your letters and writing to you about my life here in Bombay. It has been beautiful with you these last days, and seeing you again in six months will be all the more joyful because we will have had time to miss each other. So then we will realize how much it means to be together. But don't miss me too much; I'll be feeling enough of that for both of us.

August 18

Dearest G.,

Talking to you on the phone in those three-minute fragments only reminds me how much I miss you. Maybe that's a good reason why we have to be together, so that there won't be so much pain between us.

I think of you all the time. I think of us laughing, playing cards together in my little room with my parents coming in every ten minutes, or being naked together in your house with no one to bother us at all! What fun to think about a beautiful woman while I'm at work pushing silly envelopes around!

I think of how it will be when we are together again. Every night, I will kiss you for every time that you missed me while you were away from me. And I will never let you go away again.

Late September
Dear G.,

Last night I had a dream that I was at the airport to meet you. So it was just a few hours ago that I last hugged you! Now I am awake and I feel that something is wrong because you're not beside me like in the dream, talking about your teaching and all the interesting young people you meet over there.

You told me that I am always in your thoughts. I feel glad that I have an important place in your life. I would hate to fall through the cracks in your busy timetable.

I've been trying to think up pet names for you . . . I love your name, but I don't want to call you something that other women have screamed out when you slept with them!

The next day
My dearest G.,

I felt I had to tell you something that I have been keeping inside. I loved all the time I spent with you in your house before you left, except after your aunt came back from the hospital and you told me you didn't want to share the same room with me any more, because it made you feel strange to have your aunt know we were sleeping in one bed, even though she does not know we are lovers. It disappointed me because our time was so short anyway, and I was upset that I could not understand why it was important for you.

You do not see that those nights were everything I had, since you spent the day time with your family. And sometimes I think it is all I will ever have, because eight more months seems almost as far away as never. I find it hard to depend on a future when events we can't control somehow separate us.

When you and your aunt discussed all those details of ancient philosophy, and I understood nothing, I felt so small. And I was in your house, so I couldn't escape anywhere. I couldn't hide from you, and I wanted to so you wouldn't see how hurt I was. What was I supposed to do, tell you how I felt? (A little joke—you know my wicked pride too well, I could not have told you).

But I'm telling you now about this because I do want you to understand, even if a part of me doesn't. It was not easy being in a house which wasn't really ours. I really want us to live together in a place of our own when you come back. Do you want that too? I know it will have to be a very small place, and certainly not Cuffe Parade, but we said we could undergo some sacrifices to be together.

Can I tell you something else? I think that your obsession with philosophy is very sexy. At the same time that I felt left out of your conversation, I also felt proud because you matched wits so well with your aunt. The way your eyes lit up when you mentioned Plato! Maybe I should buy myself a Plato disguise to attract your attention and bring you back soon.

October 15
Dearest G.,

I miss you so much. It seems to be easy for you to be in a relationship where we're far apart. But it's not for me. I need you, because you're the only one I can talk to about our love and how much it hurts when you're away. Though I think my mother could have guessed, I'm so sad all the time, except when I get a letter.

But you're not there to comfort me. When you tell me you've tried to call and can't get through, and you laugh about Bombay phone lines, I get even more upset, because I start feeling that the world is somehow against us and I can't fight any more.

I know you will feel helpless when you read this. I know you love me.

Just come back to me soon.

Happy Diwali!
Dear Girija,
    Have a lovely Diwali!
    Miss me lots!

November 16
Dear G.,

You say you found my Diwali card cold and impersonal. But I can't be sentimental and trusting in my letters to you any more.

I've known for months that you don't want to come back, whatever you said in your letters or on the phone, whatever your excuses were for delaying. So I am not surprised at what you are saying now. 'Why is it my fault we're apart? You could easily join me here, and Dubai is so open.'

But you promised you would come back. Sometimes I think you are just like a man.

(submitted by Girija, with the permission of her ex-lover K.K.)

The Pugglee and the Budmash

Angina d'Pectoris

I
some girls have a vital gift
for using others
pressing life from them
and pouring it into a cup
spreeing on blood like beer
but not getting drunk

II
i knew one such lady once
her name was monica
she wore thin dresses
the colour of baby skin but
printed with ghost flowers
and her urgent body made them
skim on top of her surface like
milk floating up its cream
near-black hair dripped from the
top of her head to her back
like slow rain trickling from
arches of old muslim houses
dripped into beggars hands
like misers coins though
her promises flowed freely
her hand would be curled
softly around a handkerchief
that smelled of
real eau de cologne

white lace stained blue-green
with years of dabbing

III
when i lie here in the dark above me
lunatic ideas fly like hellish bats
suck out my blood like she who
cut out my heart with sawlike
caresses dragged at the web of my
meat and tore the texture until it could
not know itself without her help
i scratch myself and every flake
under my gory nail is a midget her

IV
your femme fatale dont make fun
it is too ridiculous for
a woman to say that really
you blare like a sweet fossil hero
from an old romance said
monica memsahib laughing
in english laughed again said
passion was not in fashion
and if thats what those
repressed irish nuns
used to teach in convent schools
in africa then no wonder
the blacks did not get developed

V
the night watchman slamming
his lathi on the railing
twenty feet away
behind a shuffled stack of firewood

each blow trembled loud
in my backbone
pressed to the cold iron
monica flared out
on my chest
both of us drenched
in the monsoon
of her hair
her sharpened teeth
chewing the corner of my mouth
tongue shoveling moans
into my gullet
while her wet hole
ringing my finger
in lecherous squeeze
sucked me in
with the calm totality
of swallowing mint sweets

VI
she did not want someone
more man than me lovelier
or of more cunning lips
she simply tired
and now perhaps
she spills out her
haunted thirsty self on a
chowdry of chowringhee
a nautch-girl or a nabob
or another stupid beggar
just like me but for that
one small distinction
of being unexplored and
in good working order

Glossary

from *Hobson-Jobson: A Glossary of Colloquial Anglo-Indian Words and Phrases, and of Kindred Terms, Etymological, Historical, Geographic and Discursive*, by Col. Henry Yule and A.C. Burnell. [1886]

Budmash – One following evil courses.

Poggle, Puggly, & c. – a madman, an idiot.

Chowdry – (from Hindi *chaudhari*) In a paper of 'Explanation of Terms' furnished to the Council at Fort William by Warren Hastings, then Resident at Moradbagh (1759) chowdrees are defined as 'Landholders in the next rank to Zemindars.'

Chowringhee – (from Hindi *Chaurangi*) the name of a road and quarter of Calcutta, in which most of the best European houses stand.

Nabob – Applied in the 18th century, when the transactions of Clive made the epithet familiar in England, to Anglo-Indians who returned with fortunes from the East.

Nautch-girl – In India and the East dancing girls give a fascinating performance called a natch, for which they are well paid.

Rekindle Hope All Ye Who Enter within These Gates

Sagitta

On a quiet street in Chelsea,
through an unpretentious door,
down a steep, unlighted stairway
to a smoky cellar floor

Painted, grotesque glass mosaics,
half-sawn barrel for a chair,
dim blue light above one corner,
yellow pitchers everywhere.

Here I drop the guarded posing
while the juke-box moans or blares,
and couples in their private world drift by.
I am one with all these people—these unaccepted people,
these people with their lonely, searching eyes.

Watch the boy whose airy fingers
arabesques weave as he speaks,
speculative glance soon lingers
on a new man—him he seeks?

There a butch with one gold earring
drinking beer, waits by the bar
for her femme who's late arriving,
frowns, and lights a big cigar.

Now an eyebrow lifts and quizzes—
it's the age-old, wordless pass,
sparkling champagne flows and fizzes
into casual tourist's glass.

As he gapes at all the queer ones
in their intimate, small world,
the oft-repeated question nags his mind:
How do they love, these women—these charming,
                                        wasted women,
these women with their lonely, searching eyes?
Heedless of all others they are
locked together, every pair,

dancing to the plaintive tune of
'You don't know how much I care!'

One's a crooner, one's a poet,
one a Negress, one a Jew,
dancer, shop-girl, writer, artist,
intellectuals, quite a few. ˙

Leave them to their dreams, oh leave them
you who censure, you who blame,
in their twilight they are happy,
nor do they see need for shame

as they smoke and drink or tango
laugh or argue, boldly kiss,
each craving love, few finding constancy.
The masks drop from their faces—these lonely
                              searching faces
of gay folk in their own unbiased world.

(for Gina and Ted Ware with gratitude and nostalgia)

Fateful Encounter

Pia

I have been attracted to women right from my early teens. But
it was difficult to express my feelings amidst a very Victorian

family setting. I was nurtured in an environment where middle-class values reigned supreme, and all the women around me recommended marriage and children as the ultimate fulfilment.

However, I rebelled and held on obstinately to my secret desires. In spite of their consistent brainwashing, the women in my family couldn't curb my fantasies or control the wild streak in me. I passionately craved unspeakable intimacies with women of unknown names and from unknown places.

I was beginning to doubt whether any of this would ever be possible, when our family moved from Calcutta to Kenya. I was sixteen. Africa was an unknown and compelling continent about which I knew very little.

I started school soon enough there, one of the few Indians among a crowd of different nationalities. I was drawn immediately to a girl in my class. She was at least half native, with her shining dark complexion and gleaming teeth. Her sharp features and her long slim curvaceous body spoke of a mixed descent. Her movements reminded me of a cat's. She looked elusive, mysterious and sensuous at the same time. She dominated the entire class, making us pander to her playful moods. Each time she spoke to me, I experienced unimaginable thrills. But did she really notice me, this unsure, silly new classmate?

You can imagine my surprise when one day after school she walked up to me and said, 'At last we're alone.' She touched my hand and I felt dizzy with a sensation that penetrated my entire being. I told her in a controlled and contrived tone to meet me at my house the next day.

I never expected her to come, feared she wouldn't, but she did. We spent the whole day walking in the drizzling rain, touching each other briefly and teasingly. We were under a spell. We ran around like children, laughing, joking, mocking, until we entered a secluded wood. A long, winding path beckoned us over the hills. The rain moist on our faces, we came closer and kissed.

After that things went a bit dim, and we staggered on blindly, following a trail which led us by chance to a wooden shed with a bed of sorts and a broken door. We stumbled in and undressed each other and made passionate love in the middle of nowhere, with the sound of the rain outside.

I can hardly find the words to describe that first time with a woman. I had waited so long for this. We explored each other hungrily and discovered every pore of delight. I wanted to weep in this woman's arms. It was like being born again.

We woke up dazed and exhausted, and yet terribly aware of our strange surroundings. The whole world had come alive suddenly.

We stayed together for a year and a half, until my family had to leave Africa due to some political crisis. We still talk on the phone sometimes. She is married and has migrated to the West. I live in Calcutta with my partner who is a woman. I will always cherish that initiation by my African lover. Our love is still burning, despite the distance of years and oceans.

Break-up of a 'Boston Marriage'
(for JV-R)

Ashwini Sukthankar

I arrived in Boston last Thursday to meet my girlfriend. I settled into her apartment, tried to think of it as 'ours' and tried to like it. By Monday evening, we had broken up; it seemed the right thing to do.

She is enamoured of my absence. We could not be less suited to each other. She would call me when I was away from her in Bombay, at 4:30 in the morning because of the time difference, we would talk for hours, me sometimes rolling my eyes in boredom and longing to sleep. She thrived on the feeling that if only I were there, everything would be perfect in her life and mine. And me? In the plane, I felt a little sick at the thought of seeing her again, of being re-enveloped in the inconvenience of a relationship. It was so easy for me to forget her when I was wrapped up in the events of my life far away. But when we met at the airport, and she strode towards me, her dark hair swinging against her face, her whole body exuding capability, I melted. Whereas she became increasingly aware of what it would mean to have someone intrude on the solitude she had come to cherish.

I think she is in love with my lack. And yet, it was I who developed that Theory of Asexuality long ago, with its witty idea of enacting a desire for Nothing. It is not the same thing, of course. My girlfriend desires the specificity of my absence, a space to be filled with her yearning for me, whereas I in my days of asexuality desired a nothing which was more generally negating: I simply wanted to be without, aching for the void.

Desire for a gap, a friend remarked, was a peculiarly lesbian asexuality. But I did not want a gap, which suggests something missing. Oh no, I wanted the pureness of the Void, an encompassing nothing.

Though when I say things like that to her, she says I theorize so I won't have to feel. I met her barely days before I graduated from college, on the verge of leaving Boston on the note of forever . . . she says I fell in love with the idea of getting on a plane and looking back over my shoulder with a sigh of regret for what-might-have-been.

Maybe we are both right.

So we broke up forty-eight hours ago, with perfect amicability, though we were barely a few days into a visit that was meant to last five weeks. What does that mean? She was my first love: I resent the fact that the three trite little words she teased out from me, words I had never said before to any other woman, are to be thus wasted on a relationship that has not even lasted four months.

I am also not quite sure what I have lost. I told her once that for me, when it was over, it was over. That a lover could never be a friend. A relationship has an inherent instability that is incompatible with my idea of friendship.

And now? Mentally I refer to myself as her Playmate of the Month: for the four weeks of October we will fuck each other's brains out, to use a favorite phrase of hers. And then I will go home to Bombay.

I no longer know how to entertain her. She asked me to tell her stories, and stumblingly, I told her of the rooster that was my pet when I was fifteen or so, adopted as a chick. I told her about how small and fluffy he had been, how I fed him with corn and oats and other wholesome things, until one day I borrowed a handful of professional chicken-feed for him and found that my baby grew a boisterous red comb and shed his yellow down for stiff white feathers almost overnight. About transferring him from the spare room, where he would shit up a storm, to the yard, where he pecked about in a contented fashion and, to my jealousy, followed my father's every movement worshipfully. At night my father would open the door of one of the downstairs storage rooms, and the rooster would mince inside with perfect docility. And in the end? Well, we came back one day from visiting friends, maybe six months after I bought him, to find him fluttering about, mortally wounded by a knife. When we hurried closer, the rooster gazed at us bleakly and, with a final effort, flung himself at my father's feet and died. And no, we did not eat him . . . I can't believe she even asked me that; typical Chinese-American assumptions about starving Indians, I think resentfully, conveniently quelling memories of sitting at the family dinner table in Bombay and listening with squeamish superiority to stories of heartless Orientals eating their pet dogs.

How could it seem already as though I care nothing for her, this ex-girlfriend of mine? In a certain way, it is aesthetically pleasing, this loss of her that informs the essay I am writing on desire and renunciation. I had thought I could continue to long for her for just a few more days, but her annoyance with my yearning stopped me in my tracks. She was angry with me, when I found myself crying luxuriously at the fact that our love was gone. She said things which—things which have faded into oblivion, praises be, but the look on her face, of contempt and sheer irritation, continues to poison my memory and makes me despise my own weakness.

I told her a story once about irritation. He was one of my flat-mates in college, and one particularly hot summer weekend, he had played with the dial of the thermostat and switched on the heat in the apartment, so that for three days we were all awash in our own sweat and dazed by the searing warmth. When the rest of us figured it out, we were so pissed off we could have killed him seven times over, I remarked. She ignored the story itself and took me to task for the looseness of my language, for the ease with which I swear and speak of violence, and, to my literary dismay, urged me to strive for Universal Truth. The quest for Universal Truth, I told her snidely, makes a pretence of impartiality, of objectivity, in a way that obscures difference. That when she makes a sweeping claim like 'We are both Asian', she ignores the fact that I am not an American, but she is. That, as a Third World lesbian, my concerns are perhaps a little more visceral than hers. That there is a history of distrust between Chinese people and Indians . . . what equivalent of the redemptive *Hindi-Chini, bhai-bhai* can there possibly be for the two of us? The discussion escalated quickly into an argument about whether or not she could cope with being around so much careless viciousness, and on my side, I wondered aloud if the self-censorship I had to exercise in her presence would not be wearying. She pays less attention to what I say than to the way I say it.

She saw everything that I have written so far in this particular document—by mistake, she says, and I believe her, for her scrupulous honesty is not to be doubted, alas. I, on the other hand, would have read her diary if I had come across it, but would have referred to my awareness of what I was not meant to know with obliqueness, with glancing blows where my certainty masqueraded as intuition derived from a flatteringly close knowledge of her.

But she read what I had written, since Moka the cat knocked over my laptop while I was away for the weekend in New York, and she switched it on and opened a file at random to make sure that it was still working. And she realized something of what I felt, and wondered, half in bitterness, why I wrote in my diary a despair and diffidence and thwarted wanting that I had never expressed to her, and asked whether, perhaps, I write these emotions as a substitute for living them.

And then, in spite of everything, she asked me whether it was too late for us.

That is why I am writing out here in the living room with half an eye on the door waiting for her to come back from work, with one cat on my knee and the other at my feet, dog-like. And perhaps it is better this way, since lesbian melancholia depresses and exhausts me. I have no desire for endings . . .

Ending . . . why must there always be an ending? I find myself writing again, but only now that it is over . . . happy women have no need of pens and keyboards, I sometimes believe.

This time I was the one to break up with her. We were so full of young hope when she took me to the airport. But my flight had been canceled—we had a reprieve (or so I thought) of a whole day, a whole twenty-four hours laid out before us in the late October autumn, to be savoured like an unexpected treat. But then what? I woke up the next morning to hear her on the phone with her ex-girlfriend, and realized . . . I'm not sure what I realized, but I know what I felt, like a knot in my throat, another in the gut. I grasped no words, but the tone of her voice—a childlike pleading, low and painful to hear—required no interpretation. She had never used such a tone with me.

What did she tell me when I asked her why she couldn't have waited just a few more hours to make that call? That she had managed to bury all her panicked anxiety about me leaving—never to return, perhaps—for the month of my visit, but had been unable to keep it inside her for that extra twenty-four hours. That I was the one who was leaving, and to whom could she run for comfort but her ex-lover, who was always there?

What had happened, I wondered silently, to the ragged old dyke joke we had so often shared . . . that I would never really leave, I would simply come over and over again.

But what did I tell her? That I would not have cared how much she loved that woman, since I located their relationship in the realm of impossibility, as unthreatening to me intrinsically as my passion for twentieth-century French feminists could be to her. But that, unlike my literary love, her love for her ex-girlfriend had begun to trespass on our life together, had begun to make her take me for granted. That I had begun to believe nothing she said, since she could make two completely contradictory statements with full conviction within moments of each other: *I love you . . . No, I love her.* That I felt distaste at her making a fool of herself over her ex, and that I would not be telling her this if I had not already relegated her to the position of a friend, since, as a friend, I could talk to her with a bluntness I could never have allowed myself before, when I was a lover treading gently on her past.

All this, only hours before my plane left Boston for Bombay. All this, while she and I meandered through Boston pet shops in such a conjugal fashion, buying tropical fish for the newly-purchased fish tank. We said very little consecutively, we simply exchanged sentences here and there, between comparing the relative merits of pool comets and telescope-eyed goldfish.

And then at the airport, with both of us having coffee and biscotti while watching *The Simpsons*, the TV set dislimning the image into reds and greens, she asked me if I was dumping her.

'Well, that's so indelicate,' I sighed. 'When I was trying very hard to be as circuitous as possible.'

Boarding had begun for my flight, but we hurried to the ladies' room, kissed hungrily, I wept. I had not meant to; surely I could have sustained the cool diplomatic civility of the exercise? I gathered the shreds of myself for departure.

'You don't have to do this, you know,' she said, off-hand, as I reapplied my smeared lipstick.

'Better now than later, don't you think?'

As we walked slowly to the gate, she exclaimed, 'How can you throw all of this away?' twirling in front of me in her sleekness: burnt-orange blazer, grey vest, white shirt, jeans.

'Pure spite,' I retorted lightly. 'I don't want you to have your cake and eat me too.'

She smiled. I smiled.

On the plane, seated next to a soothing soul named Adam, I wrote her a letter, and opened my ramblings of farewell with two morsels from our horoscopes in that day's *Boston Globe*.

> *Taurus: A calm discussion will provide answers while defusing tempers.*
> *Gemini: Cut your ties to people who drag you down. Their company is not worth it.*

> *Don't worry, this is the last letter of yearning you shall receive from me, my lost darling. As the imprints of the kisses you gave me at the airport flake off my lips, desiccated by this damned climate control, and the purple bruises—tiny vacuum-seals of possession!—fade from my neck, I will learn to consider you with that clean ache of friendship, to miss you without the frantic anxiety of a lover on her own. Right now the tears are still close to the surface, rendering my nose red and my eyes puffy. (Charming, no?) I have just read the scrap of paper you tucked into my pocket this morning, which did nothing to pacify my rebellious soul.*

> *On a final lustful note, I pay tribute to your body, especially those breasts which you rather disliked me touching, I know. Still, they are defenceless against my mental fingers, which must salute each nipple in tactile memory one last time before I release you. It's dark outside; I kiss you good night. My lips veer sideways from their accustomed perch on your mouth, to settle chastely on your cheeks—twice on each side, of course, in memory of our brief time together in Paris.*

How consciously heartbreaking, trying to be brave through a choking sob . . . How despicably manipulative. And thus did I take my lover's story—her story indeed, for how could she adhere to me, a woman who would never be at home with her but always in exile, offering no treaty but a heartstring?—and turn it into my tragedy.

Glossary

Boston Marriage – defunct American term for lesbian relationship
Hindi-Chini bhai-bhai – Indian-Chinese brotherhood

Thanksgiving

Abu Mansoor

I
Accidentally
as the silhouettes
of gliding riverboats
our skulls touched
when we stooped
to read a plaque
nailed to the case
of a lifesize bronze
Tibetan tantrik yogini

lustrous as the full moon
sky-dancer of the three realms
rider of the wind-stallion
honey-tongued corpse-devouring flame
vase of nectar ocean of red seed
bliss-bestowing diamond-limbed
lotus-eyed destroyer of illusion

the clear square walls

Facing the Mirror

of her glass world
swiveled on the axis
of incomparable thighs
parting the crossbeams
of bright hot lamps

II
Hunched in front
of thousand-year-old
clay pots vast enough
to house Ali Baba
and the Forty Thieves
he photographed me by
a long-necked narrow-waisted
two-handled Phoenician jar
as tall as a woman
we set timer and flash
rushed to pose beside
an exquisite royal firman
calligraphed in red and gold
stamped with the giant seal of

Abdul Muzaffar Muhiuddin Aurangzeb
Bahadur Alamgir Padshah Ghazi
Shadow of God on Earth
Protector of the Kingdom
Refuge of the Poor
Light of the Faith
Slayer of Infidels

III
He said we're like the man
selling mirrors in the city of the blind
he said we're both sleepwalking

through the same dream
he said once he was so drunk
he woke up two days later
flung up on an empty beach
of broken oars black rock white sand
he said watch me drive
with only my thumbs
and handed me his triple scoop
of almond cherry bonanza
his eyes trembling green as new leaves
my tongue chased the last drops
along the rim of the pulpy cone
sweating ice blunted my teeth
like a syringe of morphine

IV
Dagger-thrusts of cold air
seething arctic stars
muddy bootprints straggling
up the path to the house
soiled bandages of snow
on the porch and flakes
brushed like crumbs
from our limp jackets

logs settling drifting
into thick mats of ash

one brother tousled as a dahlia
wilting on the piano stool
salutes me from a halo of bourbon
and glimmering sawtooth jazz
says he loves the black rainclouds
the wings of parrots the maidservants

and conspiring messengers in paintings
of 'the blue guy with the flute'

V

His firelit old mother
whetting her solitude
like a knife on a stone
tips back and forth
in a hundred-year-old chair
that has raked its corner
of the fat yellow rug
into a stubble of threads

she had been trimming
a pink sugar rose
in the frosted garden
of a son's birthday cake

when her husband clamped
the cold unforgiving mouth
of a double-barrelled shotgun
between his waiting lips
as casually as a cigarette

flung across the red halves
of that spliced instant
she watched the lid
of thin grey hair
rise immaculate
as the curve of an egg

before she called anyone
she fell to her knees
and dipped a finger

in the sudden delta
of his pouring mind

VI
This evening tightly shawled
in years of rage she grabs
and hurls a new ten-dollar
rawhide barking bone
across the room past
dozing backwoods partriarchs
and silent pregnant third cousins

it bounces under the sofa
and the three slavering dogs go mad
and we go deaf and she laughs
like a box of damp matches
struck and flaring all together
she uncaps a sixth beer
with her teeth and lets
the plume of a frenzied tail
sweep bottles off the table top
her voice spiked with broken glass
as she snarls above the baritone
woofs dying at precise intervals
in the choked unseen throat

'I don't care where she's from
but son why in god's name
do you always pick girls
who look like boys?'

Yo no soy Mexicana…!

Extranjero

'Yo no soy mexicana, yo no soy mexicana!'

I kept exclaiming this like a joke, a promise, a threat, a curse, those first few hellish days. And then I'd swear I was not Mexican en inglés, ravaging those despotic palatals and fricatives, stumbling against distrust as solid as a fence while we scoured and mopped and swept, till the other cooks started to believe me. I was so glad when the questions and suspicions died, because after all those smoky greasy endless hours, with my legs turning to water and my arms to rubber and that long taproot of pure fatigue smouldering from neck to hip, I didn't have the strength to do anything except yearn to somehow, somewhere, sit down.

Felipe, Juan, Diego, Miguel, Estefan, José Maria and the one they called Loco, his head cowled in fleece like a dark lamb's. Bony as a broom, propped in the narrow angle between the sinks and drowning me in the dense black of his Aztec eyes. Like others up and down the beach, not one of these cooks would say where they were from, and I never asked, or asked their real names. All that mattered to them, and to me, was that they had made it over the border to el Norte, and were able to eat every day, and sometimes sent money home to their villages, and were not going back.

At least not as long as they continued to ease the earthly burden of our employer, Hamilton Hamm, owner of the snack shop. Bald as a melon, stubble peppered around mare's nostrils and mossy half-inch canines. Spasming irises stoked to fever heat impaled me in the murk of his basement office. I stepped delicately over the crippled objects expiring everywhere—a banjo with its neck snapped, a church pew, sunglasses, rosaries, fishing poles, steering wheels. Guatemalan blankets, those blood-tipped plumes wrenched from birds of paradise.

I slid my application across the overflowing desk, watching it pick up oil, ink, dust, ash, crumbs, while Hamm scalped a wart off his finger with a paperknife.

'Mexicano?'

'Indian.'

He scribbled on the form. Didn't ask for identification, or blink at my accent.

'Well, well, whaddya know. My first real Indian. Didn't like the reservation, eh? You a fullblood?'

'One hundred per cent.'

'Not lying to me, are ya? You sure do look like all my guys in the kitchen. Wetbacks, each damned one. Hablo español?'

'Inglés con facilidad,' I said boldly, but he had stopped listening while he gouged inside his ear with the pen. He dislodged something. Reluctant bliss trembled over his face.

'Sign here. You can start right now. Go upstairs and ask that fairy Loco for a uniform. Anything happens to it and I take it out of your pay. And his. Comprendo?'

'Si, señor. Gracias.'

I couldn't resist that, but it was truly absurd, the way I felt las palabras balloon from my mouth like a cartoon blurb, trailing me into a sawn-off closet next to the asthmatic freezer crammed with meat and french fries. Loco threw clothes over the top. The trousers sagged at the crotch like some giant's fraying underwear. I cringed as the zip screeched and bit. The shirt was ketchup red, with CORAL PALACE stitched in mustard arabesques on the pocket over the heart. It smelt of minimum wage and a thousand illegal aliens.

At the end of the first week, as soon as I got paid, I strolled down the boardwalk until I found a haircut shop. The hairdresser was styling the mohawk of a punk whose gang lived by the pier. This kid looked a true nazi—sharp as a dagger, studs and rings pocked like measles over his face, ears, lips, nose, hanging off his eyebrows. The radio was set at some weird station—no songs, not even a tune, just the side of a moody thumb smacking the strings of a double bass. I sat down on a bench by the door and began to turn the pages of old magazines. *Flip flip.* Sounding loud as a bomb. The hairdresser's hands moving the scissors along the nazi's ferocious crest. *Scrunch scrunch.* Blades like a shark's jaw.

'Enough,' the punk said, slamming his boots onto the spotless floor. *Thud thud.* He hitched his leather pants up around his skinny waist, yawning. Knobs flashed in the lining of his cheeks. He pulled ten bucks from his wallet.

The woman went to the counter to ring up his change. I slid into the empty chair. It was still warm from the nazi's butt. I turned to check the clock above the door. La hora diáfana. The dazzling sea calm as glass. The sky a cloudless, painted, stainless, sinless blue—lustroso, diamante. A boy sucked a strawberry ice as he revved his skateboard off a ramp. His sneakers crashed down in perfect rhythm. *Wham wham.* He coasted away, his head a small sunlit crown.

The hairdresser strode back, looking right at me looking at her in the mirror. Smooth fabulous skin, as if she'd been dipped in bitter chocolate. Sleeves of a denim shirt rolled up almost to her shoulder. Lovely ropes of muscles corded along her arms.

'How you doin', girl,' she said. 'Seems like you spent the mornin' in the tiger's cage.'

She pumped a pedal and the chair began to rise. I tore my gaze from her leg. New black jeans. Silver buttons in the fly.

'They got tigers where you come from?'

'Mostly dead or locked up.'

She gave me a sideways glance. Quickly I nailed my gaze to the posters in the shop—those smart stylish joyful heads smiling as though God himself had just served them a free smoking hot Triple Cheese Krispy Krust sandwich from the Coral Palace breakfast menu. Despair still throbbing from the radio. Swift hands around my neck tucking a plastic sheet into my ketchup-red collar.

'How would you like it cut today?'

'Any way you'd like to cut it.'

I sat in a daze while she angled combs in my hair. Her touch the breath of a feather along the tip of each burning lobe.

'Say goodbye to those pretty curls!'

She pinned them up and got to work. I watched her pick an eyelash off my cheek and shake it loose. It spiraled onto the blue cloth of her breast pocket. I clenched my fists to keep from reaching for it.

'These punks!' she exclaimed, trimming carefully along my temples. 'Lord, let that be the last greaseball before lunch. You won't believe what the wind blows in here. Yesterday, some stompin' maniac in a wetsuit, right from the waves. Actin' like he's surfed up from Hawaii. Drippin' all over my floor. Knocks over half my shampoos with his fuckin' board. Wants his head shaved for less air resistance, some crap like that.'

'It doesn't suit white boys,' I said. 'Right off they all grow that milky-green fuzz.'

Again she gave me a sideways look. Ran fingers across my scalp. The bones of my face were taking shape within the cropped thatch, like the contours of an egg in a nest. She leaned across me, took electric clippers from a drawer, plugged them into a socket. My pores prickled into avid bumps.

'I don't know if this will work,' she said. 'You really have to have Black hair for a good fade.'

'My hair *is* black,' I said. Then my heart began hammering

as I realized what I'd said surely was the stupidest remark to have been made, at that unforgiving moment, up and down the coast. She flicked her wrist and bent towards my ear as the clipper whined over the back of my neck like a crazed metal insect.

'No, sugar. I mean Black hair. Like—Black. Know what I'm sayin'?'

She switched the clippers off, pulled the plastic sheet from my ketchup-red collar and shook it. In the silence I could almost hear my cheeks flame under their tan. Quickly I pointed to the mess littered around our shoes. All the people who'd been in the chair before me. Sunshine yellow, rat grey, sandy, carroty, ginger, honey, platinum. The nazi's rainbow spikes—emerald, turquoise, saffron, indigo.

'You should get the kid to weave himself a wig from all that,' I said. 'Save you a lot of trouble.'

She laughed for at least a minute. Voice deep and glorious. Smile that could charm the honey from a bee. Teeth white as the moon. And no pins in her tongue.

She wanted to buy me lunch, and I said okay, anywhere except the Coral Palace.

We shared a banana split and a mocha. The buzz from the coffee kicked to the roots of my newly-shorn hair. The ice cream melted so fast, we had to drink it through a straw. Her mouth to mine and back, twice.

'Want to see somethin'?'

She took me all the way out to the headland. Leaping surf smashed against the seawall. A few people leaned over the rail, staring at the seals spread over the rocks. A thick sleek brown whiskery quilt, saucer-eyed. The air smelt powerfully of wet dog. Suddenly, out of nowhere, they turned like soldiers, a hundred of them all together, and flopped down facing another direction, shifting and settling, closing up the cracks between their fat gleaming bodies. We watched for a while till one of their huge old rancid grandfathers lurched to the edge of the rocks and slid into the water, and immediately the rest flopped around together, all of them, and ploughed into the current. In a few seconds all I could see were dark heads in the shimmering blue distance.

My lunch break was almost over. We walked back. The nazi sat with with his gang by the pier, preening his incandescent mohawk, chief rooster of a barnyard fenced with sullen boots and the reek of urinous leather. Sometimes the lifeguard strutted across—square-jawed, bronzed and slick with suntan lotion, bulging out of his little red-white-and-blue swimtrunks, some peach-assed bikini babe hanging off his sculpted shoulder. He'd glare as if he wanted to knot the punks with their own belts and chains and sling them into the car wash. But they'd just cruise on to the next pier and lie down and smoke and sleep in the fishy green-black shade of diseased wood cloaked with slime and barnacles. And how Hamm detested the punks coming into the snack shop. He'd slouch nearby as they wolfed down the crisp hot junk I'd just fried, and look at them as if they were squirts of pancake syrup on a snowy tablecloth.

'What the hell is it with these kids?' the hairdresser said as we passed them. 'Wearin' boots and jackets and all this other crap, and in the fuckin' sun all day? Live all year on the fuckin' beach and never once go into the water?'

A thread of sweat raced towards her collar. I itched to lick it off. Start on that bitter-chocolate skin and keep going.

'I can't stay now but I'll be back,' I said as we reached the door of the haircut shop. She glanced in. A woman stood by the counter, clutching the hands of two fierce towheads scarlet with anger, sunburn and cherry soda.

'Don't let me stop you, sugar.' She gave me that sideways look and laughed. 'But you hardly got any hair left. What else can I can do for you?'

She was taller than I am, but things are different in the ocean, so one day I grabbed her, just like that, and managed to struggle upright while the waves crashed against my spine and the undertow dragged at my legs and the sand racing under my feet slipped and plunged. But I lifted that bitter-chocolate body for a minute and before she fought her way out of my grip I kissed her mouth, right there with the sun beating on the back of my neck where my fade began, and some kid's forgotten rubber whale winking at me with a painted eye, and a pregnant Mexican asleep on the beach under a striped umbrella—that was one of the best moments of my life, the one I turn inside out over and over, like a pocket I can't believe is empty.

I rode that feeling all the way into the night shift, scraping and scrubbing the dishes while Loco dried and stacked, his hands tenderly cradling each plate as if it were a white dove. We shoveled muck from the drains with a baseball bat Hamm kept hidden below the cash register. His mind was waiting for the day he'd take a swing at the nazi's ravenous troupe. Or a crewcut turnip-head sailor sweating tattoos and vodka. Or a barefoot surfer boy peeling his wetsuit down his silken chest. Or some sultry Saturday-night Latina in murderous high heels, blotting her maroon lipstick with two dozen paper napkins and ramming them down the throat of a Coral Palace styrofoam cup.

The air in the kitchen used to get so full of water and grease that Hamm allowed us to rip holes in garbage bags and wear them over our uniforms. But we got soaked anyway—as much with our own perspiring efforts as from the venomous pipes that crawled from sink to sink. Each time Loco saw me in my plastic tunic he leaned over and hooked a thumb into my belt loop, gently tugging.

'Qué bonita! Nuestra Señorita de la Cocina!'

And I'd reply, 'Bailamos, querido Montezuma . . . ?'

And we'd laugh, no matter how tired we were. We muzzled the night's sacks of trash and hauled them outside to the dumpster. Rats as big as kittens savaged the innards, and sometimes we found homeless winos camped in the stink between the corroded bin and the Coral Palace kitchen wall. Breath you could have sparked with a match, and ursa major claws that ripped our leavings from the rats' wet snouts. Loco was as slim as a lily, but very strong. The sacks burst as he pushed them in. I reeled back from the putrid exhalation. He curved his arms around my dripping waist. And there we stood, garbage bag pressed to slimy garbage bag, in weak starlight, the ocean dimly roaring, and all the neon vowels in C R L P L C gone like rotten teeth. His mouth hovered and settled, chaste as a dragonfly's wing.

She liked the way I tanned to glowing copper like the Mexicans. Sometimes we leaned against the rail by the headland and gazed for long minutes at the rows of white bathers slapping on suntan oil, emptying bottle after bottle as they revolved in blistered agony under the noon sun like kababs on a skewer.

'Praise the Lord,' she laughed. 'Us Blacks, we just stay—Black.'

Every once in a while she'd come up behind and press into me and inhale, as if I were a dewy winter rose unfurling in the Mughal Gardens.

'Why are you growing your hair out?' I asked, grabbing a fistful and releasing it just to watch it spring free and mushroom into an ecstatic Afro. Water slid off it for a long time before it got wet. I could sink my hands in it right up to the wrist.

'So I look different. To these asshole cops all Black folk are the same, but just in case.'

'What did you do?'

She flipped me over, laughed and tunneled a long thigh between mine. I watched the dark core of her pupils dilate like the circle of a target in an archer's eye.

'Nothin' serious, lovergirl. Don't worry.'

But I did.

I took her to the boarding house where I was living. The very cheap rent was collected each week by the landlord of this ark of derelicts, Tío Angelito. Leathery as a turtle. Tough as the root of a hundred-year-old tree. Jaws that crunched Spanish like broken glass. We passed him snoring in a furry armchair, ankles awash in empty beer cans.

'Christ,' she muttered. 'He must have been tossed overboard by that fucker Columbus himself.'

A honeycomb of cells, each with a bunk bed, upper and lower. A stool. A light bulb. That was all. If you stretched your arms you could trace graffiti with your fingertips, each wall a garbled testament of our hallucinations, deliriums, manias, frenzied births, mortal wounds. The corridor ended in a slimy toilet where I scoured burger grease from my vegetarian pores. No one except Tío knew who arrived and who departed. When I was on the Coral Palace midnight shift, for weeks the only tenant I saw was a bozo from down the hall, skinny as a pencil, sleepwalking in butter-coloured pajamas, crucifying me with alcoholic eyes. Sometimes when I lay awake and listened to the surging ocean, floodlit under a white-hot moon, it seemed as if the whole house was cobbled together with our brutal cadences—sighs, groans, yells, snarls, the rasp of agonized lungs, the atrocious grinding of teeth as we plunged from dream to dream.

'Hallelujah,' she said, returning from the bathroom, 'the shower works.'

I pulled my towel from her dripping shoulders. As soon

as our skins touched, her mouth seized mine and it made my head whirl, the way her breathing quickened and roughened and she seemed so eager and young; but when her body slid over me she was instantly voracious, her desire exact, her muscles seeking and plundering, her strokes more than slightly cruel, which I love in a lover. And within, despite her swallowed moans, despite her exquisite shudder on the brink, despite the urgent naked self that pulsed and vanished, delicate as a gill, she let those fierce walls unclench and liquefy beneath my fingers.

That weekend people poured in from the beach like sand, like rain. At one in the morning we were still swabbing down the counters and floors and stacking the chairs on the tables, while the kitchen repopulated itself with new citizens—giant roaches annihilating each other like the legions of the Kauravas and Pandavas. Antennae bristled from cracks in the wall and behind the stove. Velvety growths twirled their pleats on the bathroom ventilator. The Coral Palace had never passed a sanitary inspection, but it was never closed down.

Then Hamm crashed in through the front door, almost bulldozing Loco who was lining the trash cans with fresh garbage bags. The boss was coked up to his spermy eyeballs. He circled us, pointing his forefinger like a pistol as he ranted on about seeing his head on the shoulders of a man in the audience of a talk show that featured a hermaphrodite, a dog-faced boy and a stump who played the xylophone with a stick between her teeth.

He lurched to the end of the kitchen where I was siphoning coal-black oil from the deep-fryers. Breath as torrid as a dumpster wino's scalded the back of my neck. My fade prickled alive in terror.

'Ain't you got nothing to say!' he screamed. 'Indian! Big Chief Little Cook! Fucking motherfuck!'

By the time I snatched up the spider-legged wire brush we used to rake hamburger crud off the grill, Loco and the others had surrounded me. Closer than a ring on a finger. Hamm kicked over a mop and a bucket of suds and lunged swearing through the door into the lurid carnival of his detonating mind. I stood dazed within that swift sudden wall of muscle and bone, as Loco murmured consolation. Spanish syllables fluttered around us like tiny iridescent birds from the rainforest's steaming heart.

I told her about Hamm going for me.

'He's dumber than the hole in a donut,' she said, yanking her 'fro from its band, a vein ticking in the middle of her forehead. 'Goddam pendejo.'

Sudden as the edge of a cliff. The only time I ever heard her swear en español, la lengua sinuosa, tumultuosa, vertiginosa.

'Where did you learn that?' I asked, astonished.

'Lord knows, lovergirl. Maybe I read it in a book.'

How we laughed, even Loco, embers glistening in the drenched night of his Aztec eyes. And after that whenever I saw Hamm I had to chew my grin back into the shape of my lips, because it is just not possible to be nervous of anyone your lover has called a pubic hair.

I watched Loco drift away, his shadow uncrumpling as he guillotined the towers of some idiot sandcastle. Always like this, tangled in himself like a leg of the pier in fugitive seaweed. The sun was setting, round and brassy as a coin, igniting his rim of hair like a Byzantine halo. The waves rushed in higher and stronger, the ocean dark and wide as some unknown terror. New moon curved as a rib, sharp as a fang, hauling our secret tides. The seabed pitch-black, freezing. Yet creatures swam in those depths, blind sacs spawned between the huge silent weight of infinite water and the earth's barbaric, flaming, roaring womb.

She pulled me into the water, further than I had ever been. The waves slammed against my spine, hungering. No sand or rock underfoot, only a swirling trough. I kicked in fear.

'Take it easy, girl,' she said, as my flailing body twined around hers. 'There they are, they come in real close some days. See them?'

And for a few minutes the dolphins did play right next to us, leaping and diving like God's own toys in the day's dying light, nudging the lunatics still out on their surfboards. Then a huge wave flung us gasping all the way back onto the beach. Bonfires glimmered where the punks were camping by the barbecue pits. We lay till we were almost dry. Her legs locked mine in a scissor-grip as she kissed the salt off my ears, my neck, the slope of my collarbones. Each time I opened my eyes I traced another segment of the zodiac wheeling dimly from horizon to horizon.

Exactly a month till my birthday.

Again I woke lathered in sweat. Each warm drop fat as a pea. Always the same—Loco and the rest like ragged snakes on empty bellies, trailing their sloughed skins across gashed frontiers. Dictators' boots that outshone the sun. The screams of the tortured erupting everywhere, lush poisonous corollas of blood. Swamps fertilized with human bones. Rivers of corpses. Platoons of rapists. Villages of orphans. The shattered tongues of church bells. The helmet of the jungle, dark as the inside of my dreaming brain. Trees tipped with bayonets, strung with luminous garlands of animal eyes.

That evening—how was I to know it would be our last—we met by the pier and tore up stale Coral Palace burger buns, throwing them to the frantic shrieking gulls. The nazi and his gang lay nearby, sucking deep drags from a cigarette they passed from mouth to pierced mouth, as they watched a man from the shop next to the haircut place arranging equipment to take a picture of a couple against the sunset. The sky blazed like the inside of a ruby. Groom sweltering in a tuxedo, giggly bride in a long white veil and gown and foaming lace. Blissful homeloving arms, toothpaste smiles that flashed on and off as the waves galloped to devour all our shoeprints. The photographer kept adjusting the camera. The legs of the stand wobbled treacherously whenever a kid rattled past on a skateboard.

'What a fuckin' pretty pair we'd make, you and I,' she laughed, that deep glorious laugh, as she held out the final crust of bread. A divebombing beak snatched it, almost nicking her fearless thumb.

I never saw her after that night. Loco and I searched and asked everywhere for a week, up and down the beach. Everywhere, till we noticed the pendejo lifeguard watching us through binoculars from his high chair, and Loco became nervous. She disappeared, just like that, as if she'd swum out after the seals and the dolphins. Hamm was sure the cops had nailed her for dope or stealing a car. Loco thought she'd been picked up by la Migra because she knew so many illegal aliens. I kept going to work, but the stench of ripe meat and bubbling grease made me throw up over myself and the clogged Coral Palace sinks. Loco hosed them out. And when Hamm, eager nostrils flared in anticipation, was busy with a dollar bill at his funky desk, laying lines of bad coke onto a mirror, Loco stole me another uniform.

The fuses had blown at Tío Angelito's. My cell was as dark as the seabed. I kicked off my grease-soled shoes, dropped my clothes on the floor. I groped through the tenacious hieroglyphs of exhumed hysterias, stillborn rage, abysmal rites, festering intimacies, the narcotic braille of our delusions. The wall seemed fragile as a playing card. When a voice spoke from the lower bunk, I almost screamed.

'I took your pillow. I hope you don't mind.'

A woman's English accent. Crisper than a cornflake.

'No problem. I don't use a pillow.'

I fumbled into the upper bunk, nauseated by the despair that fell upon me like a humid shroud. But it could not muffle that voice. She was waiting for friends, she said. Traveling elsewhere, they were going to meet at the hissing edge of this continent. They planned to arrive from different hemispheres, along different meridians, reading different maps. Folding the world like the corners of a handkerchief.

'I had an operation for a tumour. I was going to die, but the doctors managed to get all of it. So here I am. I'm celebrating. I'm going to be on holiday for a long time. For as long as I want. Here, it's covered up now, but feel this...'

A warm palm guiding my elbow through the dark. My fingers in strange fingers, forced under a dense crinkled sheaf. The scar writhed all the way across the back of her head like a hideous smile, its ridges and weals clamped over the spongy lobes, the seething fissures, the charred voltage, the marsh of palpitating juice. Sanctuary of the fetid fibrous lump, the size of a tennis ball, anchored in a boat of blood, glistening.

'Take my address, come and visit,' the voice murmured, shawling itself in a drowse as my thumb stroked the grimacing sutures. I traced the chasm to its butchered tip, squirmed my hand from the moist glove of hair. Quickly I touched my fade, now stubbornly curling.

'Thanks,' I gulped, choking on tears and saliva and the words splintering like fishbones in my throat. 'We'll have tea with the Queen. And make her wash the cups.'

By the time I woke in the morning the woman was gone, leaving my towel splotched with grime and the musk of her scalp caged in the teeth of my comb. Staring down at the two pillows in the rumpled lower bunk, I realized I didn't know her face or her name, though I would be able to pick out instantly, if I heard it anywhere, the voice that slithered like a blind rope into the churning storm of my grief. And when I think of all that I try not to remember the grip of those bitter-chocolate thighs, or the molten surrender to an insistent tongue, or the lovely muscles in the arms that pinned mine. I think of other things. That scar, twitching its tough flesh. An intolerable ache, raging like the mind in a deaf ear's stony canals. The pounding crimson surf that still floods the sealed dome of my skull.

Glossary

Bailamos, querido Montezuma? – (lit.) Shall we dance, beloved Montezuma?

Comprendo? – (lit.) I understand?

diamante – radiant, perfect

el Norte – the North (Mexican term for the United States)

Hablo español? – (lit.) I speak Spanish?

Extranjero – Foreigner

Inglés con facilidad – (lit.) English with ease

la hora diáfana – the diaphanous hour

la Migra – Mexican term for the United States Border Patrol

las palabras – the words

lengua – tongue

Loco – Crazy

lustroso – shining

Qué bonita! Nuestra Señorita de la Cocina! – (lit.) How beautiful! Our Young Lady of the Kitchen!

Si, señor. Gracias – (lit.) Yes, sir. Thank you

sinuosa – supple

tumultuosa – tumultuous

vertiginosa – whirling

Yo no soy mexicana – (lit.) I am not Mexican

Cherokee Driver
(for TLR)

Zebunissa Makhfi

I have long viewed treaties with the Indians as an absurdity not to be reconciled to the principles of our government.

> — General Andrew Jackson,
> letter to President James Monroe, 1817

If the savage resists, civilization, with the Ten Commandments in one hand and the sword in the other, demands his immediate extermination.

> — President Andrew Johnson,
> Message to Congress, 1867

The only good Indians I ever saw were dead.
> — General Philip Henry Sheridan, 1869

Hours since the last tree
sprang like a soldier
into the headlights

new moon raised high
as an assassin's knife

horizon of brimming sand
rougher than a bull's tongue

gaunt cacti fierce
millenial prophets

baptized in a drift
of thorny stars

wind in a sheep skull
gnaws the caged thirst
of salt   rain   blood

sloughed edge of avid lips
beneath a rattler's jewel eye

the hissing river
parts dark miles
of convulsed stone

hoofbeats and thunder
arrows and eagles
stormcloud drums

ebb from the canyon
lashing the noose
of echoes hurled

over the lake of breath
the forest of syllables
the disbelieving rasp

of trouser seams.

laipai

Julia

did you know that my inner sky
was wet with emotions of a thousand years?

i first saw you
on the 'roof on the world'
when i was in the first year of my teens
you were young—

too young
to understand
the longing of the heart

too poor was i
too obedient too
to defy the writing on the wall . . .

the years at the monastery were wasted

if you ask the aged walls
of the ruined monastery at laipai
they will tell you the story
of how

love turned to anger and to tears

of how
i burnt with fever
and writhed in pain

until
my flesh was torn to shreds

how
time after time
the walls received
the kisses meant for you
and heard
the words meant to fall on your ears

in the thirty-first year of my life
they took me
outside the gates to die
you stood beside my body
as they chanted—
buddham sharanam gachhami

in my mind
i can still see
the confusion in your eyes
when in the dying light
you caught the intensity of my heart
and then my breath was gone . . .

was it not the same confusion
you felt around me this time too
when first you saw
the glimmer in my eyes?

i have been waiting for you
wet with emotions of a thousand years

Lesbians in Indian Texts and Contexts

Mina Kumar

There are innumerable references to and ideas about lesbian practice in the Indian context, but this essay will only focus on two streams of thought which have been particularly important.

The first is the influential discourse of orthodox, post-Vedic Sanksrit literature. The texts created to disseminate brahminical ideas, ranging from the epics to ayurveda, regard lesbianism as beyond the permissible—illegal, immoral and/or diseased. This discourse has long been regarded as the irrefutable locus of Indian culture by the Orientalists as well as the nationalists whom they unwittingly sired.

The cultural stream that draws more directly on popular, non-brahminical traditions, however, has generated more positive images of lesbians. Tantrism's valorization of women and sexuality provided a religiously sanctioned role for lesbianism.

The first late Vedic text to explicitly mention lesbianism is the Jaiminiya Brahmana. In verse 1.3, the quality of jami (excessive resemblance) is compared to homosexual sex. 'An improper pairing and unproductive is jami, as is fruitless coupling of two men or two women . . . What is uniform is incapable of copulation and is unproductive' (*qtd in* Smith, 52). This disapproval of non-procreative sex pervades later elite cultural attitudes.

If on the one hand, sex outside of its reproductive uses is evil, it is also precisely the activity that women love best. The great Sanksrit epics, Vyas's Mahabharata and the Ramayana of

Valmiki, like the Laws of Manu, repeatedly describe sexual desire as a particularly female obsession. As Manu says, 'Good looks do not matter to them, nor do they care about youth; "A man!" they say, and enjoy sex with him' (199; *see also* 38-39). Lesbianism demonstrates the depths of female voracity. As Bhishma tells Yudhisthira (Mahabharata, Book VIII, 38.43) in a diatribe against women, 'when they cannot come to a man at all, then they even fall on one another'. The medieval commentator Nilakantha notes, 'They put on an artificial penis, and so come to coition, and this is known to all—when the husband is away, that is' (*qtd in* Meyer, 498). Lesbianism is symbolic of the corruption of women, and therefore of corruption in general. In the Sundara Kanda chapter of the Ramayana of Valmiki,[1] Hanuman witnesses Ravana's wives embracing each other at night:

> Some of his consorts, in dream, savoured the lips of their rivals again and again, deeming them to be the king's. Passionately devoted to their lord, these lovely women, no longer mistresses of themselves, offered their companions marks of affection. Some, in their rich attire, slept leaning on their arms laden with bracelets, some rested on their companion's breasts, some on their laps, their bosoms, their thighs and backs, and under the influence of wine, clinging amorously to one another, those women of slender waist slept, their arms intertwined. Those groups of damsels enfolding one another, resembled a garland of flowers visited by amorous bees (357).

This extremely erotic scene occurs in the demon-kingdom of Lanka, where Hanuman witnesses much that is unacceptable in Lord Rama's ideal city of Ayodhya. This passage is set between descriptions of the beauty Hanuman first sees in

Lanka and his dawning realization that Lanka is evil. Thus lesbian relations are textually postulated as the gateway into degeneracy, a meeting place of good (beautiful women) and bad (lesbianism).

Despite the fact that the Buddhist canon was formed in opposition to brahminical ideas, it tacitly accepted many of the brahminical views of human behavior and social order which decreed that women should be subordinate to men, and which explicitly associated women with sexuality and evil (Lang, 65-67). Asvaghosha's life of the Buddha has a scene very similar to the one in the Ramayana. In Book V. 54-55, Asvaghosha describes the Buddha seeing his wives before he leaves the palace:

> Others, lying as they sat, with their limbs oppressed
> by the weight of their bosoms, shone in their beauty,
> mutually clasping one another with their twining
> arms decorated with golden bracelets. And another
> damsel lay sound asleep, embracing her big lute as if
> it were a female friend (57).

In this passage, descriptions of arms 'tender like the shoot of a young lotus' (56) and a 'lotus-face' (57) precede more sinister visions of women lying 'without any beauty as if they were dead', with 'mouth wide open, saliva dropping, and her person exposed . . . every limb distorted' (58). Furthermore, this whole scene is staged by the Akanishthas to induce revulsion in Siddhartha and thus assist him in leaving his wives to seek enlightenment.

The orthodox texts at least offer the hope that women can become virtuous through marriage and breeding male babies, since 'hav[ing] sons [is] the legitimating factor for a human woman' (O'Flaherty, 118; *see also* Leslie, 43-44). A wife who stays home and serves her husband 'like a god, even if he behaves badly' (Laws of Manu, 115) can redeem her female sinfulness. And to that end, the Laws of Manu and Kautilya's Arthashastra are replete with prescriptions to limit female autonomy. In these two texts, lesbianism is a manifestation of illicit sexuality, and has a stipulated punishment. Verses 369 and 370 of Book VIII of the Laws of Manu read:

> If a virgin does it to another virgin, she should be fined 200 (panas), be made to pay double (the girl's) bride-price, and receive ten whip (lashes). But if a (mature) woman does it to a virgin, her head should be shaved immediately or two of her fingers should be cut off, and she should be made to ride on a donkey (191).

In the Arthashastra,

> a woman having sexual connection (prakartri) with another woman who desires such connection and belongs to the same status has to pay 24 panas and the latter only 12 panas. The text connotes mutual sexual passion between women. But for her own pleasure a woman ravishing an unwilling woman is liable to pay 100 panas in addition to the payment of the bride price (Chunder, 128).

If the Laws of Manu are much more stringent than the Arthashastra in penalizing lesbian sexuality, this is because Manu has a stricter attitude towards female sexuality in general. The Arthashastra, for example, permits widows to remarry after the passing of seven menses (Kautilya 1992, 183) even in cases where the husband is missing abroad (182), but in Manu, widow remarriage is forbidden expressly and at length (116, 205).

The injunctions against lesbianism are also part of a broader pattern of policing sexuality that threatens to disrupt the norms of societal relations. Both texts penalize sexual relations that veer away from the prevailing social hierarchy,[2] and make strong distinctions between hypergamous and hypogamous relations (e.g., Kautilya 1967, 267; Laws of Manu, 192-193), describing the latter as 'against the grain' (Laws of Manu, 234). Clearly, the criminalization of certain sexual acts arose out of the need to institutionalize social hierarchies. Sexual relations are deemed proper only when a woman is of the same caste as a man or lower, because she is then clearly his inferior. Where a woman is of a higher caste than her prospective husband, she is in an ambiguous position, superior by caste and inferior by gender, and their relationship has the dangerous possibility of equality. As the Kshatriya must be kept in a position beneath Brahmins, and a Sudra even more so, women must also be kept from the possibility of pleasure outside the domain of the men who have power over them. Lesbian sexuality is dangerous because it allows women to escape the social hierarchy. This interpretation is buttressed by another dharmashastra, the Yajnavalkya:

> a young woman (kanya) who pollutes another kanya becomes yoni-akshatavim; i.e. the yoni becomes invulnerable, unblemished and permanently in the 'virgin' state. By virtue of this eros, she becomes blemished with the disease of Kshetriya and thereby is the wildest woman (*qtd in* Thadani 1991, 175).

There is also the social imperative for all sexual unions to produce children. For the act of anal intercourse, the Arthashastra prescribes the same punishment whether the recipient is male or female (Kautilya 1967, 268) because it wastes the precious resource of semen. As Wendy Doniger

O'Flaherty points out in her translation of the Laws of Manu, the text conflates impotency, homosexuality, transvestitism and being a eunuch in the word 'kliba'(328), marking male homosexuality as transgressive primarily because it is non-procreative. Lesbian sexuality, by analogy, may be punishable because it does not result in pregnancy. Lesbianism does not provoke the same extended discussion as male homosexuality, which is punishable by losing caste. This could well be because Manu's primary focus is the brahmin male[3] and a woman, who is already equivalent to a Sudra, does not have caste to lose in the same way as a twice-born man.

While the epics and the shastras treat lesbian behavior as available to all women, the literature of ayurveda offers essentialized descriptions of lesbians.[4]

In the Susruta Samhita, the explanation 'lies in the mother having played the male role in the conceptive coition (the same origin as the anal-receptive male), leading to the consequent stereotypically male gender-role behavior' (Sweet and Zwilling, 597). In the Caraka Samhita, Book XXX.34, the following pathology is described: 'due to genetic defect, if in female foetus vayu [wind] destroys the ovary, the woman has aversion to males and is devoid of breasts. This is known as "sandhi" and is incurable' (506). Verse 6.38.18 of the Susruta Samhita further describes the sandhi individual as incapable of menstruation, which may refer to hermaphroditism, but in the Caraka Samhita there is no particular reason that a hermaphrodite would be averse to males, making the allusion more clearly lesbian.

The Susruta Samhita, like the Padma Purana,[5] also states that lesbian sex can produce children, but the children will be abnormal: 'When two women approach each other sexually and somehow ejaculate, emitting semen (sukra), a boneless thing is produced (Susruta 3.2.47)' (Sweet and Zwilling, 597).

This text's description of the causes of lesbian behavior

clearly implies that the subversion of the gender hierarchy inherent in the woman being on top during intercourse produces monstrous children who further subvert gender-appropriate behavior. In addition, it is important to note how abnormality is constituted. The sandhi woman is devoid of breasts and incapable of menstruation, and therefore infertile; two women who attempt procreation do not create human children. And as female worth is inexorably linked to fecundity, lesbianism is correspondingly devalued.

The post-Vedic Sanskrit epic, legal and medical texts define lesbianism as improper because it violates the hierarchy that is supposed to be implicitly coded in sexual encounters, and because it defies the reproductive imperative. Furthermore, lesbianism is interpreted as an outcome of the naturally promiscuous and corrupt female temperament.

Following the lead of Orientalists from Max Mueller onward, nationalist writers turned to precisely these same Sanskrit texts in their search for the basis of an 'Indian' identity. Ram Mohan Das, in *Women in Manu's Philosophy*, glosses Manu's verse on lesbians as follows:

> As the offense in such cases is quite unnatural Manu treats them with more seriousness. But here also we find that when the offender is a maiden the punishment is lighter but when she is a married woman the punishment is heavier . . . An unmarried girl being brought up within the four walls of her father's house is quite inexperienced and unaware of the consequences of her own doings. Naturally, therefore, she is swayed by her natural passions which are strong enough at the time of puberty and which she has no means to assuage. Hence a lighter punishment is prescribed in the case of the lapses of

a maiden. But married women have got their husbands to keep their sexual propensities in balance. So when they violate a maiden the crime is of a greater enormity and consequently the punishment is heavier (18).

For some, even punishment was not enough to compensate for the fact that the ancients knew of woman-loving women. L.N. Rangarajan notes that earlier translations of the Arthashastra omitted the passage on lesbians: 'reticence [was] . . . shown for reasons of puritanism. Some translators are unwilling to face the fact that a virgin could be deflowered by a woman' (Kautilya 1967, 26).

Or at least, these scholars are unwilling to address the possibility that such an act could take place without helpful hints from Westerners.[6] A.L. Basham remarks in *The Wonder That Was India* that the lack of homosexuality in ancient India proved that it was 'far healthier than most other ancient cultures' (*qtd in* Chunder, 129). This opinion gained currency in the innumerable texts that aim to instruct the middle classes on how to integrate Western modernity with Indian tradition. Books like Mayah Balse's *The Indian Female: Attitudes Towards Sex* and S.N. Rampal's *Indian Women and Sex* relegate lesbianism to the world of educated, Westernized women, particularly those in urban, single-sex hostels.[7] To declare that homosexuality is a Western phenomenon is the modern equivalent of Manu's proclamation that homosexuality makes one lose caste.

But as Sures Chandra Banerjee notes in *Crime and Sex in Ancient India*, there are 'a few cases of aberrations in connection with sculpture' (142).

A sculpture in Bhubaneshwar (Sakhi Archives, plate 2) is a case in point. It depicts a woman kneeling, her face at the mons veneris of a standing woman whose right hand is raised in the abhayamudra pose that signifies her divinity. Devangana Desai reminds us that 'the period when the Tantras came to be accepted by the literary class coincides more or less with the period when the reproduction of the sexual act began to appear on temples' (136). While the temple sculptures may, like the Kama Sutra, represent gentrified manifestations of Tantric thought, the poses and compositions hint at important popular themes: goddess-worship, sexual rites and veneration of the yoni.

Tantrism conceptualizes the 'female organ [as] the sole seat of all happiness' (Bhattacharya 1987, 111), and cunnilingus as a left-handed Tantric practice that violates conventional brahminical thinking. The 'Tantric text Kaulachudamani . . . mentions the rajahpana or drinking of rajas, the female discharge, as one of the . . . eight modes of love of the Tantrikas' (Desai, 142; *see also* O'Flaherty, 38). A similar sculpture in the Rajarani temple at Bhubaneshwar (Desai, plate 42) shows a man kneeling before the pubic mound of the goddess. This paralleling suggests that both male and female supplicants are in the same position with respect to her.

A different kind of parallelism is seen at Khajuraho: one sculpture depicts four women having sex while 'other images of sex between four people are dominantly heterosexual with the central focus on the male' (Sakhi Archives, plate 4). Since Tantrism drew on a complex system of non-brahminical beliefs that negotiated with divinity through erotic rituals, lesbianism may have been perceived as the paradigm of human female relations with the female divine.[8]

Similarly in Keith Dowman's biography of Yeshe Tsogyal, sexual relations are the method and the metaphor for spiritual learning. Tsogyal's spiritual apprenticeship begins with her playing consort to an important guru, Kuntuzanpo, and Tsogyal in this role 'asks disciples to take her as their consort, either incarnate or metaphysical, so that she can give them the pure pleasure of gnostic awareness' (xiv). When she and the goddess-figure Mandarava meet and teach each other, their interaction is also described in sexual terms. Tsogyal describes Mandarava's body 'danc[ing] in the sky like a rainbow' (147), and she hopes that she and Mandarava will 'be one with Kuntuzanpo's pure pleasure' (149). Mandarava replies:

> 'May I be one with you, Mistress of Powerful Magic.
> Hereafter, purity suffusing the sphere of purity,
> In your field of lotus-light,
> You and I will project emanations of Buddha's karma'
>   (150).

Just as medieval Hindu temples drew on the non-brahminical discourse on sexuality, Buddhist caves were also 'shaktic sites and often have lesbian imagery' (Thadani 1994).

As a philosophical system that is less comitted to the preservation of hierarchies (Bhattacharya 1975, 13-14) than brahminical religion, the Tantric schools accomodate more fluid and flexible categories, differentiating between biological sex and constructed gender. Tantrism celebrates and permits all kinds of role-playing, as O'Flaherty discusses in the case of Caitanya:

> Once, after a quarrel, Krsna himself dressed like a woman in order to be close to Radha; Radha embraced 'her' passionately, whereupon Radha became Krsna (Bilvamangala 2.75). The worshipper who images himself as female, and dresses like one, in order to be with Krsna, is expressing the explicitly heterosexual (and perhaps implicitly homosexual) erotic relationship with god; but that god himself is also imagined as participating in an explicitly

homosexual embrace (he, as female, embracing the female Radha) with his actually heterosexual consort. The tension is then resolved by yet another transformation: Radha becomes Krsna. For most Vaisnavas, direct identification with Krsna was forbidden; Caitanya was an exception. But any worshipper might identify with Radha—and, as she becomes Krsna, her own transmutation forms a mediation for the worshipper, her own androgyny linking the male worshipper with the male god (299).

The rigidly prescribed sex roles of post-Vedic orthodox texts give way to gender ambiguity, at least on the level of discourse.

The religious context that allows these expanded roles for women and women's sexuality, however, disappears as Tantrism travels up the social ladder. The Kama Sutra, a major text of medieval urban culture, describes how 'the nagarakas (cultured citizens) treated fertility festivals as sports' (Desai, 5). Modeled on the Arthashastra and deeply influenced by the Laws of Manu (Bhattacharya 1975, 69-81), the Kama Sutra derives many of its sexual positions from yogic asanas, but only after depriving them of their religious significance. Sexuality becomes the signified, no longer the signifier of non-brahminical rites. Vatsyayana describes lesbianism as the last resort of languishing harem women, who satisfy each other with dildoes: 'the nurse's daughter, female companions, and slaves, dressed as men, take men's place and use carrots, fruits and other objects to satisfy their desire' (376). Lesbian behavior is explained as a variation of male sexuality. The yoni, central to non-brahminical rites, is displaced by the aupadravya, itself a substitute for the absent phallus. Still, there is no insinuation that lesbian sexuality is socially taboo.

To the extent to which they describe indigenous practices,

contemporary anthropologists counter nationalist and orientalist discourses. Thribuwan Kapur's *The Sexual Life of the Kumaonis*, for example, documents several incidents of lesbian sex (34, 65) via case histories. Since the author's main focus is the inability of the men to satisfy their wives, he does not comment directly on lesbianism among the Kumaonis except to remark that 'evidences of homosexuality were however very meagre in all castes though not completely absent' (75). It is striking that there do not seem to be any moral concerns about lesbianism within the Kumaoni community. Similarly, Margaret Trawick's *Notes on Love in a Tamil Family* describes lesbian practices which do not evoke any condemnation. Of course, these cases might merely suggest that lesbian behaviour is permissible where there is no threat of lesbian identity. Nevertheless, such examples also demonstrate the existence of a lesbian sexual expression, without fear of punishment and without suggestion that it is abnormal.

To some extent, contrasting attitudes to lesbianism, as expressed in cultural images, hinge upon the postulates of genre. Thus, ancient and contemporary texts which are prescriptive—the epics, medical/legal treatises, philosophical tracts and scripture—present lesbianism far more negatively than descriptive texts such as sociologial or anthropological studies. But the latter genre has focused on the cultural elite, and there is some relationship between social status and attitudes towards lesbian sexuality. After all, the Arthashastra (which represents the views of the Kshatriya class) has a lower penalty for lesbian sex than the brahminical Laws of Manu.

Notes

[1] There are other lesbian episodes in the Ramayana tradition. The 'Mohiniyattam exponent Bharati Shivahi once mentioned that there

was an old number in this dance form which depicted one of the rakshasis making advances towards Sita while she is in Lanka' (Muraleedhara).

2 This doesn't perforce necessitate the criminalization of homosexuality, but the injunctions of Manu and the Arthashastra take place in a context which does not seem to support institutionalized forms of homosexuality that replicate the prevailing power structure, in the manner of the Greek teacher-pupil relationships. Later, when the Kama Sutra discusses male homosexual relationships, one partner is clearly feminized, bringing male homosexuality into alignment with the social hierarchy. Compare also the difference between the harsh attitude in the Saddharmasmrtyupasthana Sutra towards men whose partners are other men, to its more sympathetic attitude towards those whose partners are boys (Zwilling, 209).

3 Similarly, the 'far fewer references to homosexuality in the Bhikkhunivinaya (the monastic rules for nuns) than in the Bhikkhuvinaya (that for monks)' (Zwilling, 207) should be regarded in the light of Buddhism's focus on male spiritual life (Lang, 65).

4 Interestingly, Vinaya literature prohibited pandakas (pathics) and itthipandakas (butch lesbians) from being ordained, but considered homosexual activity among monks and nuns a minor offence (Zwilling, 207-209). Those with defects are worse, apparently, than those who volunteered for homosexuality.

5 '"When one of the two wives of a king ate a consecrated pot of rice boiled with milk and butter, and the second then had intercourse with her in the manner of a man, the child born without male semen lacked bones and was a mere ball of flesh (PP Svargakhanda 16.11-14). This is the natural consequence of the mating of females," says the modern Indian editor' (*qtd in* O'Flaherty, 50-51). Mythological accounts about pregnancy without women, however, do not depict offspring as abnormal (50), but the medical texts do not discuss this variation. Lesbian motherhood also occurs in Vedic hymns that refer to Heaven and Earth as the 'two mothers' who 'create gods, as well as create men' (Hopkins, 59).

6 This is in sharp contrast to the attitudes of Westerners, from Burton onwards, who produced 'repetitions of the old European belief that the East is the world's fount of luxury and vice' (Karlen, 230). In the

infamous 1810 Woods-Pirie trial of two Scottish schoolteachers alleged to be lesbians, 'Lord Meadowbank insisted . . . that no woman [in the United Kingdom] would have a big enough clitoris to commit the kind of penetrative tribadism he had heard was so common in India' (Donoghue, 37). In classic Orientalist fashion, the literature of the Sexual Revolution examined the sexualities of other cultures as a way of legitimizing variant sexuality through its universality. Edwardes, for example, depicts harems full of women with oversized clitori where 'lesbian passion in women [sic] was . . . acquired to supplant heterosexual needs' (Edwardes 1960, 107), and opines that Tamil boys are addicted to fellatio. Similarly, Western lesbian-feminists also discussed lesbian culture in India to legitimize their movement. Susan Calvin posits amazons in ancient India (35), but Judy Grahn goes further: she writes that in Kanyakumari, 'homosexual relations are taken as everyday occurrences and a major basis of social relationships' (110).

[7] As Renuka Singh notes, in a climate where women are reluctant to discuss their sexual behaviours, the hostel is often the only permissible locus of lesbian sexuality: 'We also raised questions regarding lesbianism, but the respondents avoided this area of discussion. Only one woman tacitly referred to it and only as a phenomenon which involved others during her days in the hostel. It seems women are not yet ready to discuss issues regarding lesbianism' (200).

[8] O'Flaherty writes that the male devotee 'must become female in order to avoid mating with a female god' (89), and Bhattacharya notes, 'Every [male] aspirant has to realize the latent female principle in himself, and only by becoming a female is he entitled to worship the supreme being' (Bhattacharya 1975, 13). Perhaps female-female is permissible because male devotee-female goddess is too threatening.

References

Asvaghosha. *The Buddhakarita: or Life of Buddha*. Trans. Edward B. Cowell. New Delhi: Cosmo Publications, 1977

Balse, Mayah. *The Indian Female: Attitude Towards Sex*. New Delhi: Chetana Publications, 1976

Banerjee, Sures Chandra. *Crime and Sex in Ancient India*. Calcutta: Naya Prokash, 1980

Bhattacharya, N.N. *History of Indian Erotic Literature*. New Delhi: Munshiram Manoharlal Publishers, 1975

———. *History of the Tantric Religion*. New Delhi: Manohar Publishers, 1987

Calvin, Susan. *Lesbian Origins*. San Francisco: Ism Press, 1989

Caraka-Samhita of Agnivesa. Trans. Priyavrat Sharma. Varanasi: Chaukhamba Orientalia, 1983

Chunder, Pratap Chandra. *Kautilya on Love and Morals*. Calcutta: Jayanti, 1970

Das, Ram Mohan. *Women in Manu's Philosophy*. Jalandhar: ABS Publications, 1983

Davies, Nigel. *The Rampant God: Eros Throughout the World*. New York: William Morrow, 1984

Desai, Devangana. *Erotic Sculpture of India*, 2nd edition. New Delhi: Munshi Manoharlal Publications, 1985

Donoghue, Emma. *Passions Between Women*. London: Scarlett Press, 1993

Dowman, Keith. *Sky Dancer: The Secret Life and Songs of the Lady Yeshe Tsogyal*. London: Arkana, 1989

Edwardes, Allen. *The Jewel in the Lotus: A Historical Survey of the Sexual Culture of the East*. New York: The Julian Press, 1960

———. *The Cradle of Erotica*. New York: The Julian Press, 1962

Grahn, Judy. *Another Mother Tongue*. Boston: Beacon Press, 1984

Hopkins, Edward Washburn. *The Religions of India*. Boston: Ginn & Co., 1887. Reprinted New Delhi: Munshiram Manoharlal Publications, 1983

Kapur, Thribhuwan. *The Sexual Life of the Kumaonis*. New Delhi: Vikas Publishing House, 1987

Karlen, Arno. *Sexuality and Homosexuality*. New York: Norton, 1971

Kautilya. *The Arthashastra*. Trans. L. N. Rangarajan. New Delhi: Penguin India, 1992

Kautilya's Arthashastra, 5th edition. Trans. R. Shamashastry. Mysore: Mysore Printing and Publishing House, 1967

Lang, Karen Christina. 'Lord Death's Snare'. *Journal of Feminist Studies in Religion* 2(2), 1986. pp. 63-79

The Laws of Manu. Trans. Wendy Doniger O'Flaherty and Brian K. Smith. London: Penguin Books, 1991

Leslie, I.J. 'Strivabhava: The Inherent Nature of Women', in *Oxford University Papers on India*, Vol. 1. Ed. N. J. Allen, et al. Oxford: Oxford University Press, 1986

Meyer, Johann Jakob. *Sexual Life in Ancient India*. New Delhi: Motilal Banarsidass, 1971

Muraleedhara, T. Letter to the author. May 31, 1994

O'Flaherty, Wendy Doniger. *Women, Androgynes and Other Mythical Beasts*. Chicago: University of Chicago Press, 1980

The Ramayana of Valmiki. Trans. Hari Prasad Shastri. London: Bownehall Press, 1969

Rampal, S.N. *Indian Women and Sex*. New Delhi: Printox, 1978

Sakhi Archives. *Jami Memories: Archaeologies and Archetypes of Desire Between Women*. New Delhi, 1994

Sharma, Parvez. 'Emerging from the Shadows'. *Statesman*. July 3, 1994

Singh, Renuka. *The Womb of Mind*. New Delhi: Vikas Publishing House, 1990

Smith, Brian K. *Reflections on Resemblance, Ritual, and Religion*. New York: Oxford University Press, 1989

Sweet, Michael J., and Leonard Zwilling. 'The First Medicalization: The Taxonomy and Etiology of Queerness in Classical Indian Medicine'. *Journal of the History of Sexuality*, April 1993

Thadani, Giti. 'Anamika', in *What Lesbians Do In Books*. Ed. Elaine Hobby and Chris White. London: Women's Press, 1991

———. Letter to the author. March 9, 1994

Trawick, Margaret. *Notes on Love in a Tamil Family*. Berkeley: University of California Press, 1990

Vatsyayana. *The Complete Kama Sutra*. Trans. Alain Danielou. Rochester, VT: Park Street Press, 1994

Zwilling, Leonard. 'Homosexuality as Seen in Indian Buddhist Texts', in *Buddhism, Gender and Sexuality*. Ed. Jose Ignacio Cabezon. Albany, NY: SUNY Press, 1992

Differences

A Controversial Sexuality

Pia

In the early eighties when I was entering adolescence and first getting off on women, unbeknownst to me, a hot debate was raging in the lesbian community. The appearance of SM or sadomasochism on the sexual scene created much dismay among the strict lesbian feminists, who interpreted it as an abuse of power along the lines of heterosexual patriarchy. As a result, the rest of us were denied our fantasies: leather straps, silk ropes and sex toys.

In the liberal nineties I found, in contrast to the predominant ideologies of feminism, that SM can liberate our sexuality and strengthen our own identity as lesbians. After all, as someone remarked, 'It is what we do in bed that makes us different.' Our sexual choices are weighted with many political implications.

SM is not merely a matter of wearing black leather outfits and carrying chains and whips. These are external trappings which no doubt help in eroticizing the expression of power and can intensify sexual arousal, but they are not the essence of SM. Therefore it does not follow that someone costumed in such paraphernalia is an SM dyke. Nor is SM a simple matter of 'getting off' on someone else's pain.

It can often be a cleansing and cathartic experience, working out imbalances and inequalities in a relationship through pure fantasy. A way of making our dreams of power come true, in a mode of make-believe.

It is not, as some people believe, women imitating men and abusing other women. If men are supposed to be violent, aggressive and power-hungry, then SM actually purges the man from a woman's body.

Also, two people indulging in SM are in a contract of mutual consent. When the game reaches a point beyond physical or psychological endurance, either individual can use a 'code word' or a 'safe word' to stop the activity. Both participants are in control of the reality beneath the fantasy, to some extent. I have found that people participating in SM are quite tender and open in their dealings with the outer world. This is because they have enacted their cruel passions in SM rituals, and are therefore less repressed and frustrated. It has also been suggested quite logically that the person 'abused' comes out more strong. Having experienced pain, humiliation, having sunk to the lowest depths, she emerges emotionally empowered and without fear.

To experience the thrill and danger of SM, one has to know the rules well and select a trustworthy partner. Practice makes it easier to come up with settings and situations and renders expression easier. You shed your inhibitions along the way. Lesbian SM is just another way of telling the world that lesbian sexuality refuses to be manacled to the insular politics of contemporary feminism.

➤◄

Love Me Cruel

Nihila

The creeping dreams of love-time come
To chill my skin to soft and slick.
The hard black stroke of your wet lashes
Scores my cheek with sweet, sharp gashes.

We kiss lip-deep, the candle's wick
Grows short, our love grows numb.

Beloved, come when dark is kind
to the sad grey mist of my shorn hair
The slim red welts that I bear—
Let love at midnight make you blind.

❦❧

Loving to Hurt You

The Slut and the Whore

Slut: Talking is the ultimate sexual experience for me. Because now, after all these years, I understand the depths of my passion, and it doesn't frighten me any more to think about it or talk about it freely. I used to fantasize secretly about SM. Every now and then I'd ask a lover whether I could slap her or tie her up, pretending it was only a joke if she said no.

Whore: So what is it that turns you on about SM? In all frankness . . .

Slut: You say it's not about inflicting pain, it's about power—it's about the mind and not the body. But it's both. I'm also exploring the limits of what I'm comfortable with physically, what kind of pain I can bear to give you and what kind of pain you are capable of taking.

Whore: For me, giving in to a woman physically is a luxury, after spending all my time dealing with creepy men on the street who want a free feel, and having to use all my energy

237

looking after what happens to my body. Doing what you tell me to, and surrendering to you completely—it's a relief and it's incredibly erotic.

Slut: And I enjoy the sense of total domination over another person. It's a part of me I've always known was there, but I've always been ashamed to think about it. You know, in real life I'm such a pussycat! It doesn't have a place in my daily existence.

Whore: For me, giving up physical control becomes a way of *gaining* control. Since I'm handing over my body to you completely, my idea of control has to be transformed radically. The definition becomes more and more refined, so that it's not about bodily control anymore but about a kind of self-control where I try to face my emotions, deal calmly with what is being done to my body, and not get disturbed.

Slut: And you know I'm doing my best to disrupt your self-control and break down your barriers and boundaries and get to you that way.

Whore: Yes. I find that tension between you as a lover and you as an adversary totally exciting. It's really in the mind for me. Very Indian, isn't it, this kind of SM play? Developing the mind by scourging and denying the body.

Slut: But it's also a celebration of the body.

Whore: Of course. Unfortunately, most of us never test the limits of how much the body can take.

Slut: And how much a relationship can take.

Whore: That as well. And it's safe, because I know that I can always step back before I go over the edge and start feeling negative things about you, like anger or resentment. Hey, when I think about this American statistic that lesbian couples stop having sex after a year or two, I think, well it's not because they've tried everything and become bored. It's because they only go so far in their encounters with each other. One woman might play around with a whip once or twice, but then she'll stop, not because her lover says so but because she feels ashamed of herself. And the other woman might be quite thrilled, but then she'll only take a certain amount of pain before she gets guilty because she's enjoying it so much. So they keep to those limits and of course they get bored. And that's when the passion dies.

Slut: And when passion is gone, what is there to hold on to?

Whore: There is this idea among lesbians that having fantasies is a bad thing which takes away from the sanctity of the relationship. I told someone that the time I felt closest to my ex-girlfriend was when we both dressed up in frilly, lacy dresses and went into a gay men's bar in San Francisco. She thought I was joking, she thought it was ridiculous. Jinnie and I were both pretending to be gay men, and I had to swagger up to her as though I didn't know her, and pick her up! Those gay men thought we were totally crazy, they didn't know what was going on.

Slut: So cut the crap and tell me, what's your scenario for tonight? Tell me.

Whore: Let's see, I'm pressed back against the wall and I'm taking it from you, taking everything you give me. It's this incredible encounter between Woman's ultimate ability to take—because I'm like a black hole, a taking so perfected that it's a passivity that's active, I'm sucking you in, consuming you—and on the other side, there's Woman's ultimate ability to give, because you're giving me everything of yourself and not holding back.

Slut: And I'm trying to fill you up, pouring myself into all the hollows of your body you thought would never get filled completely . . .

Whore: Your wetness in all my orifices, your fist and tongue filling my womb and mouth, the sound of your orders and commands in my ears, you running inside my veins when you cut your way in with a razor blade. And you can feel yourself getting swallowed up and coursing through me. Can you feel it? And there's a point where everything hangs—I don't know if in taking I'm going to get drowned in you, and you don't know whether in giving you're going to get absorbed by me.

Slut: But in the end it doesn't matter.

Whore: No, not really.

Slut: But the 'I' on each side—that's what's afraid of crumbling. That's what's fighting.

Whore: It's a game of wills. I obey you because I know you have the power. But I'm waiting for your guard to slip and for you to become . . . cocksure . . . just one moment when you're not on your toes and you're seduced by my meekness. And then you're lost to me.

Slut: But whatever happens to you or me, the 'us' remains intact.

Whore: Anyway, when both the giving and the taking climaxes—your body with mine—and we're both sweating and dripping every possible fluid on the floor . . . in the intensity of that moment, in that second right after it's over, no one knows who's won and who's lost.

Slut: You always keep your options open, don't you?

Whore: I like the uncertainty of what happens. That's my thrill. But you're turned on by very different things . . .

Slut: I'm very visual. So I make you walk around for me, and seeing you strut turns me on. And seeing me turned on by you is a thrill for you. I see you wearing black leather, it's cut so it shows your breasts, your cunt. It fits you so well that it's not clothes any more, it's a part of you. And it's not ordinary leather, which is just there, you know, matter-of-fact and crude . . . this is black and soft, the blackness that touches your soul. And there's a gold chain which goes around your waist, it's very fine, and if I slid my hand under it, it would cut my skin. But it's made for you, so it doesn't hurt you—though it would if you tried to take it off. So it's what keeps you under control.

And your neck is absolutely bare except for a black collar with animals embossed on it in gold—lions, tigers, leopards—very sleek, very dangerous if you . . . rub them the wrong way. And at the back of the collar is a loop for a leash, but there's nothing there. You have a collar on, but really you're free. And on each of your fingernails there's a metal dragon's head, like fire, breathing fire. Because that's the heat coming from your ultimate coldness, a cold that burns like flames.

Whore: And when you blindfold me I'm tense, ready for anything. The sting of a slap, or maybe the gentlest kiss. But at some point it all explodes, and exactly what it is that you're doing to me becomes irrelevant, whether it hurts or whether it's a caress. We're just drowning in the space of pure sensation, pure emotion.

Slut: And that's the moment we've both been waiting for.

➹❦

The River

Shaka

How does one write a letter to two women one loves and who are missed so much that it is like an all-consuming ache?

My dearest Rafaquat, you came into my life like the sun itself and I just could not turn away. I did not even wait to question my response to you, it was so wonderful. You brought out in me the child of my dreams who wanted to fly. We've known each other such a short time, but my essence has taken root in your being.

You are pure no matter who has touched you, because for me you are unchanging as fire. You once said that you feel 'folded' within me and that even if we never met again it would not matter. Perhaps you were right, except that I want you around for as long as ever is. I love that smile, the tilt of your head when you are caught on the wrong foot, the way you run your hand through your beautiful hair, the way you yell at me, the way you sit close to me and talk about yourself.

Two beautiful nights I have spent holding you and waking up with you feeling a completeness without having made love to you. If I have made you happy, if I have soothed you, if I have been able to chase away some of your grief, if I have given you just one more reason for living—my dearest, then I want to give you so much more.

Beloved Aangad, you are all that is earth for me, all that I can touch, and all that I cannot hold back. I can never and will never lie to you because then I would not be able to look into your trusting eyes again. You bring out the mother in me and the woman in me. I want you to laugh with your eyes and your heart and I want you to know that I will always protect you.

My two beautiful women, I am saying that I love you both. What are we in the system of this world? You two are halves of a whole, yet whole within yourselves. And you have made me see the wholeness in me. I feel I have always known Rafaquat because she is within me; I will always be what she wants me to be because she brings out the best in me. With her I have peace and time to grow. Perhaps, Aangad, I will always want to know more about you, even though I may get to know you as well as I know myself.

I am in a beautiful cave deep in the heart of a mountain and all around me are precious images, each gleaming differently for me. I am weaving the web of this enchantment. A subterranean river flows beside me and I tremble at what I see reflected. These depths belong only to both of you. If I plunge in, I can never reach the bottom. I can swim in this river, it can engulf me, it can absorb my warmth but it can never be part of me nor I a part of it. All I can do is float, or perhaps drown.

I let myself dream of leading this river to an opening in the mountain from where it could gush into the world, brilliant in the morning light. Then, I could forever lie by its sunlit banks, allowing it to caress me as it spilled forth endlessly.

Follow the light you see within yourselves and let me take you out of this hidden cave to a place where I can grow old with you flowing by my side. I do not want to drown in darkness.

❖

Threesome

Anasuya

Today is a new day.
I have surely been refashioned
In last night's supple intermingling.
Two women, two friends, two where
      one should be enough for me:
Can there ever be enough such love?
Six breasts in a bed
Oceans of flowing hair
Three soft pelts
Thirty weaving fingers
My left hand deep in Ila; Mona's in me
Did a bolt of electricity run through us, eager for joy?

One sleeps, the other rises:
'i needed to get that out of my system'
I clench hurt.
Was it just sex?

❧❦

For the Third

Shaka

We look at each other
Our eyes searching
Reaching for what
We do not touch

My woman is in your arms
My woman is kissing me
My woman is ours
But you are hers alone

The music enters
I come
I am whole
My woman within me.

❧❦

Two-in-One

Nasreen

To all the women who tell me I want the best of both worlds—or that I can't make up my mind—or that I'm too weak to say I'm a lesbian: actually, you're all bisexuals too. Everyone is bisexual. See, I knew I'd get your attention that way. *Now* are you listening?

I have always said I am a bisexual, although I have never had sex with a man, and more than twenty women have known pleasure in my arms. Still, I am not *just* a lesbian.

My strength of commitment to women is fierce. I love women with all my heart. I often wish that all men would simply die, because they have given so much pain to women I love. However, I am still a bisexual through and through, not a lesbian.

Most lesbians do not trust me for who I am. They believe that I will abandon them for a man one day. They think that because I am open to men, I am a potential carrier of AIDS. These women do not want to waste their energy on a person who could give herself to a man. They look at me exactly as their straight friends look at them—and they see a sick and filthy human being.

A man who knows that I am a bisexual will see me as someone he can just have a fling with, he has only to ask. 'Bisexual' sounds like 'highly-sexual' to his ears. He thinks about me being in bed with him and his wife, all together, and he drools.

Lots of lesbians want to have sex with me. They are drawn to my attractiveness to men, though they will never confess it. They like seeing the way men react to me. But these women just want sex from me—they act surprised when I fall in love with them. They think we bisexuals can never fall in love, because all we know is sex, sex, and sex . . .

But I am happy that I have the strength of mind to call myself what I am. I think we are all at some level bisexuals, some of us just come to terms with it. I know a man who looks at cute men with clear longing in his eyes, but would he ever admit to desiring a male? Never! I also know 'lesbians' who stare at good-looking guys from behind their sunglasses, and act defensive when I catch them at it.

I believe that we should all be bold enough to declare our most secret cravings. What's the point of talking about gay pride, after all, if we're so ashamed?

As a bisexual I know what I want and I dare to say it aloud. I sometimes like to lie in bed and hold a man close to my body. Muscular men feel good to caress, why should I pretend I don't enjoy them? But I know also that I do not like anything about the penis, it makes me sick to even think about it. I have never touched one! But most of the lesbians I know have had sexual encounters with men and have actually had a penis pushed into their bodies. So who is more subject to the 'power of the penis', them or me?

So I tell anyone who asks me, that I am a bisexual. 'I like to kiss men, but I don't like cocks, and women turn me on completely.' I am in tune with my feelings. But if I had to call myself a lesbian, then all I would find myself doing would be repeating like a parrot, 'I hate men. I love women.' It is not so clear-cut for any of us.

If I tried to explain my reasons for being bisexual, most people would tell me, 'Oh, what you really want is a man with a cunt.' I don't want any such thing, in fact I am very put off by women who pretend to be men and think that they are entitled to act just like one of the boys (except for the crucial fact that they have no penis).

I enjoy men because they are men, I enjoy women because they are women. I like men because we can discuss matters of the world.

I like women because we don't even need to talk, we connect through our hearts. A woman can see my troubles written on my face and she will understand, and know how I feel inside.

Maybe being a bisexual *does* mean that I want the best of each world. But don't you?

❧❧

Looking Different

Lesley A. Esteves

A lot of gay men and lesbians say they encounter little or no homophobia in Bombay. Some of them have then gone on to say that they see no need for activism, or even community organizing, because we don't have any 'serious' problems to face. While it is hard not to get upset when I hear these things, I am increasingly trying to find the patience to deal with these people, and for very selfish reasons. I need them. Though I face a slightly different reality then they do, I need the support of the gay men and women around me to help me survive that reality. Those of us who look 'different' must undertake the responsibility of educating those who don't, about the constant overt homophobia we face in public spaces.

I have wasted the last couple of years lambasting anyone who has shown impatience or ignorance about our problems.

While they haven't changed their views, I am still being taunted, hounded and threatened on the streets.

I don't want my sisters and brothers who look different to feel that I am asking something difficult of them, when the world takes so much from them all the time. I am merely searching for ways to help us survive, without having to 'unchoose' the way we look.

When I was young I believed that other people were justified in mocking me, because I thought I was indeed a freak and a pervert. I had had no exposure to gay culture, and assumed I was the only person in the world who wanted to marry another of my own sex. Dealing with my sexuality was limited to cursing the powers that caused me to miss being 'happy' by a single Y-chromosome. I would daydream for hours, dancing in the Kashmir Valley with Helen, and then shiver with guilt every time I passed a church. That is what they call internalized homophobia. When I was first called 'lesbian' by someone in school, I did not know that this was the name for my difference. I thought it was a curse, like 'chutiya' or 'bhadwa'. It was only a couple of years later, in college, that I accepted the term and made it part of my own language.

Recently I met someone from my class in school, who walked up to me on the street and came out to me. He said he had known back then what I was, and that it had disgusted him. He said that he hadn't realized then that, maybe, he was projecting his confusion and denial about his own sexuality onto me. Then he went on to tell me that he had a lover, and that he was so happy, etc. But he was not interested in getting in touch with any gay group—he didn't think he and his lover needed any support, since 'we won't really have any problems, as long as we don't flaunt it'. Looks like society is ahead, so far, in the battle for that one.

After meeting this man I started thinking back to those

years—something which has always been difficult for me and which I have usually avoided. I thought about why I hadn't recognized that this guy was different, when he had been able to tell that I was. The only reason I could think of is that although I wore the prescribed uniform for girls, I had never really conformed to society's notions of how girls should appear and behave. I had a crewcut even then, wore boots and cannot count the number of times I was punished for swearing. This guy didn't look or act any different from the other guys. He 'passed', but I didn't. This is the point of difference between me and women who, though they are no less lesbian than I am, fit into society's ideas of what women should look like. They can pass as straight in public spaces, as well as in their homes, if they wish.

This is not, however, what separates me from these women. I feel my difference most acutely when a lesbian who can pass, questions my 'need' to dress the way I do, and refuses to accept the idea that I cannot wear dresses or saris any more than she can sleep with men. My reaction to questions like, 'Why do you try so hard to look like a man when you claim to love women?' used to be angry and abusive. But a response like 'You are the most homophobic homosexual I have ever met!' is bound to put someone on the defensive. Which makes it that much harder to communicate, and thus the barrier is built.

When I travel to work, I have to take the train. I do not feel safe entering the ladies' compartment alone, as I have had some very bad experiences with the women's reactions to me. I prefer to sit in the general compartment. This does not solve the problem, however. If the men realize that I am a woman, the best thing I can do is get out at the next station, or I will have to deal with male hands all over my person. Given this, and the fact that there is very little that some of us can do to change the way we travel, many homosexual men and women who look different have to deal with physical abuse and mental tension very frequently. These are only a few reasons why it is particularly hurtful to have to deal with homophobia from within our own community.

I am not trying to negate the other forms of homophobia that gay people face. We must accept, though, that some of us carry an added burden that others don't. So I would like to suggest to those of us who are not obviously different in appearance, to think very carefully the next time they say, 'Gay men don't want men who look like women,' or 'lesbians don't want women who look like men.' The bottom line is, who should we turn to, if not each other? While some of us have understanding parents or friends, a lot of us do not, and therefore need to have spaces that are friendly. We all know how much our lives have improved now that we have other gay friends, that special camaraderie that exists between two gay people. At the end of the day, when I come home from work having survived a torrent of homophobia, at the end of the month when I come for one of our parties, I want to be loved in my own space. I want to belong.

Changing My Body, Changing My Mind

Sonu

When I was in the nursery, when I didn't even know what I was doing, I used to go lift the little girls' skirts, hit them on the bum, pull down their underwear . . . my teacher went and complained to my mom, saying, 'Do you know what your child is up to?' And obviously when I was at that age my mom couldn't scold me.

As I was growing up, I began to think that there was something different about me. I wasn't girly, growing my hair and painting my nails and wearing pretty shoes or anything. I wouldn't want to play with dolls—I still have all my dolls, absolutely intact! I used to play with toy cars, with boys—I thought girls were quite stupid, sitting in one corner and combing their dolls' hair. They were just too boring. I was very comfortable with boys. We used to run up and down the stairs ringing people's doorbells . . . go down to the cars and puncture their tyres . . . play cricket in the street . . . climb the trees. I've done everything. Played in the rain, got beaten up, got into fights with other guys. It never made any sense to play with girls.

But when the girls were at that age when they wanted to talk about boys, I starting wanting to talk about other girls. But I never opened my mouth around them because I knew they would not want to hear it. So sometimes I used to talk to the guys. 'Hey, what about that chick?' And none of them ever really thought I was strange. They accepted me, I had no problems with them, so I thought, they are like me.

The girls in my class used to be very frightened of me, as though I would rape them or some such thing! I must have been just eight or nine . . . Once one of my friends went and complained to my cousin, saying, 'I don't know why she's always chasing me, and she keeps on calling me up, and she keeps on touching me.' And so my cousin said to me, 'You'd better behave yourself, you shouldn't be doing things like this.' Still it didn't register inside me that I was otherwise inclined.

I started boarding school at the age of thirteen, at an all-girls convent in Panchgani, and soon I became a hundred per cent sure that I was a lesbian. There were many other girls who were obviously lesbians, and it was so good to know that I was not the only one. Finally I started feeling happier about having girls around me instead of boys.

Oh, I used to have a ball in school! I said to myself, well here I am, now I can pick and choose the girls I want. I needed a new one every month. I needed variety. One steady girlfriend was too dull! I was wild in those days—wild means wild! I'm still a legend in that school. The lights would go off at 9:30 because there was a major electricity shortage, and that made things very easy for us. The nuns used to parade up and down watching us, but we would lie quiet pretending to be asleep until 10 or 10:30, when they would go off to their own rooms. And unless someone made a loud noise, they would never come out just to check on us. So then our mischief would start. In a dormitory of sixty girls, no one bothered about what was going on in the next bed, we couldn't have cared less.

When I came back to Bombay at the age of seventeen, I was put into Nirmala Niketan College. After the convent, it was a culture shock to be in a vernacular institution where most of the girls couldn't even speak English properly. They were such horrendous women! I didn't know what was happening to me. And then I met Tina . . .

Tina and I became friendly because she was lonely and I was lonely in that place. We started taking an interest in each other, spending a lot of time together. She came from a very good family, but they were having a lot of problems so she often came and stayed with me. We started a relationship and were together for five years.

Looking back now, I guess the problem was that she was very young. So was I, but she had never been in any kind of relationship before, while I was sexually experienced and was sure that I was a lesbian from a very early age. She couldn't face being with a woman because society—what would society say? She started treating me like a man—that was okay, but to the world I was not a man. So we started having a lot of misunderstandings, a lot of fights, and then one day she just walked off.

Maybe she had started to feel that what she had got herself into was wrong, and she couldn't face it. Or maybe she was pressured by her relatives. She didn't say a word to me, so I don't know, I'm just guessing. But at that time, thirteen years ago, I thought, 'Why did she leave me? Because I'm not a man.' I hadn't met any other lesbians in Bombay. So I decided, you have to be a man to keep a woman in your life. When she took off, I was about twenty-two—I was that young! I was so hurt, I was so shaken up—all of those years with her, what was I doing, where had it got me? I thought, 'The next time I'm in a relationship it will happen again, the woman will just leave me for a man. There's no way out.'

One day I went for a haircut to this lady close by—she'd had a sex change from a man to a woman. So I started thinking, 'If she can go through it, why can't I? I would love to be a man—have hair all over my body, shave, wear pants. Oh, *yes*!' So then I started reading about other women who had had a sex change, and I thought, 'They are like me, maybe they've been through what I have been through, and if this is what they have done in order to be happy, maybe I should do it, too.'

I am religious, but any religion first says, 'Do good, be good.' God didn't say that you can't go in for a sex change. I don't believe that if you're born a woman there must be a meaning in it, that it is your final destiny, that you can't interfere with nature.

I spoke to very few people about the sex change. My family didn't say anything about my plans. Most of them know I'm gay, and those that don't, are actually only pretending that they don't; deep down they're aware. My brother and my aunt, the two people I'm closest to—they never put me down, they never made me feel like I was a freak case. My brother said, 'If there's no other way for you, then do it'—he was very supportive. I told my father and my granny as well. In fact, my granny had read about all this sexuality nonsense several years back, in the newspapers. She told me, 'I know that these things are possible. I used to think that you are like a man, but I see that you have some traits that are very feminine, and I know this change is not meant for you.' But I think they would all have accepted it. They wouldn't have treated me like the plague or anything, and finally they would have given in.

I was looking for an entire sex change—hormones, a penis, removing the breasts, all of that. This would be my New Look: a man! I was prepared for everything, body hair, having to shave every morning. I decided that I had to look like a man, I had to be enough of a man to get a woman. I do believe in honesty, I would have told her that I had grown up as a girl, and from there, whether she liked it or not, the decision would have been hers. As a man, I would definitely have wanted to get married. And when it came to kids, I would have adopted.

So I spoke to my doctor and she started giving me tablets. Because of my health problems I couldn't take allopathy; I was on homeopathy. So first and foremost, she had to make my resistance far stronger—otherwise she thought that maybe my health would give way and my kidneys would just stop functioning—they're so powerful, all those injections for the change. So she made me physically more fit, and then she started giving me hormone pills. After that I was ready, I was strong, healthwise I could take all that surgery. That took eight or nine years.

Mentally also, I was prepared to think of myself as a man. Meanwhile, I had had my crushes, I used to fall for some woman and every time it would backfire and I would go into depression again. These attractions didn't lead me anywhere. So I never had a reason to change my mind, and carried on with the pills.

I went to a psychiatrist when I was in Hong Kong in 1990, only because one of my cousins insisted. This woman said that something had gone wrong with my upbringing, that I had not had enough exposure. She was completely against the idea that there was such a thing as a lesbian, and she said, 'You should meet men, you should go out with men.' I said, 'I do go out with men, but as friends.' And I tried to explain to her, '*This* is what I feel for a woman and *that* is what I feel for a man,' but she said, 'Try and divert your mind.' I said, 'How do you expect me to divert my mind, remove it and keep it aside and say, OK, I'm not what I am? This is me, my life in this life.'

After that I thought that she was the one who needed therapy, more than I did.

And then one day, after all those years of not knowing any other lesbians I met Polly, through a straight friend. One woman who changed my whole life. From the first day she was against the idea of me having the operation. She said, 'Why do you want to go through so much pain? If it's not successful, then what? You're playing with something that could be disastrous.' And she said, 'I'm going to introduce you to other women so you'll feel more comfortable being the way you are.'

When I met the lesbian group, I was convinced of what she had said. I thought, 'There are so many other women like me, why should I waste a fortune and torture myself? Suppose I just conked off in the middle of some operation, with my kind of health problems. Or I could land up in a position where I'm messed up completely, if the surgery isn't successful or they don't do a good job. I don't have to take that kind of chance now, there are people like me who can get by. If I don't have to go through all that, then hallelujah!'

So I changed my mind.

Today, I feel like I can do anything I want to do, so what's the difference between a man and me? When I see a handsome guy, and there's a woman with him, I say, 'He's good-looking and he can get women—well, so am I and so can I!' Today, I am very sure of myself. I've gone through a lot of hardship, a lot of pain, and now I've made up my mind that this is what I want—just to be the way I am.

I am quite butch, happiest wearing a shirt. OK, so I don't wear pants, but I wear skirts that come to the knee. All the time, I face that comment, 'Is that a guy or a girl?' It doesn't bother me one bit—maybe when I was much younger it did, but not now. In fact, I turn around and say, 'Come, meet me tonight and I'll show you what I am.' Anyway, I'm too confident now to get upset. I'm very proud of myself—if God has made me this way, then why shouldn't I be?

When I was much younger, I always felt very suffocated inside this body, feeling that it didn't belong to me, that I had to be released from it. I wasn't comfortable with wearing a bra and other female things. Now I've come to terms with it. Gradually I gained more maturity, met more people, and I became convinced that the change was not worth it. I was doing it for what, for whom? I didn't want to go through it just for a woman. And not for myself either any more—when you're younger you're irrational, you look at things from one point of view.

I mean, if I take these strong injections, with my kidney problems the next thing you know I might be on dialysis—and *then* how am I going to enjoy my great new body?

(*as told to A.S.*)

❖

Will I Ever Be Free?

Sophie

I opened my eyes in this world twenty-nine years ago. The wail was normal, so were my fingers and toes. I wasn't deformed and everything seemed okay, so I was put into my mother's arms. The doctor declared, 'You have a fine, healthy and normal baby girl.'

If only they'd known better. I'd really like to know by what yardstick they measure normality. I've heard this word so often—'you are not normal'; 'this isn't normal behaviour'; 'these are abnormal feelings'.

Worst of all, 'this is not a normal lifestyle'.

I am thoroughly sick of this word and of the people who utter it.

I grew up like any other girl, though I wasn't interested in playing with dolls. I preferred my aeroplane. I enjoyed doing things that nice little girls weren't supposed to do—flying kites, catching worms and running after the girls to frighten them. I was a happy child till my first crush on a girl when I was around twelve.

Boy, was I confused!

I felt as if I was a sinner; this was not how one was supposed to feel towards someone of the same sex. I could not even talk to anyone about it. It is such a horrible thing to be ashamed about something so pure as falling in love. Yet it wasn't so bad, because it was just puppy love which died a natural death.

But calamity struck when I was about sixteen and in my first year of junior college. I met this wonderful person and got totally infatuated with her. I used to wait outside her classroom and we would go home together every day. She was in her third year of B.A. and I was just starting college. The year passed very quickly but we had become good friends by the end of it. I never ever told her how I felt about her, nor that I believed I was a transsexual. I didn't know how to tell anyone, so I just took each day as it came—hoping to finish college, take up a job, earn money. The first thing on my list was to have a sex-change operation and get married to the girl I loved. Never once did I think that my fantasies would not simply and undeniably become reality.

Anyway, I used to go to this girl's house regularly and shared a good rapport with the family too. I was present at every function or occasion in their home. Six years went by like this, till one day she stopped taking my calls. Finally I went to her house, we chatted for some time and then I asked her point blank. She first said, 'No, there's nothing wrong. I really wasn't in when you had called all those times,' but then she decided to tell me the truth. Till today I remember every detail.

'Actually, Sophie, I was there but Mom doesn't like you calling up and meeting me. She says it's not normal, you seem to be obsessed with me.' I was so dumbstruck, holding back the tears that stung my eyes. All I could ask her was, 'What have I done? Why now? Why after all these years?' I got up and told her that I would never call her place or visit her there again. But she kept in touch with me and after nearly a year invited me to her wedding. I had started working by then and it was just one of my many dreams to be shattered. I went to the marriage ceremony because I had to see for myself that it was actually taking place, and that she would never be mine. I met her just once after her wedding, and I do not know where she is now.

It took me a good two years to get her out of my system. Her mother's words stating that I was 'not normal' kept haunting me. I decided to change, saying to myself, yes, maybe

I'm not normal. Maybe it's just because I dress up in trousers and jeans and walk like a man, that I feel I am one. If I start dressing up like a woman, wearing frocks and skirts, adorning myself with make-up and mixing with guys, I could change.

I did this for nearly a year. You can alter your outward appearance, but what can you do with what you feel within? It was no use. And I was just as miserable as I had been before. It was then that I realized I was different. I decided to lead my life the way I chose and not how others wanted it.

The period of self-doubt is the most trying one. You doubt your very being. 'How is it possible for me to feel this way? Maybe I *am* a freak.' It is even worse because you cannot share your feelings with anyone, because you feel there is no one you can trust. 'Will they understand? I am sure their attitude towards me will change.' I am extremely close to my mother, she is the one good thing in my life. And my sexuality is the only secret that I have ever kept from her. I will tell her one day because I need to let her know. I hope and pray she understands me. Please, can someone tell me what is so wrong with falling in love with someone of the same sex? Why are we made to feel as though we are perverts?

I find myself caught in an even worse situation. I can never imagine myself with a man, and a woman could never imagine herself with me. I can never get into a relationship with a lesbian either, because even though I appreciate a woman's body, I cannot deal with the idea of a woman touching me. I do *not* identify with my breasts and certain other parts of my body: I consider myself to be a man. I cannot believe that any woman would let herself be touched and loved by me without getting anything in return.

I continued my existence in the same way without letting a soul know what I was going through. I joke a lot—I am the clown of the group so, sadly, no one takes me seriously. This mask that I had put on to mislead people when I was younger, has today become so much a part of me that people know me by it. So I have failed miserably once again, because now no one is ready to see the real me. They think I am incapable of deep emotion—I can erupt into spasms of laughter at the drop of a hat, but never break down and cry. Oh God, how wrong could they be?

I decided that I needed to tell someone from my family that I am a transsexual. I am very close to my older sister, and I finally plucked up enough courage to talk to her. She burst out laughing hysterically, tears streaming from her eyes as she rolled on the floor. Stunned, I forced myself to laugh along with her. Who wouldn't have, seeing her collapse like that? After she had regained her composure she told me, still laughing, 'That is why I kept telling you to dress like a lady. This is all the outcome of your tomboyishness and there is nothing more to it. You can still change the way you live and you will realize all of this was crap.'

I heard her out and tried explaining that this wasn't the case, but she wasn't ready to listen. Neither of us has ever brought up this topic again. And now I'm worried about how the rest of my family will react. I hope and pray that they understand and accept me. I will only tell them about myself when I have taken the final decision to go ahead and have the sex-change operation.

My problem, you should know, is that I fall in love with so-called straight, 'normal' women. Read on, my dear friends. Find out how a woman can manipulate your feelings, play with your emotions, and give you a taste of what could be, leaving you in the hope and anticipation of what you just might get if you play the game according to her rules.

Let me call this certain lady Miss X. We had been friends for about eight or nine years. She had been married but the marriage had not worked. She, her sister and I decided to rent a flat together. Things were really good, we shared our secrets, our hopes. She was the first friend to whom I opened up—her sister was very supportive, but Miss X herself wasn't too sure that she understood. According to her, it was all in my mind and I had simply convinced myself that I was actually a man. Still, I was at ease with both of them and with myself. I cannot explain the kind of relief I felt at being able to discuss being transsexual with someone. To talk, to reveal my fears and to know that my secret was safe. After all those years I got some feedback on what I could expect from the world—I had confided in two friends, one supported me and the other opposed me. And, as luck would have it, I fell in love with the wrong person.

As usual I did not let the woman know, since I was sure it would ruin my friendship with her and I did not want to take that risk at any cost. In the midst of all this the sister got married and left, and Miss X and I continued to stay together.

I felt I was leading a life of lies and wasn't being fair to her, so I decided to tell her how I felt. Since I did not have the courage to say it to her face, I wrote everything in a letter and added that I would understand if she felt that I should move out. She rang up at my office in the evening and spoke to me very casually, which got me wondering whether she had read my letter or not. I asked her and she said she had, and then asked me when I was coming home. When I put down the phone, all sorts of thoughts started running through my mind. I said to myself, 'Maybe she finally understands how I feel, maybe she too likes me—or even loves me.'

Anyway I left work on a note of euphoria.

When I reached the flat, Miss X looked at me and laughed, and demanded why I had felt that she would not want to see me again after what I had just disclosed to her. She said that she had suspected for some time that I was in love with her. Then she went on to tell me that we were very good friends and that she liked me a lot, but could not imagine the two of us together as lovers even after I had my sex change.

I accepted her decision and was just happy that she was not disgusted. But then there were changes in her behaviour. She wanted to have total control over me, which I was at first only too glad to give. We would fight if I made any plans to go out on her day off. She would tell me, 'I get just one day a week at home, how can you leave me alone and go off with your friends?' So I would meet my family and friends only when it was okay with her. All my space and time was at her disposal. We would have tiffs like any other couple would, and I would enjoy making up with her. She knew that she had me to herself, but somewhere she was still insecure.

Miss X started tormenting me mentally by saying things like, 'Baby, I really love you, but not in that way' or 'Kiss me on my lips, but not how lovers do.' But after a certain point I just could not handle it. I mean, here was the woman I loved so dearly, in my arms and asking me to kiss her, and I was supposed to perform this act in some mechanical way, devoid of any emotion! This was putting me through hell.

I finally told her that this could not go on—either she had to tell me that she was ready to wait for me until I was through with my sex-change operation, or she simply had to let go of me, because this behaviour of hers was driving me insane. And I told her I needed time to think and wanted to go home for a few days. She refused to allow this, saying that I could not make such a decision for the two of us, and that if she felt the need, she would come and meet me any time she wanted to. I managed to convince her, but the next time we met she asked me if I was willing to settle down in a new place with her, again without any sort of commitment or anything from her side. Then almost immediately, she said, 'But if you find a woman whom you love and who loves you back, I am sure you will leave me for her.' I said, 'Obviously, because you have never said you love me, but if I knew for sure that I would have you in my life, I would never want any other relationship.' But things just went from bad to worse, with her trying to get a hold on me all over again, and me trying to break free of her shackles.

So after two and a half years, I finally moved out. I still cannot understand this woman. I was so concerned about our friendship that I never made any advances towards her or let her feel uncomfortable around me, while she on the other hand would throw herself all over me and still hold back. Her sister laughs at me and says that I frightened Miss X away because I was too serious and far too much in love with her, while she just wanted a fling with no strings attached, where she could still lead her own life and get married eventually to someone else. She had one standard line: 'I just can't think of you as a man.'

So I was miserable, even wanted to end my life. I hated her for a long time. As James Baldwin puts it, 'I imagine one of the reasons people cling to their hates so stubbornly is because they sense, once hate is gone, they will be forced to deal with the pain.'

And yes, Miss X did cause me deep hurt. I felt totally used, a mockery had been made of my feelings. How can women just overlook all the love and attention that I have to give? It seems as though true love means nothing, intensity counts for nothing.

When I hear words of rejection it feels like someone is hammering a nail through my heart. I want to break things around me, scream out loud or just attack myself with something sharp because surely that would not hurt as much as this brutality.

At one point in my life I was so confident that that I wanted the sex change, but I am no longer sure. What if women still turn away from me on the grounds that I am abnormal? Somehow I convince myself that if I have a man's body things will be different. But I would never want to hide anything from the woman I loved—I would want her to know the truth about my past. And I'm afraid that if I tell her about me at once, she'll run as fast as she can, and if I tell her after a period of time, she will feel cheated and hurt and may not accept it. I really do not know what to do.

Why can't I be accepted for what I am? When will I be free? Will I *ever* be free?

➤⬅

Born in a Man's Body

Miss Kokilaben

I am a drag queen from Gujarat in my mid-forties. At the age of eighteen I had my first affair with a saheli of forty-two, a Bharata Natyam dancer. She was my neighbour, staying alone. I used to see her practice every day, and once she asked me, 'Are you interested in dancing?' I told her 'yes', and from that moment my whole personality changed.

She first put a long-haired lady's wig on my head, then make-up on my face—red lipstick, eyeliner, mascara—put a big nathni in my nose, clip-on earrings, big round red bindiya on my forehead, gave my eyebrows shape, shaved my moustache, applied sindoor in the parting of my hair. Then came a gajra of rose flowers for my hair, small-small ghungroos for my ankles, a padded bra, bangles, five rings on each hand, nails brightly polished, my palm decorated with alta. I was suddenly afraid that the colours would not go, so I started crying. She told me everything could be taken off with soap, and she showed me by washing her hands. I smiled.

Then she took me in front of a huge mirror; I was shocked to see my reflection opposite me. I was totally a woman, a beautiful woman, better looking than my friend. I was in half-pants so I laughed, and then she removed them and brought a chaniya choli and then again stood me in front of the mirror. Still I remember, I looked like Mumtaz in the film *Do Raaste*. She started clicking photos of me in different poses. Today I can bet that if I had taken part in a contest, I could have been a beauty queen. (A drag queen, that is).

Now for the main point of my story. Instead of teaching me classical dance, she seduced me. She used to kiss me, pamper me, hug me, pressing my breasts. She would make me lie under her with my legs raised high, insert my penis in her vagina, and give fatkas—thrusting like a man with a woman during sexual intercourse. During this period she would say, 'You are my wife and I am your husband, that's why you are below me and I am using you like a woman.'

This was my first affair and it went on for more than nine years. We were separated when her mother fell seriously ill in her village in Andhra Pradesh. I was left in darkness, I went for more than twenty days without food, I was mentally broken. But a woman was born in my body.

Here a different story starts. A lot of trouble came from the world of men, since in trains, buses, parks, urinals, many men used to find me and try to stick their penises into my buttocks or put their hands into my shirt to press my breasts. (If I remove my shirt, you will see that I have breasts like a girl of sixteen, with small nipples).

In my office there was a Parsi executive, and one day he gave me a lift in his car. As I was getting out, he offered me a coffee in his home. I refused, as I was getting late, but he insisted. After coffee, he came and sat next to me on the sofa, loudly saying: 'You are not a man, there is a woman in you, tell me the truth, swear upon your God, whether I am right or wrong.' Ultimately I had to say 'yes'. He told me not to worry, saying, 'What you have in mind I know, come,' and he drew me to his wife's wardrobe, pulled out a black and golden maxi, with bras and panties and a make-up box. He told me, 'Prepare yourself, I am returning after half an hour.' He came back with a beautiful lady's wig; by that time I had found a bra which perfectly fitted my breasts, and was dressed and adorned with make-up. This time I was not desi Mumtaz, but looking like Madonna Mem. He hugged me and kissed me, took me to his lovely bed and told me, 'From today you are my second wife and I am your husband.'

He removed his pants and shirt. Now I was really afraid. I got off the bed after seeing his big penis erect and asked him: 'What do you want from me?' He told me, 'What a man wants from his wife.' I said, 'But I am not a woman.' He said, 'Yes, you are,' and showed me photos of men dressed as females having anal intercourse with other men. He told me, 'They are husband and wife.' But still I was afraid. He came near and told me, 'I won't harm you, if you say no to anal enjoyment, I will leave you at your home.' Then he started kissing my cheeks and putting his tongue in my mouth. After half an hour he forced his penis inside me, and I shouted: 'Please, please don't do that. It's paining me, please, I'm not comfortable.' He was not leaving me so I pushed him away. The bra and maxi tore, and we were separated.

Then he joined his hands, begging, and told me: 'You do me one favour, you sleep below me like you used to do with your dancer saheli husband.' So once again I was in his arms like a wife-woman, he was playing with my breasts, licking my penis with his tongue. It was late in the night now and I had to phone at my neighbour's house for my mother. I told her, 'I can't come home, there's a birthday party for one of the office staff,' and she said, 'Come in the morning, then take a bath, change and go to office.'

Soon I was fast asleep. While I was sleeping, my boss ejaculated in my mouth. In the morning he asked me, 'Did you enjoy yourself?' I said, 'No.' He told me, 'While I was using you, you were enjoying it.' Then I told him that I was dreaming, wishing, thinking of my saheli, my husband. She would use me so beautifully.

From that day onwards I have hated men, they are cruel and mad at the time of sex play.

Now I hope for a permanent saheli, and I will be the perfect wife. She will have all the liberty to use me, and I will be such a tender flower, kachi kali, like an innocent village beauty.

⇝⇜

The Complete Works of Someshwar P. Balendu

Qamar Roshanabadi

This is what I have named myself, but you can call me anything you wish, because now I am not who I was on the night of my birth. As my mother shifted my hungry mouth from breast to breast, light from the full moon slid through the window bars and poured like a veil over my head, hairless as a boiled aloo, my mother told me. The next day the family pundit opened some sacred book at random. 'P' was the first letter of the first line on the page. So my mother chose 'Purnima'. Everybody in the house, and all the neighbourhood wives, agreed that it was beautiful.

Later I also came to love moons. New moons are broken bangles, half moons are smooth foreheads, full moons are shining faces. I even loved the tear-soaked light of cardboard moons in the romantic scenes of old Hindi movies. And the moon I love most of all is the crescent trembling in the matted hair of the lord of yogis, om om om.

I started to love moons when I was twelve, going to my cousin's hometown by a night train. Very crowded, people, more people, more and more, climbing on, people climbing over each other. Shouts, shoving, ma-behen gaalis, sharp corners of luggage. No place to sit, no place to stand. Even the air crushed between sweating bodies. Grabbed by my shoulders, hauled into a cursing tide of angry elbows, necks, backs, knees. Pushed into the corridor near the toilet. Old man drew me suddenly into his lap. Thigh fell like an iron rod across mine. Arm pointed at the new moon rising, sharp as a grasscutter's sickle. Voice said, 'Beta, I have not eaten or drunk all day, praise god. Break my fast with me. Let's sweeten our mouths.' Train whistled, jerked, swayed, lunged forward. Engine's shriek filled me like a storm. Legs stumbling over me all night on the way to the toilet. Door swinging on one hinge. Latch broken. Dim yellow bulb. Crawling yellow streams. Choking yellow stench. Old man's cactus beard, sewer breath. Next to my face a blind beggar snoring. Even dogs wouldn't fight for such bones. No ear, only a rag of flesh studded with a waxy hair-fringed hole. Deep enough to collect raindrops. All night the pissing men spread their legs. All night the old surprised claw turned inside me, a piece of glass turning and turning. Dawn a splash of turquoise in pale water. Blood in my trousers dried to stone. All night the throats of distant boys shouting chai garam chai garam laddu samosa glucose biscuit chai garam chai chai chai. In between stations without slowing without stopping all night the train wheels reciting *hilal hilal hilal hilal hilal* . . .

The family pundit kept coming to our house for something or the other, some ceremony, some ritual, some celebration, some havan, bhog, shradh, mundan, annaprashan, whatever you can think of. Hoarding his tattered shlokas, loudly belching as if he had swallowed too oily an Upanishad for breakfast. Head like a bumpy lota above a stomach round as a matka pressed into the lovely waist of a Vrindavan gopi. Whenever he saw me he tugged the lobes of his ears, mumbling 'Shiva, Shiva, Shiva', and jumped back as if my shadow would pollute him. Though he himself told my mother that our original gotra ancestor was that rishi who exhaled famous curses with each pranayama, till he was able to seize the fury writhing within him like a knot of cobras and disappear into the sudden lightning that raked his hundred-year-old brain.

One evening I was in the kitchen making tea for the neighbourhood wives who had filled up our house to listen to some katha or gatha or chalisa or the other. All of them sweating in a crowd along the wall, and the pundit alone under the fan, his chikna complexion shining like desi ghee. With one hand I was stirring in the sugar, with the other hand I was feeling in my pocket for my last cigarette and thinking where I should go to smoke it, when my mother came in and began to put cups on a tray, looking at me from the corners of her eyes. Then she whispered, 'Punditji says something is wrong with you, he says I must take you to the doctor.' I said, 'Tell your pundit that the next time he comes here I'll feed him the leg of a tandoori chicken as prasad, and wipe my hands on his dhoti. And after that I'll plait his janeyu into his pigtail. Understand?'

Then I went out, thinking let me just sit somewhere and

smoke and calm down, but I couldn't even do that, I was so angry and my hands were shaking so much, I wasted half a matchbox. One end of the cigarette got soaked with my spit and the other end from two fat tears I couldn't pull back inside my burning eyes, so finally I just broke the cigarette and threw it into the drain.

My mother saw the way I was growing up, my never-combed boy-cut, my pockets full of cigarettes, my best-quality English-medium education hanging from my wrist like a kite no one taught me to fly, and began to keep fasts eight days out of seven till she was nearly fainting from hunger and despair, looking at me as if her womb had spat out a red chili instead of a girl. She starved herself in the name of who knows how many goddesses—riding on tigers, sailing on lotuses, all the snow-covered devis of Himachal hillsides, all the large staring South Indian such-and-such-ammas whose sacred names are too long for my sinful tongue. She even lit agarbattis to the cushion-breasted smiling matas with hips like hairpin bends, produced and directed by Anant Kundalini Studios. Then she wore out the soles of her chappals roaming from this dargah to that qabar and that maqbara to this mazar, tying threads to marble lattices and flapping shawls over the holy graves. One pir gave her some soot scraped from the rim of a burning diya and said, 'Tell your daughter to apply this daily like kajal, using her left thumb; it will destroy the influence of the evil eye.' I said to my mother, 'You think that by churning water you are going to get butter? Tell your pir I'll use this kajal to dye his beard.'

After that she left me alone, but she wouldn't stop fasting and crying. I said, 'You should have done all this before I was born. No point running to dig a well once your thirst has already begun. Why don't you look for your miracle in the place where I get my shakti?' So we went to the Shiva mandir at the end of the street, carrying a thali of god knows what all to be offered. Everything from a Kerala coconut to a pebble from Gangotri. We stood behind the neighbourhood wives, all of them folding rupees into the pundit's chikna palm, and pouring precious litres of full-cream milk over the lingam, as if they wanted the black stone itself to curdle in front of their eyes. My mother could not reach the temple bell, but I was growing by an inch every month so I easily took hold of the heavy tongue and crashed and crashed and crashed it against the side. Oh the way the power of the lord of yogis filled me up, from my toenails to my fingernails and the root of each quivering hair, om om om. I felt solid brass echoes rippling out above the satellite dishes on the roof of Doordarshan headquarters. 'Stop, stop,' my mother hissed, 'everyone is looking.' 'May they all go blind,' I said. I put on my shoes and went out and stood under a cinema hoarding and smoked a cigarette between the giant boots of Ajeeb Ashiq, who was aiming a rifle at the warning light blinking red on top of the All India Radio tower. You tell me how this chutiya became a hero, with a face uglier than the inside of a crocodile's mouth.

As soon as I was old enough to find out where it could be done, I had my breasts cut off. Do not ask how I got the money, because I will not tell you. The nurse standing by my bed when I woke looked at me as if I was Yamraj himself. She kept chewing a strand of her long oily curly hair. A stupid cap sat on it like a white bird. I begged the nurse to give me something for the pain. More, I begged, more, more. The syringe pricked me once, twice, thrice, the blessed prongs of the trishul of the lord of yogis, om om om. Then I was able to close my eyes and let the agony flow into a mirror of glass, a mirror of silver, a mirror of water, a mirror of dreamless sleep, covering me like a wide moonlit wing of Brahma's swan.

I forget how long they kept me there, in the filthy general ward. The bandage became stiff as a Kurukshetra warrior's shield. Thread by thread I pulled it loose from my wound. All around me suffering people called upon deaf gods for water, for mercy, for death. Monkeys leapt in through the windows and dug into open tiffin carriers and snatched bananas from the patients' hands, but the ward boys were Hanuman bhaktas and refused to chase them away.

I was not sure, but I thought my breasts might have been thrown into the municipal dustbin, buried in mango peels, eggshells, tea leaves and crusted sanitary napkins until dogs or a sweeper's broom found them, ripening in the heat. Two small jewels, fit to blaze in the centre of any shehenshah's crown. But the nurse would not answer my questions till I told her a story that my cousin—what a girl! Slim as a creeper, eyes like a Kalidasa gazelle—told me about a villager who worked on her uncle's farm. One hand was pulled into a threshing machine during harvest. Chopped off completely. Someone picked it up from the wet red wheat, but stole the ring. The villager screamed all the way to the district hospital, carrying the hand in her father's turban. Twenty kilometres. The doctors stopped the bleeding but threw away the hand. She cried all the way back to the village. But her father managed to get her married, after the in-law family had seen her knead atta with her stump and make rotis at the speed of the Amritsar Express. Each roti perfectly round, rising, swelling, steaming at her touch. Those nerves are dead, so she can put her stump right into the flame.

The nurse stood by the bed and listened, rubbing the silver cross on a chain around her neck, her nailed-down god looking at me from under his sad eyelids as if my pain was thickening like marrow inside his hungry bones. Then she said, 'This is a charity hospital, we don't have incinerators, we throw away lungs, brains, livers, umbilical cords. What do you expect us to do—make pickles?'

After that I never asked her anything. And I would not let

her watch me heal. All night I pushed fingers under the caked bandage and stroked the gash that might have been darned by the needle of some old darzi forcing his cloudy gaze through the blurred slit trembling between hours. All night I gnawed a corner of the stony pillow, thinking my eardrum would be punctured by the howl circling in my brain like a forest bird with an arrow in its eye. All night I pressed the throbbing stitches as if they were the keys of a celestial harmonium. And even on that torn mattress rigid as the planks of a second-class sleeper, my back stayed soft as a petal, smooth as cream.

The nurse walked with me to the hospital gate. 'You are not strong enough, you should not go yet,' she kept saying. Aandhi was building up. The sky was as greyish-yellow as the dead and dying human parts the hospital threw into the municipal dustbin. The wind grabbed the nurse's cap and flung it against the bars of the gate. Quickly I stretched my leg and stopped the cap from rolling into the drain. Somehow I picked it up, nearly screaming as the agony rushed like floodwater into the flat place beneath my bandage. 'Leave it, leave it!' the nurse shouted as the wind tore pins from her hair and whipped long strands into her wet eyes. 'Here, keep this. I will pray for you.' She ran back towards the ward. I stood in the chaukidar's empty booth, looking at the card she had pushed into the pocket of my new shirt. A bright picture of her sad god. From head to foot he was sprouting thorns, nails, bones, blood. His chest torn open like huzoor-e-ala big boss Hanuman's. Pointed yellow flames nibbling a heart red as a murder.

The first day I felt I could walk for a few hours, I got up from my charpai, drank tea, smoked a cigarette, then went out of my rented room. I thought, let me go to the mangal bazaar behind my mother's house, I must get used to people, and maybe I will see her in the kitchen window. In my crisp collar, long sleeves, metal buttons, sharp crease, I felt such a prince in the crowds. I told a pavement astrologer my date of birth, and his parrot jumped out of a cage and picked some cardboard numbers from a box. Predicting marriage, money, sons. An Afghan refugee with eyes like golis of opium tried to sell me a thick root bottled in vinegar, swearing it would increase my mardaangi. 'Beta, I promise you'll be on top of her so often and for so long, you'll scrape the skin off your knees.' I almost took out my wallet, thinking maybe this man has escaped from those bazooka-loving bullet-eating chutiya Taliban who have put their women in burqas and locked them inside their houses and painted the windows the colour of night so that no one can look out or look in. I stared at my many faces as I passed a rack of stainless steel thalis, and I was just going to pose in front of the largest one and comb my hair with my fingers like Ajeeb Ashiq, when I suddenly saw ten bamboo poles strung with cheap brassieres, huge stiff pointed cones fluttering like obscene flags. Black as Kali's hair, red as Kali's tongue, white as Kali's necklace of skulls. My god, how fast that snake of bitter vomit uncoiled in my burning throat.

The summer I left my family—they pay me to be far from them, but I am closer than they will ever know—I had no job, nothing. All the surfaces in my rented room were hot enough to raise blisters. I had baths in my own sweat and dried myself with the pillow case. Each hair in each pore soaked, except where the dead tissue along the deep slash hooked my salty drops into delicate glittering chains, like the zari on my mother's Banarasi silks.

I lay on a charpai, naked. The ropes cut into my back. All day I was there, listening to the radio. Everything—lok sangeet, sobbing dramas, ghazals, bhajans, mushairas, kavi sammelans, goshthis, guftagus. Discourses on Atman and Brahman. Lectures on Marx and Engels. Film songs, from 'Chaudvin ka Chand' to 'Choli ke Peechhey'. A hundred clapping ishq-ishq and zaalim pardanashin and ghuroor-e-husn and zakhm-e-jigar qawwalis. A hundred sighing barse kajrare nain and sajna re and panghat pe and ghata ghanghor dekh naache man ka mor thumris. All the ragas you can name, from Ahir Bhairav to Yaman Kalyan. Unbroken egg-shaped hours of tabla taals *dha dhin dhin dha dha tin tin dha ge na tinaka dhi na dhin dhin dhagetirkitdhinatirdhadhita.* The news in four languages. Bulletins back to back. Same news each time. News read at dictation speed. When I listened to this news on afternoons hot enough and silent enough, I felt the gaps between the words widening to receive me. Like the earth opening to take Sita back after the agni-pariksha. But I loved the five-minute Sanskrit news that made me think of my gotra ancestor looking into the lord of yogi's gyan-chakshu, a hair of blood-red light between its carved lids, om om om.

I smoked a lot and drank tea and let my stomach juices burn all the way up into the back of my brain. I thought of all those clever people in the universities of Harvard and Oxford and Forward and Backward, lost in the space between their eyeballs and their scientific spectacles and thick telescopes. Frogs in a well trying to describe the ocean. They get infrared and ultraviolet cancers photographing those Bakasura-type inside-out holes that swallow everything, even light. For such minds the universe is stretched from a beginning to an end and still remains the size of as many zeroes as can be multiplied between nothing and infinity. These mahamoorkhs, measuring the realm of the lord of yogis as if it happened to be a blanket woven in some Ludhiana cloth mill.

By evening my body became as hot as the air boiling in my room. So I went out and waited for one particular bus which had a very long route from depot to depot so I could sit for two hours, safely. And this bus I also liked because next to the windscreen there were tin and plastic idols of every divine being your heart could desire. When the driver stopped at traffic lights and put a fresh match to his dead beedi, he touched the flame to a new agarbatti in front of one deity or the other, for keeping him alive on these roads of death. And he had a display of small cards like the one the nurse gave me of her sad god—every known and unknown guru, muni, sadhu, mahatma, acharya, saint, swami, rishi, baba, bhagwan, avatar, sai and sri sri maharaj, bald or bearded, in crippled padmasanas or erect on one leg like panchatantra herons. But the one I liked best was not a god but a godling—chubby, dimpled, dreaming. Lips curved like the new moon in his hair. Cobra, trishul and damru thrown nearby as if he had grown tired of some favourite toys. Two sparkling ghungroo bells tied to his ankles to remind me that when the destined day arrives, those mighty dancing legs will smash the spinning galaxies to less than even a musht-e-ghubaar, om om om.

This one picture makes me forget the stinking armpits and swollen crotches of all the chutiyas in the bus, flogging me with their 'what is this thing' stares from eyes like open manholes. Because by then I am already thinking Janmashthami, Diwali, moonless, useless. Karva chauth, all the neighbourhood wives climbing to the terrace of my mother's house to look at the moon through a sieve or in a thali or whatever they do—no point. But Shivratri, the marriage of the lord of yogis—thinking of that, I am able to let all my chakras flower into slow joy till body is mind is breath is thought is world and I am overflowing with light and brimming with bliss through skin blood bone hair and groin navel heart throat brain flaring lotus petals blue as the neck of a peacock, dazzling gold, jewel green, smoky purple, red as sindoor. And the one most radiant luminous burning blinding pure moonsilver pearlwhite so beautiful my ecstasy throbs like a fresh wound and I become a falling fountain, om om om.

One night I got off at the bus depot not wanting to go back to my room, so I walked till I came to the railway bridge. I sat under it and smoked. People coming and going, more and more people, crowds of lepers, addicts, runaways. It was safe because in the deep shadow no one could see anyone very clearly. A stranger came and asked me in a deep voice for a cigarette. I said, 'Why one, take the whole packet.' The woman said, 'You have a big heart.' I struck a match and held it to the tip of the cigarette so I could see her face in the glow. Then I said in proper filmi style like Ajeeb Ashiq, 'My heart cannot accommodate the world, but it always has room for a friend.' She laughed and growled, as she came closer and rubbed two false lumps against my chest, 'Sara sheher mujhe Raat ki Rani ke naam se jaanta hai!' I put my arm around her waist and blew smoke from the corner of my mouth and giggled in a high voice, 'Pyar se mujhe Som kehete hain.'

Again she laughed. Then she took me to the darkest wettest corner and said, 'Beta, stand in front of me so I can retie my sari, I have to meet someone.' I almost had to say no, the stench of piss under the railway bridge was so strong, like a knife at my throat, but I stood there keeping some chutiyas away and thinking how a hijra could be as modest as a neighbourhood wife taking a purnmasi dip on the ghats of Allahabad.

The next week I went back and some more hijras found me. God knows where they had been living, they smelt worse than tonga ponies. I took them behind the depot and got buckets of water from a dhaba handpump so that they could bathe in the stairwell of an abandoned bus. I stole some soaps from a lala's shop early in the morning when he was sitting with closed eyes and folded chikna palms, praying to Lakshmi before opening his ledger for the day. I tore off the wrappers and inhaled. All the soaps smooth and fragrant as the bodies of apsaras on beds of clouds. In the bus at night, when the hijras were getting ready to go out, they lit diyas and clapped and sang in their cracked voices old romantic songs from *Pakeezah* and *Taj Mahal,* and I lay across the seats and drank from the hijras' bottles and watched their shadows and dreamed I had a secret mantra to call a shining woman from the moon, the way Kunti, mother of warriors, had called the sun god.

Before leaving the bus the hijras prayed to their special mata for protection and lit the agarbattis I bought for them. I like the Tibetan type because it has the scent of wood and smoke, not like the lala's type which has a sugary perfume. As I told you, I had no job, nothing, so I spent time at the Tibetan basti when I went to buy agarbattis. I sat in the fermenting cloud of butter tea and butter lamps and fried pig and the chang that flows in thirsty veins and in the gutters between the shacks. Each month some new escaped Tibetans come there, hollow with fear and hunger, and peeled red and burnt black by the sun and wind. Sometimes they have babies wrapped under their jackets; those that die on the way they bury in the snow. The chutiya Chinese are still raping and shooting, even so many years after smashing the huge golden Buddhas and bulldozing the monasteries and burning the holy books. After one bottle of chang I started thinking how things were not so bad here, at least my life was not a kora kagaz in our desh jis mein Ganga beheti hai; after all, you could take any stick stone brick twig hibiscus flower and make a temple anywhere, it didn't matter if men had been pissing on that spot for seven births and rebirths; you could have a chikna pundit reciting 'Om namah shri peela chausa, langrey ka mausa' or 'Jai baba surkh mehfooz tarbooz', and people would still keep coming because everyone needs a god for some reason or other. The rich would drive up for blessings in air-conditioned cars, and beggars would crawl there for shelter on one leg or no legs, winter or summer. So I fought my tears when after two bottles of chang the Tibetans became sad and started to hide in the stony caves of their dark language. Believe me, in their homeland the air is so sharp and clear and cold and each star is so big, it flashes seven different colours, and the moonlight reflected off the glaciers is so strong, you can read a book as easily as you are at this moment. And when I remembered their lord under the pipal, his body pure silver, the universe calm as a lake under the lids of his lotus eyes, I started shivering and freezing and sweating and burning, and I had to pour the rest of the chang into the drain because I couldn't even swallow, my breath had turned to ice and my blood to fire.

Of all the hijras I know, Raat ki Rani is my favourite. I love the way she rests her arm like a heavy branch along my shoulders and says in her crow's voice, 'Kyon, Chhote Miyan, kahan rehete ho, Eid ka chand ho gaye!' She makes me read out the masala headlines from the *Sandhya-Chhaya Khabarein*. Bride Burnt to Death in Mubarak Nagar. Rejected Lover Throws Acid on Neighbour's Wife in Khidmatpur. And so on. Many such items. I don't like to think about such chutiya news, but for Raat ki Rani I will do most work without asking questions or expecting answers. She is only angoothachaap, but let me tell you she can do a lot with her karamati fingers. She is highly respected because she was born with everything of both, and they are full size, I swear, to this I am a chashm-deed gawah. And Raat ki Rani is the best dai-ma in the city. When she operates it is like an ant's bite, she says. She ties the parts with a string, very tight, then she cuts, two cuts, left and right. She lets them bleed and bleed and bleed because all the man has to be drained out of the person. Then she pushes in a stick to keep open the pissing hole. The parts she drops in a pot and buries under a tree. With her knife she makes hijras from men, the brave ones. Other chelas are fully males, in women's clothes, and she treats them worse than servants, but even if they are beaten and kept without liquor they stay in their guru's house, it is better than sleeping under the railway bridge.

One full-moon evening on my way to visit Raat ki Rani I

bought a gajra from a dwarf at the traffic light. The woman was no higher than the bus wheels and the top of her skull came to the car windows. Her maang was full of sindoor. As the red light turned to green I stood there thinking maybe the husband is a dwarf also and maybe they have a child this mother squeezed out like a sticky doll too big for her dwarf arms to hold to her breast. Then I thought my life is not so bad after all, at least my feet are not growing from the ends of my thighs, and maybe in her next birth this dwarf will be born with the mighty dancing legs of the lord of yogis, om om om.

I buttoned the gajra into my shirt so carefully that not a petal was crushed, and it scented my whole pocket. I had to weave it into Raat ki Rani's plait with my own hands because she was already quite drunk. She embraced me and said, 'Meri aankh ka noor, mere dil ka qaraar, chalo mere saath, aaj jannat ki sair kara dete hain.' I didn't know where she was taking me, otherwise I would have made sure I was also drunk so I wouldn't have to remember the legs of all the chutiyas going up and down those narrow slimy stairs. The duty policeman sat on a stool, scratching himself and yawning. One woman was pressing the keys of a cracked harmonium, another woman was making half-dead mujra movements, and a third woman wearing ghungroos on her wrists was beating *dha dhin dhin ta dha dhin na* on the floor with the policeman's lathi. As I stepped over it Raat ki Rani said, 'This dance makes it a house of entertainment, not a kotha. So don't worry, Chhote Miyan, no one can be arrested!'

We climbed some other filthy stairs to the top level. The air smelt of men and I tried not to put my hand on anything because I felt as if the chutiyas had sprayed themselves everywhere. Bulbs were so dim, the walls looked as green as the vegetables that the madam, Qatilana Bai, was chopping and throwing to boil in a degchi as big as the small naked children running like mice between our legs. A white goat tied to the charpai was eating the peels. Qatilana Bai put down her knife and lit a cigarette and pushed it first between her lips and then mine, and before the smoke had finished leaving her nose she had prepared a paan with a goli of something crushed into it for Raat ki Rani. A boy carrying a kettle stopped to stroke the goat, staring at me as if I also had hooves. Qatilana Bai grabbed his ear and twisted him around, yelling through the noise, 'Behenchot, bring some first-class chai garam right now, otherwise Raat ki Rani will make you her asli chela before the sun rises.' The cigarette made me feel sick but more than that it was all the women on the stairs and in dark wet corners and on benches and squatting on the slimy floors and stained mattresses; all so young, in torn blouses and petticoats and bright cheap saris, all dripping powder and kajal, all watching the chutiyas going behind the torn curtains and emptying themselves like overflowing mouths into leaking spittoons.

'So what do you enjoy, beta,' Qatilana Bai said, watching me like some old puppet with vulture's eyes. 'I have every kind of girl here, from north south east west; fair dark thin fat; from Sri Lanka Nepal Pakistan Burma Bangladesh and even further. Tomorrow a sheikh is coming to buy something special I have saved for him. A real bud. The dew is still sparkling on this Persian rose. She is twelve. Want to see?'

Raat ki Rani looked at my face and quickly said, 'No, tonight your gulistan is as busy as a railway station and your cigarette has made my young bulbul here very sleepy.'

She pushed me out through the crowd, holding my arm in a grip as strong as a dog's bite so that I wouldn't hit anyone on the narrow slimy stairs. And until dawn I lay awake in my room, staring through the window grille, clenching my fists and wishing I could steal an AK-47 from those chutiya terrorists who blow up buses and trains. And feed it with a cartridge belt stretching from Delhi to Bombay.

Nowadays when I leave my room in the mornings I first go loafing through the market, stealing bananas from the carts, eating them in two bites. I feed the peels to the starved cows scavenging in the municipal dustbins. If the white bull is there I feed him six bananas, best quality, fresh and firm, no dark spots, no soft pulp. He stands near the vegetable booth, waiting, unblinking, his giant hump majestic as Nandi's. I am careful of that tongue sharp as a sword. Even the flies are scared and leave him alone.

Then I tap on certain doors. If a car is parked there I stop and look in the side mirror and window glass and comb my hair and adjust my collar so that I look smart, like Ajeeb Ashiq. In my khaki shirt and trousers I could be any delivery boy, vendor, repairman, servant or some beardless tenth-standard dropout with a pocket full of stones to throw at laden mango trees. I have stopped counting the number of begum sahibas and chhoti bahus and rakhi behens and mrs major-generals I have made happy. Let me tell you, I remember each nasheeli gulbadan, each nazuk fasal-e-bahar! With one look I let them know that I don't want to be touched. Sometimes they blink at me as if I am a particle of dust torn from some howling aandhi and rubbed into the membranes of their eyes. But they love how I am quick and silent as a thief. And I love the small things about their lives, like pearls that I steal to caress when I am alone. The cold rim of a green bathtub sunk into a green marble floor. Bangles accidentally hitting the side of a cup on an afternoon so hot and so silent that even the sparrows seemed to have died in the trees. My fist opening where a baby fought towards wet breath, tamaso ma jyotir gamayah, om om om.

Only once I was almost caught. I heard the man snoring like Kumbhakaran on a sofa downstairs, then the next minute he was on the threshold, panting. Must have been the street's ugliest patidev. Furry as a Sunday morning TV rakshasa. Flabbier than five-day-old atta, in a polyester kurta-pajama as yellow as the caked vomit on the side of a Haryana Roadways bus. My god, how fast I snatched my clothes and rolled under the bed! With my chin between my knees, among forgotten newspapers and rupee coins and toy cars and cockroach husks, I lay and swallowed my spit, listening to my heart thumping, listening to the mattress groan, listening to her cries, smelling her all over my face and one hand while with the other hand I plucked loose all the gold threads fraying in her kolhapuri chappals.

So—such is the qissa of my kahani. When will you grace my garibkhana with your presence, share a cigarette, chai garam, a little ashiqi? By the time you have finished turning the pages of my bayaan-e-badmasti, and made your own meaning of my dastaan-e-zubaan, I must have become your very favourite chutiya nacheez, nothing more, nothing less. With a final back-bending, waist-bowing, floor-sweeping kathak-dancer tasleem, I will now request ijaazat. By moonlight or sunlight or the light of a leftover Diwali diya, with or without kajal, I am not the lie that I was born as, nor the illusion into which I have been carved. I am the fire that cools, the water that burns, the truth that blinds the liquid mirror of your naked eye. Look behind and you may see me following you, like the hunger of orphans, the stare of zoo animals, the smell of poor people. I have no choice but to be faithful to my nature. All your mothers must have warned you that a tick on the udder of a cow never sucks milk, always blood.

Glossary

aandhi – dust storm
agni-pariksha – test by fire
Ajeeb – strange, peculiar
aloo – potato

Anant Kundalini – Infinite Kundalini

angoothachaap – (lit.) thumbprint, i.e. illiterate

Ashiq – lover

ashiqi – romance, courtship, lovemaking

asli chela – true disciple

Bakasura – cannibal rakshasa in the Mahabharata; killed by Bhima during Pandava exile.

Balendu – young moon (crescent in Shiva's hair)

barse kajrare nain – (lit.) eyes darkened with kajal are raining, i.e. weep

bayaan-e-badmasti – (lit.) testimonial of debauchery

behenchot – sister-fucker

bhakta – devotee

bulbul – nightingale

chalisa – devotional verses

chang – rice beer

chashm-deed gawah – eyewitness

chikna – oily, greasy, slippery

chutiya – fucker

dai-ma – midwife

damru – small drum

dargah – tomb

darzi – tailor

dastaan-e-zubaan – (lit.) narrative of my tongue

desh jisme Ganga beheti hai – country through which the Ganga flows

gajra – small string of flowers braided together

garibkhana – (lit.) impoverished room, humble abode

ghata ghanghor dekh naache man ka mor – (lit.) seeing the dense rainclouds, the mind's peacock begins to dance, i.e. become sexually aroused

ghuroor-e-husn – (lit.) arrogance of beauty

goli – lump

goshthi – gathering

gotra – Vedic category denoting all those who descend from a common male ancestor in an unbroken line. There are supposed to be eight primary gotras

gulistan – flower garden

guftagu – discussion/conversation

gyan-chakshu – (lit.) eye of wisdom, third eye in Shiva's forehead

hijra – eunuch
hilal – new moon
huzoor-e-ala – supreme sir
ijaazat – permission (to leave, enter, etc.)
ishq – love
janeyu – sacred thread worn by brahmins
kahani – story
karamati – miraculous
katha – discourse from epics, etc.
kavi sammelan – gathering of poets
kora kagaz – blank sheet of paper
kotha – brothel
Kumbhakaran – brother of Ravana in the Ramayana, who slept for six
    months of the year
Kyon, Chhote Miyan, kahan rehete ho, Eid ka chand ho gaye – (lit.)
    What, young fellow, where are you these days, you have become
    the Eid moon (i.e. rarely sighted, much anticipated and desired)
lota – small brass vessel
maang – parting of the hair
ma-behen gaalis – (lit.) mother-sister obscenities
mahamoorkh – great fool
mangal bazaar – (lit.) Tuesday market
mardaangi – virility
maqbara – mausoleum
matka – earthen waterpot
mazar – shrine
Meri aankh ka noor, mere dil ka qaraar, chalo mere saath, aaj jannat
    ki sair kara dete hain – (lit.) Light of my eye, solace of my heart,
    come with me, I'll take you on a tour of paradise
mujra – courtesan's dance
mushaira – poetry recital
musht-e-ghubaar – fistful of dust
nacheez – (lit.) non-thing, i.e. insignificant
Nandi – Shiva's bull
nasheeli gulbadan – (lit.) intoxicating flower-bodied
nazuk fasal-e-bahar – (lit.) delicate harvest of spring
padmasana – lotus position
panghat pe – (lit.) on the river bank or ghat
patidev – husband

peela chausa langrey ka mausa – nonsense slogan: (lit.) yellow chausa
 (mango), uncle of langra (mango)
pir – Muslim holy man/keeper of graves
Purnima – full moon
purnmasi – full moon night
pranayama – yogic breathing exercises
Pyar se mujhe Som kehete hain – (lit.) Affectionately, I am called Som
qabar – grave
Qamar – moon
Qatilana – murderous
qissa – case, incident, event
Raat ki Rani – (lit.) Queen of the Night, a bush with strongly scented
 white flowers which blooms only after dark; said to attract snakes
Roshanabadi – One from the illuminated/radiant city
sajna re – (lit.) O lover
Sara sheher mujhe Raat ki Rani ke naam se janta hai – (lit.) The entire
 city knows me by the name Raat ki Rani
Someshwar – lord of the moon (Shiva)
surkh mehfooz tarbooz – nonsense slogan: (lit.) red protected
 watermelon
tamaso ma jyotir gamayah – from darkness lead us into light (second
 line of a well-known Sanskrit shloka)
tasleem – formal bow used in respectful greeting or ceremony
trishul – trident
Yamraj – god of death
zaalim pardanashin – (lit.) cruel veiled ones
zakhm-e-jigar – (lit.) wound of the heart
zari – gold embroidery

Connection

My College Auto

Juliet

I went to college in Bombay in the 1960s, and back in those days, all the girls kept autos—autograph books, to use their full name. I am told that the girls of today call them 'slam books', which makes me feel my age and listen for the creaking of my old bones.

Some auto-owners I knew of asked their friends to write prophecies of the future or recipes for keeping a man; some wanted paintings of flowers or watercolour sunsets! One girl wanted each one of her friends to catch a butterfly and stick it into her auto with a famous quotation. I was too kind-hearted to kill harmless insects, so I put in an old shell I had found, with the quotation 'Love's feeling is more soft and sensible than are the tender horns of cockled snails', because at that time we were studying *Love's Labours Lost*.

I have my own auto right here in front of me. I am so flabbergasted to see that the pages are yellowed with age—do such things really happen? I was sure that yellow diaries confessing the notorious past were only found in fairy-tales. I am now looking in the mirror to see if my hair is grey! It is not, really. Not much.

My auto is full of the sweet nothings that my old friends and girlfriends wrote for me. Oh, yes, we had girlfriends in the '60s, and you can tell your mother that with my compliments, each time she tries to say, 'When I was in college, no one thought of love at all, we were just interested in our studies . . .'

Over to you, my dear, long-gone harem girls. I hope you will forgive me for citing you. After all these years may all that young love rest in peace.

Come, dear girls, one and all,
Sweet, sour, big and small,
Leave a kiss, a smile, a tear,
So whether you're far or near,
I shall remember when this I see
All the girls so dear to me.
—With love, Juliet

These are the opening lines of my auto. They are not much different from the opening of anyone else's, for a certainty. Except my dreadful friend Amrita who wrote 'If you want me to remember you, please will you try your best to be interesting.' But let us continue to leaf through the pages of my book.

Always remember that you are
    2 dear
    2 me
    2 be
    4 gotten
Yours 10 derly,
—P.

P. was a little Parsi girl with soft white shoulders—or was she that Gujarati beauty with shiny hair? Oh dear, I really do believe that I have completely forgotten who she was, that P.! My one consolation is that I am sure she does not remember me either.

Love is like the measles—it is all the worse when it
comes late in life.
—D.

Isn't that the awful reality of it . . . all those girls like D. and P. and X., Y. and Z. that I treated so casually when I was in my adolescence. Every morning I came to college to collect the heart-broken love notes, and half of them I laughed over with the group of boys who were my friends. (In college I didn't have friends who were girls. Most of them were in love with me, and the rest of them were my rivals. I was a young thug). That was many years ago, before I fell in love. And now look at me, wrapped around my baby's little finger like a piece of string.

May your smile retain all charm
May your heart be light and gay
Some day a girl's sweet voice will whisper
Dearest will you name the day?
—A.

My heart still is light and gay. Completely and totally gay! But not A. though. She promptly forgot all of the passionate love letters she sent to the girls in college, 'Dear Juliet/Hema/Anna, I will never love anyone else but you and I will chase you all my life', and she is now a noble wife and mother in silk saris who very wisely looks the other way whenever we run across one another at the club.

Love is a golden knot
Which angels tied together
So if you never cut this knot
I shall love you forever.
—K.

The naughty lying beast! She dumped me and got married to a doctor 'boy' even before finishing college. The wound to my pride is still sore and it aches and stings when the weather is cold and I am lonely because my baby is away.

If all the girls were across the sea
What a good swimmer Juliet would be!
When you read this, then think of me.
—C.

I do think of you, C. dear. Often! What darling lips, and such legs, as perfect a pair as Mother Nature ever shaped. My regret about C. is that she always promised to model for me an itsy-bitsy teenie-weenie yellow polka-dot bikini in real Miss India ishtyle, and never did.

> To Juliet's future wife:
> Feed her well
> With bread and jam
> Tell her all the lies you can
> Don't ever give a damn
> Beat her up
> With your frying pan
> Then give her sweet kisses
> And be her darling Mrs.
> —D.

Very good advice to wives, even in the liberated era. Once you're married, the way to the heart lies squarely in the stomach. Equally true that a wife must learn to fib to her lovey with wifely dignity. Most important, in the end it is always better to stop the fighting, kiss, and make up. My baby follows this advice to the letter.

> When months and years have glided by
> And on this page you cast your eye
> Remember it was your own dear
> Who left all her love and blessings here
> —S.

That was not all she left, that S.! Also left huge teeth marks on my cheek and got me into trouble with my mother. This was on the first evening that she let me kiss her, she was trying to help me with civics or geo, and I kept diverting her attention from our studies by whispering to her names like Star-Eyes, Gazelle, Little Peacock. I was a real Romeo, and like all Romeos my lines were not very fresh.

Drink hot coffee
Drink hot tea
Burn your lips
And think of me.
—G.

Her burning passion was all on paper, regretfully. End of story.

When worlds apart
And never to meet
May on your lips
My kisses be sweet
—M.

*The ink is not so old on this page, in fact only ten years or thereabouts
. . . because M. is my baby, the love of my life, my girl to this very day.
And she refreshes those old kisses every chance we get.*

⋆⋙◉⋘⋆

womonlove

Shalini

I
The war cries do not fade.
They come back
again and again,
in familiar faces,

in loved voices.

My very own familiars
come to do battle with me,
and bring their hurts to me too.

Enemy and healer –
I have these two roles, simultaneously.
Is it any wonder that I am schizophrenic?

Every morning I tell myself, today will be different.
I will create joy, life, newness, peace . . .
I will build bridges.
We will laugh together—
my familiars and I.

But so ritualized are our greetings
that we do not need to sound the gong.
It does not end
in blood, or pain, or tears.
These are just part of the plan.

II
We did not believe that the world will love us for who we are.
But did we know it would be so difficult?
That there is nothing in the world
which makes it easy for two women
to love and live together—we knew.
That our own will battle us the most,
that friends will claw at this love,
that the pain will come from those
we are loath to fight
—what justice is this, goddess?
You give me pain but love too so I can't fight back.

You give me enough understanding to leave
me speechless to the assaults on me.
You give me enough patience to listen.

And yet goddess, you do not give me enough love
to not fight and still be joyful,
to understand anger and yet love where I will,

You do not give me enough patience
to listen to my own love,
follow my voice when I hear it clearly.

You do not give me enough
to go the peaceful way to love.

⤖◆⤆

Dyking Around

Stree Sangam

Who we are and why we came together
Two women for a long time, then three, four—and now more
than twenty-five women . . . starting to talk about being
women who love women, starting to connect with each other.
Trying to create for ourselves spaces where we can be all of
who we are. Wanting to offer such spaces and support to other
women who might be in more restricted circumstances. In
April 1995, some of us met for the first time at a weekend
picnic—an exhilarating experience. Since then, we have been

meeting socially and as an organization. Forming this group and negotiating the many difficulties is a challenging task we have undertaken. We are excited about the possibilities that lie before us . . . Many ideas, many dreams.

We've only just begun . . .
It finally happened—a three-day gathering, June 7-9, 1996, of women who love women—the first of its kind in India. The retreat was organized by Stree Sangam—a collective of lesbian and bisexual women in Bombay—and for many of us, it was the realization of a long-held dream. Thirty of us, mainly from Bombay and Delhi, came together on a beach near Bombay for three days to share our lives.

The place was beautiful, and so were the women and the spaces we could create in those three days. We walked on the sands near the water, in groups, in pairs, alone. We talked and shared, ate, danced, slept, flirted . . .

The Delhi group had brought a bunch of films and some of us spent parts of the evenings and the nights watching them. The Bombay group had moved its library and documents to the retreat and some of us found time to browse through them.

The first day we all gathered by lunchtime and had our first meal together. Then we had an informal opening, a round of introductions and a discussion on what we wanted to get from these three days here. People suggested workshops, a number of topics were listed for discussion and over the next two days and three nights we gathered together at different times to talk and listen.

The first workshop/session was on sharing our lives and experiences, especially our 'coming out' stories and processes. How we felt about being where we were in our lives today and what our concerns were. We talked at length about our various relationships, some of us spoke about coming out to parents (or parents finding out) and the subsequent difficulties, being single, breaking up, jealousies, non-monogamy . . .

We spoke from varying backgrounds and perspectives. Some of us were in our late thirties and forties and narrated our stories of pressures in our lives and choices made. Some were as young as twenty, and as we talked we discovered the differences that had taken place over time and we also discovered the things that hadn't changed. We exchanged laughter over crushes, hostel love stories, discovering 'it'. We shared the joy we felt in relating with women, in loving and being loved. But we also exchanged our disillusionments, our bitter heartbreaks, loneliness, and the trauma which also sprang also from our most intimate relationships with women.

Later on over the next two days we also talked about sexuality, sex, safer sex, lesbians/bisexuals and AIDS, looking different and androgyny, families, organizing and the politics and dynamics of collectives, networking, the importance of reaching out to as many women as we can, ways and strategies of doing this, some brief reporting on lesbians and the law.

At night we romanced, danced, fought, shared our writing and talked some more. Some of us actually got some sleep. Many of us who had worked hard to put this retreat together had to miss some sessions and do organizing, especially around food, and by the end of the day needed some rest. By the end of three days we felt that this time together had been too brief. We left affirming that there would be another such meeting soon, to be organized by the Delhi group. Though there were differences which were not always openly stated or discussed, we left feeling that we had begun a conversation. A conversation which we came to from different paths, having negotiated different journeys.

-⊷≡◯≡⊶-

The Unconsumed
(for Saleem Kidwai)

Ruth Vanita

The party is picking up.
Faces are flushed, eyes water from the smoke.
Music storms the mind.
Besieged by ageing adolescence,
Roses, too many roses, soon to die,
Put a brave face on it,
Make a space of silence.
Suddenly, quietly, you are here,
Self-contained, somewhat wistful, somewhat lost,
Immaculate.
Almost in pain, no more benumbed, I ask,
What is beauty? What distils that flavour?
Must it be thought into being?
Has it to do with grief?
Is it a gift?

It's a matter of taste, you say,
As men are chased on the roof
And moonlight stands in pillars between the trees.
The potatoes are slightly off—
Women pick at them without appetite,
While a wide-eyed, starved-looking kid
Throws up in the bathroom—
I want to say, no, it's not,
Not what you want to eat or hold or squeeze
And then spit out. But I'm unsure what made
The little-known compound of your still face,

The cocktail of your smile,
As all of us try out our recipes
Into the unsated reaches of the night.

———◦◦———

Jogtrot; or, The Not-the-Nursery-Rhyme
(for Sanju)

Ann Urning

There's a man I'm watching
solitary to see,
I'm alone too
I think he's watching me.

Sometimes I find him in the rain,
as though to wash his sins,
he saw me take the drizzle in,
I feel we could be twins.

I dreamt he stopped me at a bend,
I thought I heard him say:
'You're very queer, I'm very gay,
will you please be my friend?'

———◦◦———

A Fish on a Bicycle

Phillippa C. Crescent

Bonny, a computer engineer in her mid-thirties, an attractive, vulnerable-looking woman with long, well-maintained hair.

Heta, Bonny's ex-lover, dynamic founder-member of the Bangalore Women's Network. She is in her early thirties, wears her hair short and presents the appearance of constant tension, but under strong control.

Vicky, Heta's best friend and an artist. He is entering forty, but takes great pains to conceal it.

Mohan, Vicky's much younger lover. A flight steward still on the correct side of thirty.

Bharati, a close friend of all the others, comfortable about her early fifties.

Act One (an excerpt)

The living room of a small apartment in a shambles. Boxes lie everywhere in heaps. Set is half-lit, suggestive of the time around sundown. Bonny is folding a tumbled pile of clothes, and putting them into a box. The front door, which is half-open already, is pushed fully open.

Bharati: [*pretending to be disgusted*] What a mess! This is just like a pig sty without any pigs. No, it is even *worse* than that. I think Lord Shiva has performed his tandava in your room, and that is why everything is everywhere.

Bonny: [*laughing*] Well, at least you don't have to feel guilty about not wiping your feet on the mat! The mat which I have only just finished packing away. Come in, don't stand by the door. When did you get back?

Bharati: Three weeks I have been away. Only this morning I got back. What to do, a social worker lives like that only! Here, there and everywhere all the time. But now tell me . . .

Bonny: I cannot, cannot, handle all of this packing up. I have only this second come back from a walk in Lalbagh to clear out the junk in my head. There is so much to do. I have all of these clothes to fold up, and I don't know what else—sheets, towels, cutlery—and I have to finish packing before Heta returns. You understand, don't you?

Bharati: Come, leave it now. Let us go to my house and have some drinks. I did not have one small drop of any alcohol in Andhra. I did not have even this 'spurious' country liquor, or booze from a bootlegger. Horrible it was, talking to these women about anti-liquor movements and wanting my whisky. Such a swindler I felt in front of them . . . Shall we go? [*silence, while Bonny folds a dress with care and Bharati watches*] Have you and Heta been living together two years or twenty years, to have so much of towels and books and tables to divide up?

Bonny: Oh, so *you* at last are talking about the break-up. Not a word all these weeks, and now suddenly—

Bharati: I have been away. And what, I did not think you wanted to discuss.

Bonny: Well, you were Heta's friend first. I don't like dividing up sheets and towels, but I am completely sickened by the idea of dividing up friends . . .

Bharati: Talking does not have to be in that style.

Bonny: Do you know, no one wants to talk about it *at all*. All of the gay community is pretending simply that I am moving for some other reason. No one will say, 'Oh, so you and Heta are breaking up.' Or 'Why are you breaking up.' But everyone is talking between themselves, I know that for a fact.

Bharati: Where are you going to shift? To . . . Arun's place?

Bonny: I didn't want to live with his family until he gets here from LA next month. It would feel very strange. Not right at all. Of course, after marriage I will have to stay there until all my immigration is done. And then I will go the States right behind him, wagging my tail like a good puppy dog. Aha! You're smiling at last!

Bharati: Well, it is quite funny. Arun's mother-father don't know about you and Heta at all, hah? What is it they think, two of you were sharing a flat to give some company to each other?

Bonny: They do know we were lovers. I am sure they have guessed. But they have not said anything to me or asked for explanations. Arun says—have I told you what he says? That I've lived it up, and now I can live it down, it's fine. I told him, you wouldn't be so saucy if you were getting married after you'd told all of your friends and even your own mother that you're gay.

Bharati: So you don't have somewhere to stay?

Bonny: Actually, Mohan has that empty flat which he is waiting to sell . . . I'm staying there until Arun comes. Even though it's much too close to—to this place for me . . . I'm a bit afraid of running into Heta when I go to buy vegetables . . . knowing what my luck is like. You and the rest of our gay group think it's so simple to be good friends after breaking up. But two years of my life! She has been my whole and entire life for two years. She knows exactly how to give me pain, and I know how to give her pain. How can we just go back to being 'pals' after that, Bharati? You can be far too idealistic sometimes. I don't fit into that cosy lesbian world of yours. I'm not a part of it, it's just not me. But don't hate me because of that, because I can't so easily go back to being a heterosexual either. I don't fit anywhere, anywhere at all any more.

Bharati: Now you are tired and you are talking absolute nonsense. Look, it is almost six o'clock and any time soon Heta will be here. Don't worry, I will get things a bit more tidy here and push these boxes to the side. Just *go* now and try to rest.

Bonny: Thank you, Bharati [*hugs her*] I've always felt such a bond with you. That won't change, will it, because I am moving out of your world? I'm not a traitor, am I, because I'm giving up my lesbian identity card and getting married? I was an impostor in this lesbian life from the very beginning, don't you see? I tried because I wanted to please Heta. Now I just want to be me, and find my *own* place on this earth, without these labels. Can't I just live, live without fighting so hard to work out what this is all about and who I am?

Bharati: If you don't want to live as a lesbian, OK, fine. But why are you running into this marriage? If you want to be your own self, then you can live alone instead until you *know*.

Bonny: Bharati, dear, don't make this harder. This marriage, it is my bridge to where I want to go, it's not an escape act. And Arun is not like that, he's not a tyrant. But look, it's after six. I have to rush, right now.

Bharati: OK, go now, go! But we will talk soon, promise me.

[*Bonny laughs and goes out, shutting the door behind her. Bharati picks up a piece of clothing and folds it absent-mindedly*] Now whose is this, Heta's? Or Bonny's? [*goes to switch on the radio*] The lamp must be Bonny's. Leaving it in the middle of the floor like this so carelessly . . .

[*The door is unlocked with a key. Heta enters*]

Heta: Bharati! Exactly the one person whom I've been searching for all over town, and now look where I find you, in my own back yard. Helping Bonny to pack, are you? Anyway, what I wanted to tell you is that I've just now found the perfect location to run the women's helpline from, wait till you see it—it's on the first floor of that green building near the CTO, lovely view of the park, one small room for record-keeping and administration, and then another one for operations, just right, hah?

Bharati: Yes, Heta, yes. But will you *stop* talking about the Network? Look, this place is on its head, such a mess. Look after all the women in the world, but charity starts at home. The Network can wait, na, until your life is more settled?

Heta: I have been waiting to see this helpline happen for how many years now? It's been my dream ever since I arrived here from New York. It *is* my life. So many women, so many, feeling alone and helpless.

Bharati: What about Bonny?

Heta: Bonny? What about her? Is she here?

Bharati: No, a few minutes ago she left. Because she said, just now, it would be better to not see you. Which you probably know, na?

Heta: Hmmph. Yes. We have talked about it.

Bharati: It is difficult for her—

Heta: Very difficult. [*shaking her head, once more in control of herself*] Isn't it shocking, Bharati? Poor Bonny, when I think about her fate, and the impossibility of escape, I feel so angry at this heteropatriarchal culture in India. In spite of being in contact with the lesbian community—whatever small community we have in this city, four-five of us—there was still unceasing pressure on her to get married. And she cracked, of course. I knew she was going to crack, you have to have superhuman strength to be a lesbian in this country and not go insane. It is just so hard, so hard. No public role models to look up to so that we know that we lesbians can actually be happy living as lesbians!

Bharati: Heta . . .

Heta: What are the reports you read in the newspaper, tell me? It is significant that they are all about lesbian couples getting murdered at the hands of the family, or being forced to separate by the police under the threat of imprisonment and public exposure. There are no stories of lesbians living happily together, because that is simply not news.

Bharati: [*gently*] Heta. In her heart, inside, Bonny was always denying to her own self that she was a lesbian. To me she has said this many times—when she was drunk—and she has told you this also, I know, many times. She did not ever really believe that the relationship between two women could be normal and healthy . . .

Heta: How *can* a lesbian relationship be healthy here, in this country of colonial and Victorian mores? There is no acknowledgement from the family or the state, we have to expect all our strength to come from each other! That is such a strain, as you are only too aware—you and Shakuntala have had so many troubled times. It is hard for lesbian couples to survive, almost impossible.

Bharati: Heta, you think everything is about being visible to other people. Getting approval or acceptance from these other people, whoever they are. Other people! Some problems are from inside—inside you, inside her. You have always known that Bonny is attracted to men, and still you—

Heta: She was free to explore the possibility of her bisexuality within our relationship—it was open, I was open to her sleeping with men if that was what she wanted. But she did not want to have any sexual interaction with a man while we were together. [*pauses, while looking out of the window*] But you know, Bharati, I think this helpline will serve as a very important resource, and we can only hope that it will be a small step towards preventing *other* lesbians from seeing marriage as the only solution.

Bharati: Heta, I am not talking about other lesbians—

Heta: [*ignoring her*] . . . because I called Aditi in Bombay, and she is very ready to be one of the first staffers on the helpline. It is so important to have an identifiable lesbian presence.

Bharati: Why Aditi? There are women in Bangalore, no, who could counsel.

Heta: Not lesbians. Can you think of a single lesbian who would do it?

Bharati: But many committed feminists are there, as you know.

Such as Lily—she does very good work in counseling. And what will a Bombay person, even someone like Aditi, know about realities of Bangalore women and family politics of the South?

Heta: What have your precious Bangalore feminists done for us? They won't even say the word 'lesbian'. They are in complete terror of the world—and their husbands—thinking that they are lesbians too if they support lesbian rights.

Bharati: But how will you justify this, a women's helpline run only by lesbians?

Heta: [*lightly*] Why not? Lesbians are everything that women are, and then a little bit more.

Bharati: [*laughing*] Hopeless! You are hopeless.

[*A cheerful knocking at the door, voices murmuring. Enter Vicky and Mohan; they pause for a few seconds on the doorstep*]

Vicky: [*kissing Heta on both cheeks*] Hello, love. Sorry we didn't call before dropping in like this, but we were supposed to meet Bonny here.

Mohan: [*aggressively*] We're taking her out to dinner.

Heta: Well, she is not here, Mohan, my boy.

Bharati: Bonny told me she is moving to Mohan's empty flat. She is there, maybe?

Vicky: No, she can't be there yet. Mohan and I wanted to give her the keys tonight, which is why we are so set on finding her!

Mohan: [*taking keys out and shaking them loudly*] So, where is she then?

Heta: She will have to come back here to collect you, so *I* will go out of the flat for an hour, since she feels it is a good idea that we don't see each other at all for a few months . . . by which time she will be in America anyway, I am sure! So, unless she invites me to her wedding—!

Mohan: For Christ's sake, Heta—

Heta: So I am going downstairs to buy groceries. There is nothing in the house at all, except some bread. Help yourself to a slice if you're hungry, boys. Or have a drink or two, at least we're not short on the essentials. Bharati, do you want anything?

Bharati: No, I must be leaving too, really.

Heta: We'll walk together, then. We'll catch you later, boys.

[*Bharati and Heta leave. Mohan and Vicky wait until the sound of conversation fades, then stare at each other*]

Vicky: What will I do with you, my cranky loverboy . . . Why can't you be just a little sweet with Heta? She is also very hurt, as you know.

Mohan: I cannot stand her at all, that bitch. She has ten thousand silly airs and graces. Hey, Vicky, why did Bonny want to meet us here? I would think this is the last place she'd want to be when it's not necessary.

Vicky: She lived here for two years, didn't she. I bet she's very fond of this flat, it must be the closest place to a home that she has . . . whatever ugly business is going on with Heta.

Mohan: [*crudely*] Good riddance to bad rubbish. You know it's true, Vicky, so don't make that face, babe. At least this time Heta did not start talking that bullshit about how much she pities Bonny, who is so *confused* and *misguided*.

Vicky: Maybe she *is* confused. What do *you* know about it, little love? All said and done, Heta is right. This is not a country where you can easily feel glad to be gay. You runaway child, you fly off two weeks each month to all these gay-happy places like Paris, London, Amsterdam—

Mohan: But you know Anil? He was saying just yesterday how he knew Heta when they were both in New York. And that woman was not at all who she is now. She was a total shadow, going nowhere in her life and doing shit with herself.

Vicky: I wish you wouldn't pay attention to gossip—

Mohan: Will you just listen? . . . I don't know why Heta is so fucked up, but she is. Anil thinks she left New York because it's far too easy to be gay there. He says, it might be hard in

India, but here at least gayness still means something. Because here, you can still go through a lot of shit if you try to be open. So Heta felt like she was really someone who was doing something, just because she went around holding hands with Bonny and kissing her in the middle of a restaurant for no fucking reason.

Vicky: Heta was in love with her . . .

[*The door opens silently while Vicky is talking, and Bonny comes in unnoticed by Vicky and Mohan*]

Mohan: She treated her like a bloody prop, you mean. She was a gorgeous accessory, and so Heta could make a statement to the entire city, 'Look, not all lesbians are ugly women with short hair—'

Bonny: Mohan, you insufferable creature!

Vicky: Oh, sweetie, you startled me. And you were not supposed to hear that, you eavesdropper!

Mohan: But it's true, isn't it? She took total advantage of you, that woman. You met her when you were not feeling secure about yourself after a string of loser men, you slept with her a couple of times—

Bonny: But wait, how do you know all of this?

Mohan: Everyone knows. It's a small city, baby . . . yah, and then when you wanted to go back to men, then she started a relationship with you, because she hated to see one get away.

Bonny: My god, so now I am truly the one that got away. Ha, it's so perfect. You gay boys always call us women 'fish', don't you? I wasn't a lesbian for two years for nothing, you know! I know all the terms by now, especially the vulgar ones. Fish! I *feel* like a fish, too—a fish out of water. Fitting in nowhere. Can't go back to the sea, can't survive in thin air. I'm a fish out of water! Hey listen, if it's true that 'a woman needs a man like a fish needs a bicycle', what d'you think happens to a fish out of water?

Mohan. Bonny, Bonny, Bonny, Bonny . . . what have you been drinking, baby?

Bonny: Whiskey and soda. But I'm not drunk, it just helps me learn to love myself without these crazy labels. Don't you think these labels are crazy? I mean, I love who I want to love, why do we need to give it a name? Why? Hah? Me and Heta, it was not what you think, Mohan—god, what a sick cliché—a voracious lesbian taking advantage of a straight woman who has her defences down around her ankles . . . [*walks over to Mohan and holds onto him for support*] I was the aggressive one, can you understand that? I looked at Heta at Mithi's party, so sure of her place on earth and like a flash I knew I wanted to make love to her. She was like a cat, with those lines of . . . force . . . under the soft fur on the outside. God, and all this time you thought I was the typical straight woman in need of gentle loving after a bad patch of . . . patchy men with bald patches. I got to tell you, though, lesbianism sounds like the answer to all the modern Indian girl's problems—it tells you exactly who you are, and—and why you've always thought men are dogs . . . who just want to sniff your crotch . . . and why you've gone through life feeling like you have to try to be the lady next door . . . who is trying to be you but you never guess it. Heta said there were lesbians who didn't realize what they were until after marriage, even . . . Heta said that with everyone telling women that they are put on earth to be with men, it was not shocking that lesbians often don't discover ourselves—themselves—at all . . . Heta said, just think about all your friendships with women, and couldn't they easily have grown into something more? . . . it sounded excellent . . . [*she turns towards the window, stumbles, and Vicky quickly moves to steady her*] I felt purified, like purging away tired norms and seeing my true personality for the first time. She never pushed me . . . never pushed me, I jumped. Right off the cliff.

Vicky: [*after a pause*] Now—

Bonny: [*laughing*] That is a very good idea, if you were going to talk about eating. Have you decided where we are going to have dinner?

Mohan: Perhaps you'd like dinner at our place? I'll make you chicken, from a recipe I learned in Gay Paree.

Bonny: —and we'll have a gay old time—for the last time! [*Their laughter is interrupted by a loud, showy series of knocks, and Heta comes in. Bonny glances up at Heta, then ignores her, speaking feverishly*] —though when I consider the whole thing, it's amazing, isn't it, I always thought when I went from being grave to being gay, I was going to be gay to the grave.

Heta: How much have you been drinking?

Bonny: Heta, don't talk down to me, I don't like it. And—and what are you doing here, then? No, not like that—I meant, I thought we were supposed to stay out of each other's path, I thought we'd decided, that—that if you knew I was somewhere, then . . . but still you're . . .

Heta: I came here to talk to you. Please spare five minutes for me, Bonny?

Mohan: I don't think that is necessary.

Heta: Why can't you mind your own business?

Bonny: [*almost begging*] Heta, *is* it necessary?

Heta: Five minutes. [*Mohan and Vicky go out quickly; Heta does not speak again until the sound of their footsteps has faded*] Don't worry, I don't want you back.

Bonny: [*in a low voice*] I know.

Heta: Would it matter to you if I did?

Bonny: Don't make me suffer any more. Leave me in peace, all I want is some—peace.

Heta: So . . . is your mother happy that you have come back to eat at the family table?

Bonny: Is that what you want to discuss?

Heta: No. I want to ask you, did you have to tell everyone in the gay group about our private life? I hate the pitying looks, and I feel stripped naked in front of them. Yeah? So will you have *some* respect for our relationship.

Bonny: You're going too far—

Heta: Me? *You* are leaving to marry your ex-boyfriend, you've decided you want him again after dumping him five years ago, you couldn't have made a decision to want him before all of this uproar . . . and *I* am going too far?

Bonny: You are very clever with twisting words around. But you cannot ignore my feelings.

Heta: What *do* you feel? Hah? I heard you're telling them all how you were always *feeling* uncomfortable about sex with me, *feeling* like this was not your lifestyle—

Bonny: Don't talk at me like that! You were always talking at me when we were in a relationship, telling me what to do. 'Go sleep with a guy, I won't mind, see if it suits you, maybe you're bisexual—'

Heta: I never said that!

Bonny: [*ignoring her*] I felt like an experiment for your articles on the ebb and flow of Indian female sexuality! That was how I felt!

Heta: I never said that! You're inventing things!

Bonny: And when I said I was feeling wrong about being involved with a woman, you said that some level of self-hatred was normal in women who were just discovering their sexuality, and that I should learn to accept myself.

Heta: Will you stop this?

Bonny: I don't have your courage of conviction! My life does not belong on display like that. And I want to say this for the last time: the word 'lesbian' does not describe my—my flesh. This body has been through so much, my mind through so much more. There is no one word to describe it all.

Heta: On the next occasion that I try to talk to you, please leave your speeches behind at Arun's house.

Bonny: [*starting to cry*] I thought you wanted to see me out of genuine concern for me.

Heta: You thought I wanted you back. Go, lead your wonderful new life.
[*Curtain*]

━━◉═━

XX

Gauri

No, this isn't soft porn, hard porn or erotica.

It's about ex-girlfriends. Two, to be precise.

And I love them both. One I shared four and a half years with, and the other barely one and a half, but the bond I have with them is unbelievable.

Let's call the first one A and the second one B. A and I went through a lot of turmoil in the relationship. And, as all break-ups are, it was bad. But then I met B, and she played a small role in my developing a friendship with my ex-girlfriend. 'You're very unforgiving,' she used to tell me. Well, she was right. Decided to let bygones be bygones and today A and I are great friends, even though she doesn't stay in Bombay much.

But B and I have a bond that very few people have. This kind of love is unimaginable and very rare (that's what she tells me). I tend to agree with her. The break-up was even worse than the first one. I felt hurt, betrayed and insecure. Felt she didn't respect my emotions and gave me a lot of pain. But I had sworn to myself that when the bad part was over and the sun started shining again, I would work at a friendship. Little did I guess how much time and dedication would go into it. We both kept at it and today we are closer than ever before. I think I know her a lot better now than I did when I was seeing her.

Both of us are now involved with other people, and we discuss our relationships with each other. When I'm with her, it's like going home. With ex-girlfriends, there's a comfortable understanding that you can't share with anyone else.

When A calls me from out of town, after we hang up, I have this smile on my face and I realize how much I miss her.

When B calls me at work and I'm in a foul mood and take it out on her, I know I hurt her and don't excuse myself. But I also know only she realizes where I'm coming from. And if I'm busy and haven't spoken to her for two days, I get a call to remind me that she's alive and that we must meet. Or when I'm going through a rough time with my present involvement, I call her up and hang out with her.

So would I go through the pain, confusion and misunderstandings of my relationships with both these women, all over again? If it meant a lifelong friendship with them after a bout of the bad weather, yes!

⤖≡◐≡⤖

Maqbara

Shaka

Did I think relinquishing you
would be easy?
eons have passed . . .

Did I say love
was my birthright?
illusion, memory, dream . . .

Trying to release you
trying to connect
I swallow the knot of loneliness

In cities, lanes, ancient forts
I hear echoes of voices
waves of a restless sea

Suddenly, this silent mausoleum
is drenched with your fragrant touch
my falling tears the essence of you.

⊷⟫⊚⟪⊷

The Adventures of Maheshwariya

Mita Radhakrishnan

Chapter 1

Maheshwariya was walking down the road. Doing nothing in particular, going nowhere. Just walking, breathing the smog-filled air deeply, dreaming that it was the clear crisp mountain air of her childhood. Of course, she was very much rooted in the here and now—it was just the air, that's all. She loved the city. She loved the people, the cars, cyclists, autos, the trucks. Yes, even the trucks. She would fantasize about running in between the traffic and jumping into the back of an interstate truck and seeing where it would take her.

Suddenly she pulled her dupatta over her head. 'Let me play a demure role now.' She tapered her strongwoman swagger into a staid walk. 'I hope my hips are moving just so, like in the movies.' She let her shoulders sag, pulled herself in—demure women are not supposed to take up space, you know. But strong women! Strong women are just that. Strong women take up space. Strong women swagger—as Maheshwariya had been doing till she decided to be timid.

But there was a problem: Maheshwariya—shoulders sagging, hips moving just so (like in the movies), taking up as little space as possible, dupatta covering her head—still felt strong. 'Hey! I'm not supposed to feel strong when I walk like this,' she thought. She pictured those women she saw everyday, women who were exploited, sexploited, beaten by their husbands, or just plain oppressed by 'the system'. 'They may not walk with a strongwomon swagger, but they are strong! What a revelation!' she cried. 'I suddenly feel free!'

And so happy was she at this newfound freedom that she didn't see herself walking right into a teenage tigress.

Chapter 2
'Ouch! Such manners!' exclaimed the tigress. 'Women these days just walk all over me. No manners. No decency. Can't you watch where you are going? Who do you think you are? What do you think I am? A doormat? Some kind of obscene rug . . .?'

Yes, Tigress was utterly and totally exasperated. But she stopped her grumbling when she realized that she was beginning to be uncharitable. Besides, something about this particular woman made her fall silent.

Maheshwariya was in shock. Not only had she hit upon her most wonderful idea yet, but here she had gone and bumped into a tigress, and a talking one at that! And not just a talking one, but one who was accusing her—Strongwomon Maheshwariya!—of treating others like a doormat! She forced herself out of her stupor and started apologizing profusely. 'Oh I *am* sorry. So sorry! I guess I wasn't looking where I was going. I was just struck by this wonderful thought—the most wonderful thought I've had so far. And I suddenly felt free. But you see, the story is longer than that. I am Strongwomon Maheshwariya. And I was just trying a little experiment and I was struck by this thought, see, and . . . ' Maheshwariya came to a halt. One, because she was out of breath; and two, because she suddenly realized that she was going on and on about her strongwomon self (and strongwomen are not supposed to talk about their strength, you know, since it is obvious for the world to see).

Chapter 3

Maheshwariya and Tigress looked at each other. Tigress had picked herself up from the ground and shaken the dust off her coat. Now she stood listening to this fascinating dupatta-covered apparition. Maheshwariya was a little worried and embarrassed.

'Lets have chai,' Tigress said suddenly. Now that this being had walked into her life, she was unwilling to just let her go. 'I need some chai. And I think it's only decent that you pay for it since you are the one who walked into me. I must say though, I would really love to hear about that experiment you were conducting—a demure experiment, you said . . .?' For Tigress had felt something change within her. She had been prepared to be bitchy as usual, crabby as a cat and completely sick of women trampling on her, when all of a sudden she was ready to hear anything this woman (who had after all treated her like every other woman had, she reminded herself) had to say.

Maheshwariya could only agree. The thought of a nice hot steaming chai and a willing ear was irresistible! Besides, this ear was striped! How often does one get to converse with a talking tigress? So she threw all her strongwomon caution and all her misgivings to the winds.

'Well,' said Tigress, as they sat down on two stools in front of Poonamben's Deluxe Chai Shop, 'let me tell you that I am Tigress and, while I do not usually conduct experiments here, these are my haunts. I live a few streets away with my family, and Poonamben has the best chai shop in this city.'

Chapter 4

One day Maheshwariya and Tigress were sitting together as usual, drinking Poonamben's tea and talking, when Maheshwariya was suddenly overtaken by an urge to buy her new friend a gift. She asked, 'Tigress, did you ever play with dinky cars when you were growing up?'

Tigress had never heard of this phenomenon, so they strolled together to the toy shop which Maheshwariya had once visited as a child. There were girl dolls dressed in white frilly dresses, and boy dolls, in sailor suits. There were block toys and wooden toys, woolen toys and papier mâché ones. There were puzzles and board games—Snakes and Ladders and Ludo. And there were dinky cars galore. Red sports cars, police jeeps, road rollers. There were trucks and buses and scooters. And there were engines, complete with railroad tracks and bogeys for coal with tiny signals and plastic trees, bridges too.

It was a whole little world in itself, and one new to Tigress who had walked past many a toy store in her city life and never once dreamt of looking in. Maheshwariya turned to her and said, 'Take whatever you want, it's a present.'

Tigress looked and looked, her tail twitching with excitement. Finally she settled on the big red fire engine with a long ladder and a bell which rang if you pulled the string. This would be her new toy. Already she was dreaming of fires, and imagining herself driving madly down the road to rescue women trapped in flaming houses, ringing the bell urgently so that all the tongas and scooters and autos and buses and cars and cyclists rushed out of her way . . .

Maheshwariya looked at Tigress, and could only smile.

Chapter 5

'Maheshwariya, I want to talk with you today,' said Tigress. Her voice was a strange mixture of decision and tentativeness, and she spoke as though acutely aware of the impact of her words. Maheshwariya's heart skipped a beat. Tigress had never announced conversations like this in all their friendship.

'Where shall we sit, Tigress?' she asked. 'It is so hot that maybe we should go back to my room and lie under the fan. If we go to Poonamben's she'll wonder why we are so serious,' she added, her mind racing.

'Anywhere,' said Tigress.

'Well, maybe we should go to my room because it is so hot and you must be sweating in your coat. You can shave it if you want, you know; I'll do it for you . . . ' she continued, trying desperately to change the subject.

'I really don't care, Maheshwariya, where we talk, I only care that we do,' Tigress replied. Maheshwariya's spirit sank further. In silence they walked, Tigress listening to her thumping heart.

Chapter 6

Tigress was very nervous. Never before had a conversation felt so crucial. But then again, never before had she had a soul-friend such as Maheshwariya. Scared though she was, she felt driven. The little statements made so nonchalantly, the ignorance, and moreover, that terrible condescension in Maheshwariya's overbearing nature had all pushed her to this point.

'Maheshwariya, I think you talk down to me,' she began resolutely. 'Just because I am a Tigress and you are a human, you think you know best. You are constantly making all the decisions, telling me what I should or should not do—whether it's shaving my coat or going for a movie.' She paused for a breath.

'You think that because you are past your teens and I am

not, you are bigger and older than me. You forget, Maheshwariya, that you are a human and I am a tigress. In human years, I, a teenage tigress, am over thirty years old. Really I am almost old enough to be your mother. Maheshwariya, I am tired. And more than tired, I am sad. I get this treatment every day from other people, from my family even, but I never expected to get it from you—I thought you were different, you were special. But you too think all I can do is provide fun and entertainment, a good laugh and nothing more. Why . . . ?'

She could have continued, goaded as she was by her sense of injustice, but her voice quavered as she glanced at her friend's face. Maheshwariya looked stricken. The cigarette she had lit had fallen to the floor, her mouth was opening and closing as though the words of self-justification had caught in her throat. When she looked up at Tigress, there were tears in her strongwomon eyes.

‹━━◉━━›

Chakra/Circle

Swatija

One late winter night in Delhi, we attended a dance performance of the Ritu Chakra. It presented, in Indian classical dance form, the heterosexual ideal of pranay—an eternity between man and woman. But it was also intermixed with depictions of the relationships of women amongst themselves. We were ten women from different backgrounds and contexts, but each of us enjoyed that two-hour performance enormously.

It was a really special experience for all of us, especially for our friends who had come from the First World. The programme said that the performance was designed as a way to introduce Indian dance forms to 'Soviet Russia'. All of us were intrigued by that, too: was this an old programme which had been revived, or was it a fresh attempt to address a newly transformed USSR?

The performance was a heavenly treat and we were all drunk on it. We were in such a delicately balanced and charged emotional state that the winter cold receded and it seemed like a pleasant time of year. Altogether, the atmosphere became very conducive to sharing our understanding, our concerns. Four of us stayed on, and then a very spontaneous discussion emerged, taking off in many different directions, following many unplanned paths.

We two Indian women instinctively understood each other and grew close; shared, revealed our inner cores and depths in that short period of time. That was an enriching and empowering experience for me because I was feeling rather low and wanted to talk about the many questions churning in my mind about my physical desires and my ideas of love. The weight of old and new commitments was oppressing me. I was eager to strike a balance within and without. This sense of connection made a lot of difference to me.

The two women from the First World were in a relationship, it was obvious, but they also had the mental space to explore and enjoy the company of others. Their relationship was not something jarring, not a source of uneasiness to those of us who were single but never claimed to be celibate. This mattered a lot to me, because overt, explicit pairing is many a time insensitive to others. The atmosphere encouraged me to share my ideas about woman-to-woman relationships.

It was an experience that was individual as well as

collective, which pleased me and boosted my morale. I realized all over again that I am not divided into personal and political compartments. We pursued the thread of our earlier discussion around my activist interests. I began talking about gender-just laws and their rationale, underlining the need for special consideration of the particular homo-relational and hetero-relational lived realities which extend far beyond the confines of the legal structure as it stands. This brought in related topics—the situation in India, and, at another level, our personal lives.

I talked a lot in that informal meeting. Over the last few days, I had noticed a change taking place within me. All these years, I used to express myself in the form of writing. Conversations were hampered by my diffidence with spoken language. I used to struggle for words. And since this happened with all the languages I knew, it was obvious that my problem lay in the mode of communication rather than in a specific language. I had reconciled myself to the problem, and found comfort in writing. But that form has its own limitations, because when one tries to write, one often loses the sense of urgency, of immediacy.

Meanwhile, my wide and wild attempts to write letters had faltered. Diary writing has long been my way of communicating with myself, and I had opted for letter writing as a way of communicating with others. But I felt I had failed miserably, because my letters could not connect with the one person to whom I was reaching out. Today I am struggling to regain my ability to relate to people. Physical interaction has its own sweetness, but it is limited, and my need to communicate verbally has grown manifold.

That turmoil forced me to explore various genres. I wrote poetry and also some fiction. Such creative spurts come and go. But the urge remains. And the need to fulfil that urge has made me see my blind spots. Lately I have been talking, and my image of myself as a complex, opaque person is vanishing; I feel a greater sense of transparency.

The utterance that lay dead within me is coming back to life in different forms. I do not have you to thank, my dear friend to whom I have not been able to reach out; this process of returning to life has not been an easy one, and I have taken the help of many friends from all over the world. I owe it to all of them, and not to you, and this gives me a strange kind of reassurance.

I am not talking about all of this because it emerged during that conversation in Delhi; when I recollect those moments, these ideas emerge on their own in my mind. I value such awareness since it is also a kind of creativity, and brings to me an understanding of the depth and power of conversation. The act of self-disclosure allowed the sweetness of memory to come to the surface and strengthen my resolve to continue speaking. I recalled walking along the reddish-brown sand of a beach in Holland at twilight, feeling the force of the sea, something I love. As I shared my story, I was filled with the intoxicating energy of potential connection.

I got married at the age of twenty-one, by my own wishes, and from then onwards a sacrificing, giving role became an overwhelming part of me, and I submerged my identity in it. But at the same time I began to realize that this was not necessarily what I wanted. I started to live my life intensely and was exposed to a host of possible connections—blood relations and non-blood relations, all sorts of combinations of dependent, semi-dependent and independent ties. I was struggling to achieve some autonomy, and had to live through the transition from looking at myself as a sacrificing being, to becoming a self-willed entity who believed in 'take' as much as 'give'.

I became a part of collective activity at that point in time, and a new vision of 'being' started to emerge. All women are powerless in their own ways: each has to struggle to create a space of her own, and there is no hierarchy in the struggle. This world-view brought me closer to women emotionally. The ideal of power-free equations in the bonds between women drove me to the realization that I love women.

I talked to these friends about the whole question of the visibility of lesbian relationships. I said: 'I do not feel the need to demand visibility because for me, the relationship is what matters most. Close friendships between women are accepted in Indian society, even though it does not confer legal rights on these relationships, and when disputes arise, recourse to such rights is required.

'In my life, I realized after eleven years of marriage that I love women. The space to explore my orientation was created by me and my partner. This is what I value most, and for me, the question of visibility by itself is secondary. For me, the sexual is not the most important aspect; I do not agree with the norms which are maintained even in lesbian relationships.'

I was expecting a somewhat heated response to this, but to my amazement, it did not happen. Both of my friends from the First World were surprised to hear me, because the prominence given to the issue of visibility in the white lesbian movement was something they too had been finding objectionable. Visibility becomes all-important, and dominates the issues and processes of women coming together. My friends were also concerned by the kind of unhealthy atmosphere created by the politics of such groups.

I told them it was a process of ghettoization. When sexuality becomes the revolving or central point of discussion, boundaries are drawn, immediately separating women from each other. I do not consider the celebration of desires wrong, but it is not everything: the task for lesbians who do not subscribe to the traditional norms of heterosexual, power-laden relationships is a much more difficult one. We have to demonstrate the humanness of this so-called 'abnormality'—a humanness emerging out of love for humanity as a whole—without being either arrogant or insecure. It will not happen if we denounce those who are not like us and who are more like the social majority.

The task is tough, and it requires tremendous inner strength and patience.

I share all this and will share more in the days ahead. But now, with the happiness of meeting others who share my vision lingering in my mind, I fall into a peaceful, reassuring sleep.

⊷━◉══←

My Best Friend Is Gay . . . and So Am I!

Kristen

'Wow! What a babe! I swear she batted her eyelashes at me. Hey! I can see her from the corner of my eye looking at me from the corner of *her* eyes. Oh, and what eyes (sigh)!'

That's anybody's reaction when they come to the college I study at in Bombay, since it's known everywhere for its extremely hot women. But being a woman myself, I can't openly admire someone of my own sex.

'Hey! All women are latent lesbians,' I want to scream from the top of these articulated carved stone structures. Oops! Now you'll know the college I was referring to, but who cares. I did not drop names, subtle hints are enough for smart people.

It's a pity that I can't openly woo some of these women for

fear of being ostracized. Call it peer pressure or mental conditioning, it means the same thing in big bold black letters: I DON'T HAVE THE GUTS. It's not that my cuteness quotient is extremely low or that there aren't enough chicks who would like to be seduced by an attractive and charming girl like me (excuse me, this isn't a case of exaggerated self-importance and neither am I a narcissist, it's just that I don't like to be too hard on myself).

Quite simply, I don't want to rant and rave about being gay, especially if no one's listening, and being ridiculed isn't something I want to experience.

Talking about it is risky anyway, at any time. And it's tough finding friends who are like yourself. But they're around, if you look hard enough in likely and sometimes the most unlikely spaces.

In college, as in my all-girls school, there were always girls who were 'different' and girls who fell for them. The former had a large fan-following. I did too, but so did the bitch in the next row with the cropped hair and the sickeningly sweet smile, called Kimberley. She was popularly known as Kim. We never liked one another and were always competing for the same reason—girls!

If she was busy charming a long-legged, straight-haired beauty at this end, I was busy with a sexy, doe-eyed, ample-bosomed babe at that end. Both knew what the other was after, but instead of acknowledging each other, we stayed poles apart. Besides a courteous nod or a deadpan 'Hi!' we did not want to have anything to do with each other.

But the strange ways of fate . . . One day I saw her crying uncontrollably in the loo. Being a soft-hearted person, I could not leave her in that manner and began consoling her. Then I learned that she was from a rich family where everything was provided for her except love.

325

This encounter was the beginning of our friendship. As we got older we became wiser and sadly wilder; what we used to do alone we now did together. Before we even knew it, we had become the best of pals. We knew we were both 'different', but it took a long time for us to come out in the open and tell each other the truth.

As time passed, we both went into relationships and came out of them, but our best-buddyhood just kept growing. Some of my greatest times have been spent with her. We discovered this lonely place and called it Sunset Point, and we met there regularly, drank beer, smoked, ogled babes and felt very adult. Foolish us!

No friendship, past or present, compares to the one I share with Kim. These lines are a tribute to her. Right now she is going through a very bad phase, she is single and desperately lonely. I'm always there for her, but I've got a girl and she hasn't, and that doesn't make things complete.

I'd just like to tell her one thing: Love ya, Kim, and I always will! We'll be pals forever.

⊷══◉══⊶

Justine

Kimberley

I had known Justine since my school days. A change of stream did not keep us apart: me a science student and Justine an arts buff, we still debated priceless matters.

Justine—an irresistible medium-built girl, with cropped

hair, mischief-filled twinkling black eyes, slender nose, and always a heartwarming smile to top everything.

Something common between us brought us close.

'If you are gay, don't be ashamed of it. Are you . . . ? I'm happy you are not. But be what you are. Make your own identity. Try and forgive people, even when you know it hurts—you aren't God, you haven't made them. Believe me, those women you are hunting don't know your worth. Just be yourself. Tell the next woman you meet that you find her really hot! If she asks you to change, tell her, "Accept me as I am, because I am what I am", and see her go for you.'

We always had a hearty laugh over this issue of me being single.

In just two months one could make out what kind of friendship we shared. Of course it wasn't physical. We loved each other, but not in that way. We were the best of pals, 'chicklets', as we were named in our college.

Bunking college lectures to run away for 'babe watch' was what we did best. Our fave spots—the local girls' college, the brand-new coffee shop, the nearest disco club, gift shops, cosmetics shops and the beach—all of which were filled with beautiful women to the brim.

'Oooh, I lust for that woman down there in her cute shorts.' Justine was panting already. 'Slurp . . . this woman who just went by smelled delicious, just like hot chocolate fudge. On second thoughts, let's go down to the ice cream parlour.' The only thing I could do was turn my face away from her and look up into the sky, laugh, take her by the hand pulling her through the crowd, with her still yelling, 'Hey! Look at that living doll, I must make her mine.'

She put me in one embarrassing situation after the other.

But she was mature enough to understand the realities of life. She easily took things in her stride, and failure never hurt her. She dropped a year in school, and to anyone who asked her, 'Fail, didn't you?' she would shoot back: 'No! They just made a deal with me due to the lack of seats. Your best friend was so weak and ill that they asked me if I'd give up my seat for her, that poor hardworking freak, and well! I sacrificed. Wasn't that nice of me?' And there was always a grin on her face.

It was the start of a new semester. She walked up to me after her last class at our appointed place, many minutes late, with a strange look on her face. Like she might sneeze at any moment.

That dreamy look in her eyes, her fatigued walk, made *me* feel tired! I couldn't understand. She had dragged herself from the class to me and now looked like she was just going to drop to the ground.

Threw her bag down, flung her hands in the air and yelled, 'I am in love!' I should've guessed. 'Let's party!'

'No,' I said. We had made up our minds, no partying until the girl says 'Yes'.

It came as a shock to me when I realized that the woman my best pal had fallen for, fallen hard for, was the new sociology professor. She was much older than Justine, but she was still unmarried. It took Justine two weeks to get her hands on this woman.

That day, Justine asked me to meet her at seven in the evening at our usual bar for a drink. I could see her come towards me, late as usual, with a huge smile on her face. The smile of a contented woman. The place was full of business executives speaking on their mobile phones. We two were in our torn jeans and 'attitude' T-shirts, our heavy boots thumping through the crowd. We had just made ourselves comfortable in a corner seat when a straight couple walked in. We identified them as a gorgeous chick in bad company.

'Kim, if there weren't so many people around and that man with her . . . If it hadn't been such a rigid place, then maybe

I would've thrust two fingers in my mouth, whistled and: "Hey, bombshell! I gotta pack you up and take you home.'"

This was my Justine, until she was shunned by her lady-love after a year for a real man.

Suddenly she became sad, full of regret, sat in corners just thinking and repeating, 'What did I do to deserve this?'

The months passed. Justine picked up a Great Dane pup to keep herself occupied and began hunting for a job. She was about to start her final year of college.

Justine never came out and expressed her pain. She preferred it as it was, inside. She didn't want anyone to know what she was going through, and no matter what, she always wore that smile on her face. To her, the problems were hers alone and she found it disgusting when anybody invaded her thoughts.

After college, we hardly met. My job took me far abroad to Silicon Valley, Cupertino.

Justine wrote to me. She was working hard, and her current girlfriend was her own boss. Justine had developed this sudden interest in reading about the occult. Why would she want to study something which was beyond the realm of human comprehension, I wondered. What had pushed this idea into her head? She asked me to parcel her some books on occult practices. I refused, and earned her wrath.

When I returned to India for a holiday, Justine was in bad shape. W—, her Great Dane, had grown as big as she was, but she was stuck in the same rut. Her career took her hopping from one lover to the other, and she watched each of them change into straight women before her eyes. I had returned after three years to find my pal in this mess.

'Troubled by Ts,' as she put it, grinning. 'Torn, Tormented and Troubled by the pleasure-giving pain called Love.'

Two weeks of my vacation went by. I got a note through

Justine's co-worker one rainy afternoon. I had met Justine the previous night. We had had a heart-to-heart conversation. She told me that she had grown close to her older brother and his wife and had told them what she was and why she was that way. They seemed to love her regardless, to her surprise. I was thinking of that as I unfolded the note.

> *Dearest of all, Kim, I am happy today. I love you for what you were to me, still are and always shall be. Trust me, I respect our friendship a lot—please keep a place for me in your heart forever. I am going away.*
> *Goodbye.*

Was she running away from home? What was she up to? I waited for her to call me, though I somehow felt that she would not. By evening I had tried my best to locate her in all the places I thought she might be, but I failed. Even the steps of the church disappointed me—it was the one spot where I would always find her when she was disturbed.

I gave up at twilight. I telephoned her house and got a horrible shock. I couldn't believe what I was told. She had boarded a sightseeing ferry, and jumped off as it passed through a narrow, rock-lined tongue of water.

'A lot of passengers observed her praying by the rail,' the boatman reported.

That night I came back from the police station with Justine's brother and sister-in-law, weary and numb with grief. It was about nine o'clock, and W— , who had been lying next to the sofa, ran to the window and started barking furiously. Then he rushed back, put his paws on my knees, and growled in the direction of the street.

All this while, Justine's sister-in-law was telling us about the announcement Justine had made as she left the house.

'I may not be back this afternoon,' she had declared, marching out. She had patted W—, who stood quietly as he watched her leave.

According to her sister-in-law, Justine had become very grim and moody, much obsessed with death. She believed passionately in reincarnation and the spirit world.

W— ran to the window, snarling and baring his teeth. The hair on his neck and back stood up as he barked and growled.

'No one's out there, boy.' Justine's brother-in-law looked out of the window, trying to calm the usually gentle dog.

'You mean, no one you can see!' exclaimed his wife nervously as W— raced into Justine's room and returned with her cap in his mouth. He placed it at my feet.

As I sat with a drink that night, I missed her. I missed 'cheering' her glass with mine. I missed her 'Hey, what's up?' I missed her hugs when I cried. I missed her.

W— sat next to her favourite chair, resting his head on its arm as if he was waiting to be stroked.

Justine, you were crazy, girl! What drove you to the point of suicide? When did *you* forget what you had told me over and over—*love yourself, only then can you be capable of loving somebody else*?

⋯⋯⊚⋯⋯

Reflections of an Indian Lesbian

Naseem

For me, lesbianism is a form of resistance to patriarchy and male oppression, and not just a sexual preference. The experience I describe comes from having been in an open and declared relationship for the past eight years, and in having tried to break the sustained isolation of living as the only 'declared' lesbian couple in the city of Bombay.

It is not difficult to be a lesbian or gay man in India. The social segregation of men and women provides enough space for friendships between people of the same sex, which may lead to sexual relationships. But such relationships do not acquire social status or legitimacy. There is constant pressure to conform and get married. Nonconformist sexual choices have to remain hidden and can never be verbalized. While it is possible for the couple to meet privately or even be seen together in public, they cannot be frank about their sexual relationship. If they are, they will encounter hostility, and the limited space available to them may be denied. Most homosexuals are terrified of being ostracized by family and friends.

How important is the issue of sexual choice when there are more serious concerns facing women? This is the first question to confront many of us. Women lack the freedom to make even the most basic choices in their lives—seeking education, acquiring economic independence, deciding whether to get married and to whom, and whether to bear children. Women are also the worst affected in terms of broader political issues such as communalism, casteism and political instability. In such a context, feminists frequently argue that the time is not ripe to place sexual preference on the 'political' agenda of the women's movement. While not denying the abovementioned socioeconomic realities, some of us who have 'come out' as lesbians feel an acute need to create a social space to validate the personal choices which profoundly affect our existence.

In our attempt to build a community of lesbians we have come across two sets of women. The experience with both has been frustrating. On the one hand are politically active women who believe in lesbianism on a theoretical level. Some of them are from leftist political groups and contracted marriages in the late seventies; others were married first and then joined the women's movement in the early eighties. While all of them admit they are unhappy in their marriages, and some of them do venture into 'experimenting' with women, marriage continues to be the source of their strength, social recognition and economic support. For this reason, they are reluctant to be seen with other lesbians or gays and are scared of being labeled. However, relationships with other women are not a threat to their marital ties since in most cases the woman lover is secondary to the husband. Sometimes the lesbian relationship even serves to strengthen the marriage by providing a vent, a buffer or outside support to absorb and stabilize the ups and downs of wedded life.

At times it seems that these very women would like to negate our existence entirely. They have gone to the extent of saying that while they believe in the politics of lesbianism, there are no lesbians in India. In fact, we have even become an embarrassment to the women's movement by declaring ourselves lesbians. Just as in the earlier days women's issues were secondary to the agenda of the class struggle, today feminists tell us that lesbian issues have to be secondary to the other concerns of the women's movement. Some of these feminists had accepted their own lesbianism but later retracted and reversed their stands. In one instance a woman who had earlier declared that she was a lesbian, told us that she was going back on her position because in the West women had moved beyond the 'personal is political' framework and involved themselves with 'broader' social issues.

On the other hand we encountered women for whom lesbianism is purely a sexual preference. For them, there is no politics involved. Many of these women belong to the sports community, within which they are open and accepted. But here too their relationships with other women pose no threat to their marriages. Lesbian relationships are more about sexual expression than support structures for these women.

At a personal level, my relationship with Amita has nurtured both of us through the struggle with the outside world. For us, this is not just a relationship but an alternative model for a family. By defining ourselves as a domestic unit of women, we have created a space for and a sense of belonging to other women as well. We had to pay a price but it was worth it. Unless some women have the courage to be pathbreakers, how can such a precious space ever be possible? But our ultimate aim is to create not just a household but a community of women who together will validate each other's existence.

(presented at the Asian Lesbian Network conference, Bangkok, 1991)

❖

Toward a Lesbian World

Seema

I was born and brought up in Bombay, and studied at a convent school for girls, in the suburb of Bandra. As I was growing up, I found that I was attracted only to girls, and by the time I had crossed puberty, I had confirmed to myself that women are in every way better than men.

When I started college, I came across a girl who was slightly manly; when I saw her it was love at first sight on my side. Somehow I got myself introduced to her—her name was Jyoti, and she was one year senior to me. Following our introduction I tried to meet her every day, with some excuse or the other. We used to sit in the common room for hours together. In the beginning I was very quiet around her. She used to talk a lot, I would only look at her. One day, I put my hand on her thigh and started moving it upwards. I was terrified, since I could not see any reaction, and I thought, well if she doesn't like this she will definitely break off our friendship. It was almost five o'clock so I had to tell her I was getting late, but that I would see her the next day.

I went home, but I was very disturbed. The whole night I thought only of her, and anxiously waited for the sun to rise. When I got up in the morning, I immediately called her to confirm that she was coming to college. She told me that she had been thinking about me all night too. I just can't express what I felt at that moment. At college, both of us bunked our lectures and went to the common room, but since it was full of girls, we went to the bandstand at Bandra and sat on the rocks. Since it was our first date, I tried to be passive. We started talking about various topics, but finally I got her onto the right track, and we started discussing women. As I was talking, I moved closer to her. It was cloudy and windy, drizzling slightly. In such romantic monsoon weather, how could I restrain myself? I just put my hands on her shoulders and pulled her towards me and kissed her. *Everything happened within the fraction of a second.* Afterwards, all she said was, 'Thank God, finally you did it.'

I still remember, it was the ninth of July, 1971.

After the first kiss, I suddenly realized that we were in a public place and I felt shy. But she didn't care, she said, 'Chhod, yaar, hamare jaisi kitni ladkiyan hain. Duniya gai bhad mein.' But still, I felt really awkward. I was also scared that someone would see us and report it to my parents, who were not at all aware of my tendencies. But Jyoti was not ready to leave me. This time she kissed me and I responded to her kiss. We didn't want to go home, but we had to. Before we got up, she said, 'I love you.' I said, 'I, too.' We started walking towards the bus stop hand-in-hand. Neither of us was bothered that there were people around.

As we were walking, I asked her why it was that I was always getting attracted to girls and not boys. She replied, 'Because you are a lesbian.' I told her that I had thought I was abnormal because I liked only females. My other college mates were always mixing with boys—they used to go for movies and picnics together—but I never felt like joining them. Jyoti told me, 'We are not abnormal, do not ever think that way. We are perfectly normal.' This gave me more confidence.

She was often alone at her house, since both her parents worked. So one day she invited me for lunch. She stayed at a very nice apartment in Juhu, and I arrived at about 10 a.m. She had asked me to wear a sari, and a particular hairstyle—she used to love my long silky hair—and I had obeyed. She opened the door and stared at me. She was in jeans—she was always in jeans, or sometimes in shorts. She said, 'You look gorgeous.' She began showing me her house, the kitchen, the terrace and so on, and finally we landed in her bedroom. It was superb, with a double bed and an attached bath.

She told me, 'This is our bedroom.' She told me, 'This common time is ours.'

She undraped my sari and kissed me hard. She got me onto the bed and then never looked back. But while we were in the middle of our act, the door bell rang. She urged me not to worry, she would see who was there. I took my sari and went into her bathroom to hide.

Jyoti called me from my hiding place. She said, 'Don't worry, come out as you are.' I came out, not knowing that there was another female in the bedroom—Jyoti had not told me that she had invited anyone else! I tried to run back into the bathroom, but Jyoti caught hold of me and said, 'Come, I will introduce you. This is Salma.' I was feeling very uncomfortable as I was wearing just a bra and a towel. But Salma, seeing me, only uttered, 'She is sexy, Jyoti, good choice.'

So all three of us continued with the act which had been interrupted in the middle. We had a good time, a good lunch, some good music, and finally we parted in the evening before Jyoti's parents could come home. Salma told Jyoti, 'We should introduce Seema to more women.' She explained that all the women met once a fortnight at someone's house. All these things were very new to me, I had never even been out of the house at night without my parents.

One Saturday morning, Salma called at my place, saying, 'Tonight we are meeting at Andheri, so please come.' I couldn't, because I had no excuse to give my parents. This happened twice or thrice, then I decided that I must join the party. One weekend, I told my parents that I was going for a movie and would be staying at a friend's place. I was immediately asked her name, and by reflex I responded, 'Jyoti'. By this time my parents knew her. But they were not aware of the nature of our relationship.

When I went into the flat where the party was, I was surprised to see so many women. Jyoti told me, 'Don't worry, they are all like us.' I was totally lost in the crowd. They were discussing lesbian rights, women's liberation, and many other things which were unfamiliar to me. Everybody was with her partner, and of course, I was with Jyoti. The party ended almost at 2 a.m. I went to Jyoti's house to sleep. The next day being Sunday, there was no hurry to get up, but since it was my maiden outing I rose early and went back home. These parties were to become a routine part of my life.

Jyoti and I had been going steady for four years when I reached the final year of B.Com. The SSC results had just been declared, so there were many tenth standard students standing in a queue to fill up forms for junior college and pay their fees. Jyoti and I were watching them, remembering the days when we had stood in line waiting, like them. A boy approached us and asked us where forms were available. His style of talking was just like a girl's. We pointed him to the office, and when he started heading towards it we observed that even his style of walking was not exactly masculine. I asked Jyoti whether he was a boy or a girl. She said, 'Let us follow him, and we will come to know.'

We waited outside the office, and when he came out I noticed one more thing that almost convinced me that this individual was not a boy, but a girl—I could see a bra under the shirt. When I told Jyoti, she said, 'Let's ask it for a name.' The person replied, 'Champa'. Both of us were startled. The tone of voice was male, the physical appearance was like a boy, but the name was a girl's. We were told by 'her' that she had just got admission. When she went away, I asked Jyoti, 'Yeh lafda kya hai? What is this, a boy or a girl?' She replied, 'Hijra.' I was shocked to see a hijra in the college, because up until now I had only seen them on the road, clapping in typical fashion and asking for money, especially targeting scared ladies. Jyoti told me, 'This hijra is not the same as the ones on the streets.'

After Champa had left the college compound, Jyoti told me, 'We should not lose this opportunity. She could be useful to us.' I asked, 'In what way?' She declared, 'These hijras are given their birth only to serve women. They are supposed to work for us, otherwise their life is useless. They cannot have sex and so are totally harmless.' She also explained to me how, long ago, hijras were kept in harems to guard women. She said, 'Just wait and see how we will make use of this chhakka.'

By the time college reopened, news about Champa had spread through our group, and everyone was curious. Of course, both Jyoti and I were waiting for our final B.Com results and should have been at home preparing for our accountancy entrance exam. But just to catch Champa, we went to college. On the third or fourth day, I don't exactly remember,

Jyoti saw her at the bus stop and called out, 'Hello Champa, how are you?' Champa looked at us but did not recognize us, as she had only seen us once, and that too for only fifteen minutes. In addition she felt awkward, since Jyoti had shouted her name loudly.

When we came up to her, Jyoti asked her which class she was in. I still recall the way Champa replied, 'Mai FYJC mein padhti hoon.' We asked her, where are your friends? She said that she didn't like to mix with boys, she didn't think it was right. We started laughing again. Then the bus came, and she went away.

The next day she met us in the college canteen, and slowly-slowly she became friendly with us. The first few days, we tried to gain her confidence. We used to talk to her as if she was a woman, and she liked that. At first, I was under the impression that Champa was a gay, but she was so shocked when I asked whether she liked boys, and whether she had ever shared her bed with any male, that I realized that she was a pure hijra.

One day Jyoti called Champa to her residence, and when she came, asked her whether she would wear a salwar kameez. Champa, without any hesitation, agreed. She changed in front of us, and when I teased her about this, she said, 'Usme to kya hai, hum sabhi ladkiyan to hain.' Then she told us that she liked women's clothes like saris, ghagra cholis etc., and wore wigs so that she could enjoy long hair. Two other women came by to visit, so we introduced Champa to them. We requested her to dance for us, and she agreed. 'Which song?' I asked her. 'Any song,' she replied. So we put on some music. Immediately she said, 'Yeh to mardon ka gana hai, ladki ka lagao.' We looked at each other. Then Jyoti played a song by a female, and Champa danced. Later, she told us that whenever she saw a woman with beautiful long hair or nice breasts, she would miss a heartbeat and feel sad that she could not be like her.

At one party, we made Champa wear a sari. We had made a plan to strip her, just to confirm her hijra features. So, while she was dancing I suddenly caught hold of her pallu and started to drag the sari off—vastraharan, as we called it. She stopped dancing but I ordered her to continue, in her blouse and petticoat. Her hands crossed automatically over her chest like a lady, though she had no breasts to hide. We all stared at her and laughed, but Champa kept dancing. After some time, Salma went up to her and unhooked her blouse. When Champa tried to hold on to it, Salma screamed, 'Hijra, drop your hands,' and she obeyed immediately. I came to see that Champa was scared of us, and that she would do whatever we told her. Until this time, I had been very gentle with her, but then I, too, decided to be harsh—*because I realized that hijras are here only to serve women, especially women like us*. I rushed and untied her petticoat and pulled it down, and as I did this, Champa crouched like a lady, hiding her penis.

Salma slapped her on her buttocks and told her to stand up and dance. Champa stood, hiding her face. We stared at her penis, waiting to see whether the shape and size would change, but there was nothing, no erection. It was like a dead piece dangling. It was very small, too, maybe an inch or so in length—just like a toy.

From that day on, Champa was totally under the control of our group of twelve women. If we needed anything, we used to call at her residence and not request, but order her, to come whenever and wherever we wanted. Many times, as punishment, we used to put a hot spoon—not too hot, but warm—on her toy.

One day we took her to Juhu to have a ghagra choli stitched for her. The tailor was also a lady, a friend of Salma's, and knew that we were bringing a hijra to her shop. When she took Champa inside the room for her measurements, Champa asked her, 'Are you not afraid of me?' I do not know what made her pass such a comment. That lady got wild, and without wasting a single moment, she shouted, 'Maï aadmi se nahin darti, phir chhakke se kya daroongi? Tere mein kya hai darne jaisa?' When they came out and the lady repeated the story of what had happened inside, Salma immediately pulled Champa's hair, pinched her toy and slapped her. Champa started crying. After going to Jyoti's place, we combed Champa's hair into a single plait, removed her clothes, tied her plait to the bolt of the door and made her stand there for the whole afternoon.

These things with Champa went on for years—dancing, punishing, stripping—but after some time reduced in frequency as both Jyoti and I were busy with our accountancy course. I became a chartered accountant in three years; Jyoti took an additional two years to finish. When my darling completed her course, we had a very big party at her place—by that time, her parents knew that she was a lesbian, but mine did not know about me.

After becoming full-fledged chartered accountants, both Jyoti and I started working, and both of us got good jobs. We decided then that we would stay together for the rest of our lives. My parents started searching for a boy for me; when I came to know, I told my mother that I was not interested. She was very disappointed and tried to convince me that marriage was necessary. But, being a staunch lesbian and a supporter of women's liberation, I had my own ideas on how to lead my life. Both Jyoti and I decided to leave Bombay and settle in Pune, and we started looking for work there. There was no problem about a place to stay, since Jyoti's father had invested in a flat there which was lying vacant. My father had also booked a flat, but it was still under construction. Jyoti told me that she would work and I would look after the kitchen, but I said that there was no point in me sitting at home, and that too when I was so qualified. My parents were not happy with this decision but my father told my mother, 'Let her go and be independent.' Poor dad, he was so innocent.

Jyoti and I shifted to Pune. Both of us found jobs and we lived very happily for almost five years. My mother was always asking me about marriage but I used to avoid her questions. One day she came to Pune without informing me, on a surprise weekend visit. But it ended up being a surprise for her rather than for me. It was a holiday and I had gone shopping, so Jyoti opened the door and took her to leave her things in our bedroom—it was a three-bedroom flat but we were using only one . . . I think there is no need to elaborate on this. When my mother opened the cupboard, she saw a vibrator inside and read what was written on the box. When I came back with the groceries, she took me aside and asked me what that thing was for. Finally I had to tell her. She started crying. I proudly told her, 'Mama, I am a lesbian.' I was very tense, but I said frankly, 'Jyoti and I love each other and want to marry.'

My mother stayed in Pune for two days, but she didn't say a single word either to me or to Jyoti. On Monday morning she went away without telling us. That evening, I called up at the Bombay residence to find out what my mother's state was. She was okay, and she had not told my father about our conversation.

But soon afterwards, Jyoti's father told us that he was selling the flat. He wanted us to vacate it within a month, and asked Jyoti to move back to Bombay. Very sadly, we hired a car for the trip and left Pune early in the morning, at around 7 a.m. About fifty kilometres from the city, our driver tried to overtake a Maruti car. But the road was narrow and he didn't notice a truck approaching from the opposite side—or maybe he misjudged its speed. He just managed to avoid a head-on collision, but our car got banged on the rear and pushed off the road. After that, I only remember coming to my senses in the hospital in Pune. My parents were there—I don't know who had informed them, or how. I immediately asked about Jyoti, but everybody was silent. They just told me to rest and not worry about anyone else. I was recovering fast, so I requested to be discharged. But I was not permitted to leave Pune, so my parents took me to our flat. I was continuously asking about Jyoti, and one day, after a month, I demanded that they reveal the truth, I would take it. I was informed that Jyoti was no more.

I felt as if I had suddenly become a widow. I lost all my energy to live and thought of committing suicide. But I could not even get up from the bed. My legs were badly injured and the doctors had no hope of me walking in the near future.

Finally, my father took me to the USA for further treatment. As he was in Air India, our passage was free. A place to stay was also not a problem, since my cousin sister lived there. After six months, my condition improved—first I could walk with the help of a walker, then with a stick, and finally I was doing it on my own.

When I came back, my mother, even though she knew me to be a lesbian, forced me into a marriage. My father still did not know about me, but he urged me to accept the idea. So, against my wishes, I was married. My mother had high hopes that I would settle down. It was impossible for me to forget my darling Jyoti, but for Mama's sake, I tried. When we were newly married, my husband often attempted to provoke me to have sex. He would try many different things so that I would become his. He would take out his penis, but I would ignore him and read novels, or turn on my side and go to sleep. When he asked me the reason why I was not allowing him to touch me, I told him clearly that I was a lesbian and that I was not interested in men. He was shocked to hear this and thought that my parents had deceived him by not disclosing the facts. I also felt bad for him, but was helpless.

Soon afterwards, my husband got a good job in the UAE. But before we could leave, another unfortunate incident occurred. While I was climbing down the stairs of my family's residence in Pune, I missed a step and rolled all the way down. I blacked out completely. When I came back to consciousness, I found myself in the hospital. My parents and my husband were there in a state of great tension, since we were to leave for Dubai within two months. I was discharged from hospital within a week, but I still could not walk, so I was taken home in an ambulance and laid flat on the bed.

One month I was totally immobile. Nobody was willing to tell me what was happening to me. After a month, I was taken for a check-up, and I grabbed that opportunity to ask the doctor what was wrong with me. First he tried to avoid the question, but I told him I wanted to know, and I would not lose my will to live even if the news was horrible. Finally, he told me that I had injured my legs on the same spot where I had been hurt in the car accident, and my vein was damaged. I would never be able to walk on my own in the future.

I hope this was a punishment for me and my parents for not having explained the truth about myself to my husband.

Three months later, my husband called me to join him. I went in a wheelchair. I was very lonely in Dubai. It is very difficult to trace women of our particular category in the UAE—it is very strict there, it is not free like India. There must be women like me in the Arab community, or among the expatriates, but since I am in a wheelchair I cannot locate them, sitting in my house.

After a long time of being alone, I have started growing close to my maid who is only nineteen years old. Since frankly I feel that all women should be like me, I decided to convert her. I brainwashed her by telling her how sex with women is healthier than sex with a man. Slowly I trained her and she started getting pleasure from me. Today I am happy. Today she is able to give me the orgasm which I need. My husband, knowing everything, tolerates me as he has no option. I want to get a divorce, but he is still under the impression, after all these years, that he will one day change me.

Now he is planning to move to the USA and I will go there with him, to work for women and contribute the maximum possible to our cause. Of course, I shall be doing all these activities from home as my handicap has rendered me completely immobile.

My manifesto: All women in this world should be lesbians. We must all try to convert more and more women to be like us, so that our population will increase. We should fight for our rights so that one day we will dominate society.

Glossary

chhakka – (derog.) hijra, eunuch

Chhod, yaar, hamare jaisi kitni ladkiyan hain. Duniya gai bhad mein – Let it be, there are so many girls like us. The world can go to hell

Main aadmi se nahin darti, phir chhakke se kya daroongi? Tere mein kya hai darne jaisa? – I'm not afraid of men, why would I be afraid of a chhakka? What do you have that I should be afraid of?

Main FYJC mein padhti hoon – I'm studying in the first year of junior college

Usme to kya hai, hum sabhi ladkiyan to hain – What's wrong with that, we're all girls

Yeh lafda kya hai? – (coll.) What's going on here?

Yeh to mardon ka gana hai, ladki ka lagao – But this is a man's song, play a song by a woman

Milli Dreams of a Women's World

Mallika

Milli had a dream. Well, to start with it was a small speck in her small grey room in Calcutta, but it floated out of her mind and got bigger. 'It is an island,' thought Milli. And that is what it was—an island that rose like a green balloon from her mind and spread out, a big-winged bird between the stars and the ground. It went rising up, up from the dirty buildings, up from the smells, up from the violence of men, and away.

It moved south and then it stopped right above the navel of Mother India. But it did not stop there, it just thought for a while and then moved lower, till the shadow of it fell on the yoni. It was over the dot on the map where the borders of Karnataka, Maharashtra and Andhra Pradesh come together. We can call it Shaktinagar since it does not have a name already.

Woosh! There was a sound like air sucked into a straw, and Milli was pulled out of her bed and found herself flying over the hills and rivers of Mother India and onto the floating island. She lay among blue and yellow flowers on waving stems. The sun was shining.

'Where am I?' she asked the beautiful woman kneeling beside her.

The woman, draped in a white garment, bent to kiss Milli with soft gentle lips, starting from the parts of her feet made rough by walking on crowded streets in plastic shoes, all the way up to her head which was so heavy with worries about money and how to go on living.

'You are in a place made by the energy of women,' said the new friend. 'All you have to do to stay with us is to share

346

your strength which will help to keep us flying.'

'I have no strength,' said Milli, who was afraid.

She looked at the woman and saw a beauty who resembled Kalidasa's Shakuntala walking out of the forest. Eyes shaped like sweet almonds, hair woven into a long plait down her back, a waist supple as linked vines. Milli could not help her gaze dropping to the breasts like golden papayas ripening on the trunk of the tree.

'You are so beautiful,' Milli cried, covering her face which she thought was ugly, but Shakuntala drew her fingers away and held them in her own hands.

'You are also beautiful,' she said sternly. 'Your body has lived so much, you have to see that beauty.' Shakuntala moved her hands up, and laid them on Milli's shoulders. 'Your body has worked hard. It has been raped and used by a man who pays you for work but takes your body free. A child grew within you. Your body fed that child.'

'How did you know?' Milli's voice cracked with fear.

'Your body told me,' Shakuntala said. 'It screams.'

Her fingers touched the scars caused by burning oil on Milli's arm, and her big eyes blazed like those of an angry goddess as Milli, in anguish, fell into her embrace. Shakuntala held her while she stared over the rim of the island to the place below where men walked like fools, not knowing that one day women's anger would rain upon them like fiery arrows from Amba's forehead.

After Milli grew calm, Shakuntala led her across the island. Women were tilling the fields and planting seeds in rows. The sun turned their naked bodies to a darker brown. Milli was at first afraid to look, but because the women themselves were not shy, she watched them and smiled back when they smiled at her.

'We do our work by turns,' said Shakuntala. 'If I till the land today, then tomorrow I cook, or net fish from the lake.'

As they talked, the sun was beginning to dip over the edge of the island, and as it became darker there, the light slowly dawned on Shaktinagar.

A bell rang out, and all the women from all over the island gathered to share food. They drank the milk of sweet-eyed cows and ate grains pounded and cooked in ghee, and the tender flesh of lake fish. There was no need for light, because the stars were so thick and bright in the island's pure air.

'At night we build fires,' said Shakuntala.

'For warmth? To keep away wild animals?' asked Milli.

'No, we do this to celebrate the strength of women. We dance because we are moved by the shakti that is in all women.'

'Where do you sleep?' asked Milli, who was looking around for huts.

'We sleep in the open,' said Shakuntala. 'We do not want shelters which try to divide us into smaller households. We are a whole. We live as a whole, brought together by our love for each other.'

'What about the storms and insects?' asked Milli, who was very practical.

'There are no insects this high in the sky!' laughed Shakuntala. 'And the storm is our friend. You will fall in love with the night wind and the rain.'

The fire was lit. Dead branches and leaves roared into fierce orange and red flames. The dancing light and the dancing women made Milli dance too, even though she felt awkward and clumsy. The dancing became slower as the fire died down, and women lay in the grass nearby. They reached for one another. Their sighs mingled with the crackle and hiss of wood.

Milli looked across the circle of women moving like healing, life-giving waves. Shakuntala had bent her head over the naked body of an older woman and she softly kissed her breasts. Their hair flowing together in the firelight sparkled black and silver. A heavy pain filled Milli's heart. But then both women turned and saw her and stretched their arms out to her. Milli ran forward to their embrace.

Fingers light as feathers soothed her back, and lips traced the stretch marks left by the birth of her dead child. Her dizzy head fell back as a hand roamed between her legs and touched the centre of her consciousness. She began to weep with joy as the hot fire swallowed her up. Surrounded by warm bodies, Milli fell into a deep sleep.

When she awoke, she gave a great sob, because the grey walls of her room in Calcutta were closing in upon her again. A man's shadow slowly filled the doorway. She bent her head and drew up her knees, waiting for the hand to hit her and the hard penis to force its way inside. But the palm that was laid on her shoulder was very gentle. Milli looked up to find Shakuntala's face looking down at her with indescribable love.

'Wake up, Milli,' she said quietly. 'It was only a nightmare. This is reality.'

A Decade of Lesbian Halla Gulla

Amita

Till the beginning of the nineteen eighties, no one had really heard about lesbians in India. There would be some stray, oblique references in conversations, writings, films—but it was all very hazy. Lesbians must have existed before that and did exist then, but even we did not know them as yet. We did not know ourselves. There was very little sexual awareness, and no scope for exposure and exploration. These factors, along with rigid heterosexual conditioning, prevented women from realizing their own desires. Secondly, tremendous social pressures coerced lesbians to conform to the patriarchal ideal of femininity. Thirdly, an almost total lack of options regarding education, jobs, accommodation, mobility and support structures in general forced many lesbians into unwanted marriages.

The initial silence regarding lesbian issues in the women's movement as well as other progressive and democratic movements did not help matters. We knew that the law of the land prohibited same-sex relationships under Section 377 of the Indian Penal Code, though the phallocentric and penetration-oriented definitions of sex paradoxically protected lesbians from being sentenced to ten years of rigorous imprisonment.

Nevertheless, there was segregation of the sexes, there was the tolerance (if not approval) of intimate same-sex friendships, including cohabitation. These factors allowed women who loved women to deal with otherwise hostile and oppressive environments, and lead fulfilling private lives as lesbians.

But for many, it was a short-lived dream. There was a steady stream of news items about lesbian suicide pacts, about eloping female couples tracked down, forcibly separated and restored to their families to be married off or killed. There were reports of women undergoing sex-change operations so that they could live with their partners as 'normal' couples. During this period we were also to meet women who had immigrated in order to express their sexuality, to follow lovers or to find love.

There were also the brave ones who stayed on and looked for ways to survive as lesbians in India. A couple from Gujarat took advantage of maitri karar—a quasi-legal solution legitimizing a non-marital bond, which had originally been devised as a way for wealthy married men to have relationships with women who wouldn't 'do it' without a veneer of security and legality. There were Leela and Urmila, policewomen from Madhya Pradesh who tied the knot when they found a priest who believed that marriage is a union of two souls and has nothing to do with the gender of the betrothed.

The eighties witnessed the formation of women's organizations in all major cities. These were not mahila mandals or the women's wings of political parties, but independent, autonomous groups with a feminist ideology. This development perplexed, hurt and angered former political comrade brothers and husbands, who considered it a betrayal of the earlier agendas. But the women knew they were mapping their own route to the same destination. These groups networked nationally and also with international women's groups. The exchange of books and ideas brought them exposure to lesbian communities abroad, their lives and their struggles. An occasional NRI lesbian visitor, amid predominantly white ones, made some restless local hearts flutter. Who am I? What are my desires? What are my feelings towards the woman I consider my best friend, even though I seriously differ with her on the issues of reservations for scheduled castes, and postmodernism?

Our 'normality' was further certified by the American Psychiatric Association. And the hard-core leftists among us breathed easier when the status of homosexuals was legitimized in the Soviet Union.

It was not all sweetness and light, but not all gloom and doom either. The mother organizations tacitly agreed to tacitly extend tacit support as long as lesbians did not brandish their visibility, appear in meetings with 'Dykes to Watch Out For' buttons or indulge in aggressive dykespeak. There was tacit opposition to 'blatant' declaration of relationships and tender expressions of love. Women's organizations made consistent efforts over a longish period of time to get over this 'taciturn' phase.

By this time, it was already 1990. One lone ranger in Delhi—Giti Thadani—was networking and trying to trace the existence of lesbians in our own country, attempting to prove through researching ancient scripture and architecture, that lesbianism in India is not a decadent Western import. Three lesbians in Bombay braved women's meetings and gay male parties with equal equanimity. And, of course, countless unnamed (except for Leela and Urmila) women brazened it out without any support, enduring all kinds and degrees of homophobic brutality.

The first issue of *Bombay Dost* was launched with a lot of sympathetic media coverage that eventful year. The first conference of the Asian Lesbian Network was organized in Bangkok, and was attended by seven Indian women. At the fag end of 1990 the Fourth National Conference of Women's Movements was held in Calicut, during which a special session titled 'Single Women' was organized. It was a very meaningful event for those who attended it, but it holds special significance for lesbians. It marked the end of the 'tacit' era—it was the last time lesbians took public refuge under the umbrella of 'single women'.

Bombay Dost provided a forum for expression, and its male readers obliged us by introducing their lesbian friends and sisters to us through the magazine. There was a flood of letters—friendly, desperate, romantic, lustful. Letters from teenagers, middle-aged married women, women in love, lonely women; letters coming from Ludhiana, Meerut, Gauhati, and predominantly from Hyderabad (the reason for this has not been discovered as yet). They were all isolated in their own spaces, and were reaching out for support. The flood of letters continues, and now there is a better infrastructure to respond to it.

The Asian Lesbian Network conference at Bangkok brought the Indian delegates face to face with their other Asian counterparts. It was like looking into a mirror. With a few regional and culture-specific variations, our situations were fundamentally the same. The experience of partying with two hundred other lesbians the first evening and sharing our lives with the fifty delegates over the next three days helped us feel nurtured and more connected. It resulted in more focused activities back home: some participation in *Bombay Dost*, and continued interaction with our Delhi sisters (whom we had met for the first time in Bangkok).

After the Calicut conference, preparations commenced for the Fifth Conference of Women's Movements, at Tirupati. By now there were younger, braver, articulate members in the lesbian community, and the consistent efforts at visibility by the old guard were paying dividends. The issue of sexuality and lesbianism was placed firmly on the agenda of the women's movement in India at that conference. About one hundred and fifty women attended the four sessions of the two-day Sexuality workshop. There was open discussion about body image, sexual fantasies, masturbation, incest and abuse (these were touched on briefly because there was a rare experience shared of voluntary and delightful incest).

When the discussion of lesbian relationships began, there was awe, disbelief, disgust, open hostility. Lesbians were badgered with queries and allegations. The interrogators turned sympathetic by the end, while some accusers remained confused and unconvinced till local facilitators forced them to apologize to us. Their thought process was sacrificed at the altar of their leaders' overt political correctness. Despite the pigheaded hostility of hard-core leftists, the issue was launched, the silence broken, the bug of sexual diversity was planted firmly in the brains that believed sex could only consist of missionary coupling between a man and a woman.

The situation changed rapidly in the nineties. More and more women came into the group. Soon a clique of three lesbians became a crowd of thirty. Earlier we would hope to meet a new woman only through the feminist group. *This* was a new crowd belonging to different, non-conventional, professions—social worker, fashion photographer, journalist, scuba diver, professor, air hostess—you name it and they are among us. Women going to pubs and discos, college socials and sports meets, conferences and seminars.

The group has called itself Stree Sangam and has begun to shape its own identity. Not everybody likes the name, but they tolerate it since they like the group. We face the problems which dog all organizations—hierarchy, discipline, accountability. In addition there are the problems peculiar to broad-based groups diverse in class, caste, education and age. Despite all this, Stree Sangam women made an meaningful effort to come together for a three-day retreat in 1996. There was the mandatory (and, as always, the most successful) session on sharing personal experiences, the session on sex (hard core), organizational perspectives and strategies, poetry reading and writing sessions, and halla gulla pure and simple on the beach.

I suppose this is not a scholastic paper worthy of being presented at such a distinguished gathering of activists, social workers and professionals. But this is the spontaneous and heartfelt outpouring of a person who has been around from the beginning of this jhamela here in India. So that is that!

(*presented at the conference on Strategies for Furthering Lesbian, Gay and Bisexual Rights, Mumbai, November 7-9, 1997*)

Glossary

halla gulla – mayhem
jhamela – complication

⊷≡◉≡⊷

Words from the Silence

Puja

I am a lesbian like you.

But I do not enjoy the company of other lesbians because we speak in different languages, you and I.

I am profoundly deaf, as is my lover who has been with me for six years. Ours is a quiet love.

We met through our involvement in the women's movement in a neighbouring country and she came here to live with me, leaving behind all friends and family.

We both prefer the society of women who might be married, some of them with children, but who are deaf like we are.

We have thrown in our lot with them because we have more in common with them than with you, even if they do not share our sexual love for women.

We share in silence, we speak in silence with the force of our gestures. We live in a silent world that makes you shudder.

Other lesbians speak and make love with their tongues.

My lover and I speak and make love with our hands.

Learn our language, if you want to be one with us.

Love

All Cherished Loneliness Is You

Sandhya

Fifteen years ago my lover died, she was very young, and so was I. At that time I did not know another breathing lesbian in this country. I could not tell my parents, my family or my straight friends about my grief. Silence was the only possible refuge. I betrayed our time together in many ways by not talking about us, and our love. Fifteen years later, I look at these poems written in a secret diary—the only safe space for that pain. I feel rage that I let the world shut me up. And that I continue to let it shut me up . . .

Deathwish

If the wind were
one with my mind
and there never was a
moon and all the birds in the trees
fled with all the flowers
and puddles lived with no water
and spiders hung from my ears
and words written
would drift with ease
there would still be mould
in my heart and sorrow would gnaw
through friends' days and no one
would know, not you, not anyone,
any story
or the difference it made

Facing the Mirror

Leaving

I pass a gate where
a woman at 7pm leans and waits
for one who never seems
to be there and whom I'll never see
and what if I should would that
help my tears, push my feet? Explain
my next turning under
which yellow moon night, how long
this yearning, this tossing and turning
and if it should pass and leave no
sign of returning then why not
some joy

Mornings

Why then did you leave
now that three enchanted souls
dry eyed and soft love you
and your mother, ready to paint lived
quite near the sea where frilled waves
murmur no songs of brevity
and distant friends in winter nights
and long walks with hands in pockets
had no thought of no more you—
So then suddenly there is anguish and anger
and no reprieve and what one knows and pickles
in memory, waits,
to be woken up.
With flowers,
from
you

Still

Melancholia at dusk, overhead clouds
no friend or lover I dare arouse
to watch with me.
The flight of a thousand wings
This is my land, in my tongue I may speak
But I must resist
the gnawing of time
under sounds of birds heading home.

A Hot Movie and More

Sangeeta

I am a young married woman in Haryana. My husband is absolutely perfect in sexual activities, but I enjoy much more the act of making love with other ladies or girls.

Once I even taught my friend Poonam how satisfying lesbian lovemaking can be. She was alone at home without her husband and I went to her place for a night stay. She was wearing a sheer negligee, and the room light behind her illuminated her body so that I could see right through her clothes. Her little breasts were capped by impressive nipples just waiting from some attention from me, and her parted legs completely exposed what was between.

We were watching a hot movie on video when she told me that she had never enjoyed sex with men. She looked at me and asked, 'What about you?' I told her that I love to make love to women. Wide-eyed she asked, in obvious embarrassment, 'You are a lesbian?' I nodded, still smiling sweetly at her. 'Yes I am, and I am quite happy and far more satisfied,' I said.

Without saying another word, she put a hand between my thighs and gently rubbed my cunt. Her other hand pulled her negligee off her body. I also stripped off my clothes. Poonam's breasts were like two balloons, sticking proudly straight out from her body. They looked firm and full, rounded and soft. I unhooked my bra and dragged down my panties. I leaned forward, pressing my lips to hers. Our tongues made love while our hands tenderly but deeply massaged each other's breasts. She held her breasts to mine, and rubbed them together. My stiff nipples felt delightful against hers.

Our arousal was building. We were both moaning quietly. I broke off the kiss and licked my way down to her pert little tits. I took one in my mouth while I fondled the other. I kissed my way down her soft tummy. My fingers brushed against her pussy. Sparks flew up my arms and exploded in my gut.

Really, I was feeling much more hot and excited with her than I had ever felt with my husband.

We were both gasping, occasionally squealing.

Our fingers made slurping noises as they slithered in and out of each other's hungry cunts.

We continued without a break, fingering and licking each other rapidly towards another and yet another body-shaking orgasm.

We finally fell asleep in each other's arms. The next morning Poonam nibbled on my ear and softly said, 'You are right. It's so much better than any man could ever do.'

We both laughed and hugged each other tightly.

❧

etching

Shalini

memories

lie in skin
inside my eyes
etched in the threads on my palm

to close my hand is to hold her

like those first times when i touched her
and touching her was touching myself when
i did not know if she came or i did and we
come and come

and touching me is touching her
and knowing me is knowing her

moving
breathing

in silent waters

like living in moonlight
feeling silver on hair
on back on face
touching the beams
just before they sprinkle
into waves
catching rays and pulling them deep

in
deep in   deep inside the water
like breath.

≈

snippets

Shalini

I

No easy love
stretches my hand
to the soft hair behind your ear.
No fevered words strain my lips.
Leisurely, and carelessly,
my hands rest their while
on your shifting body.

You turn your back to me
in your sleep.
I spoon around you
and dream.

II

the cat crawled to the ledge
screamed her fear

now nestles her fulfilment
in my shirt

we sleep the sleep of trekkers
who have crossed the chasm.

III

I dreamt.

I dreamt that
you were a poem
you were a flower
you were a house
you were a dream
you were a book

I dreamt that you were the woman you were
before you loved me
before you accepted
your love for me.

IV

'Junk food,'
I interject between the conference sessions
and our wavering energies,
'is what you are to me.'

'I am your junky,' predictably you reply.

V

the world
returning from work
sleeps on its feet
in the squeeze-blocked local

you wedge against me and ten other women
uncomfortably we sweat.

You surprise me
in a half-empty local
by holding me so

and then letting me fall gravityless
as I absorb your moment of daring

We live on a drunken edge for days.

VI

It takes me too long to learn your love.
A lifetime to read.
A moment to know.

You Call Me Unique . . . ?

Nora

I have felt the solitude bound to my heart and I know this can never change. Loneliness is such a part of me it might well be my name. Perhaps it is. In the same way my little daughter says 'I am Nina', I say 'I am alone'. But loneliness has become almost a comfort to me. An identity which helped me to stay alive when I first realized the fact of my difference.

Men and women surround me and their similarities to each other clog the back of my throat; I am so much the odd one out. Every second my heart panics—now these people will notice how different I am, they will confront me. How can they help but notice? My daughter is not camouflage enough. I sometimes think they are too polite to mention it.

I know there are others who are different (as I am) but this fact gives no relief; they are not like me. Once I gave my hungering body and fevered mind to a woman who seemed of my blood. Tired of my raw need, I opened my arms to her. In the darkness as she slept my heart howled disillusioned betrayal.

In the refuge of her arms I had thought to find myself. But it was a stranger who had shared my hurrying heartbeat.

To what far-flung land could I carry my quest for the mirror-image of my difference? In dream-like moments I could hope for a mind pacing beside mine and in step with my thoughts. A body whose contours I knew as I know mine. I never once doubted she was real. I never once doubted I would never find her.

On tormented nights I would write her letters. My impossible love. Pouring forth all of myself. I knew there could be no one else. I wrote slow sensuous kisses, the kind to make hours fly. Lovers' quarrels resolved themselves between the lines. When I put pen to paper, images of her body clinging to mine flowed like brilliant watercolours over the page.

In a quiet stack I preserved all of my love-letters. Until the night before my wedding day when I took them all in my arms. I walked to the sea and the shreds of them I freed on the waves and wind.

One word-particle must find its way one day to the one for whom I had written it. One word will be enough for her to know. Then to her soul mine will stretch its cold hands and flee to join her. While my body continues to walk like the living dead through the light of common day.

Shairi for Hina

Harshu

I had thought to find a little shelter
Within the drape of your sari.
But the will of God is such
That I must suffer the burning sun.

Whenever I yearned for flowers,
I found only thorns.
Wherever I sought love
I met only with slaps.

I have heard that one who loves, will surrender her life,
    That after death, one will live again.
I have seen that one shackled by drink can still dance and sing,
    That wounded to the heart, one can smile.

Love does not let me die,
Pain does not let me live.
Find me someone to love
That I may give up my heart.

Though I aspire for death,
Who can say why, I live on.
My destiny lies in one direction,
I am traveling another road.

If I am alone, why should I grieve?
If friends are gone, why should I grieve?
The world is, after all, not mine.
When my own leave me, then shall I grieve.

I love her:
This, she does not know.
I live only in her gaze:
This, she does not know.

What can I tell you
Of my heart's longing?
I have only to speak of it,
And calamity will strike.

We live in the hope
That good fortune awaits.
The world does not permit
That we should survive.

(translated from Hindi by U.S.G.)

Devour

A.G.

I have turned into
an emotional vampire
by licking
other women's wounds.

My Love, My Life

Sasha

My real name is _____, and I like to think of it as meaning
. . . queen of the skies! The goddess of rain, storm and thunder.

My name fascinates me. It is my identity, and I often think of myself as 'the invincible one'. And as you can see, I like to talk—or in this case, write—about myself . . .

I remember stories from my childhood; they usually began with 'Once upon a time . . . ' They were mostly about beautiful girls, princesses, queens. I found these women intriguing, they had so much to offer. The entire plot revolved around them. I was proud to be a girl myself, for it seemed to me that in life, as in the stories I read, women commanded so much power! The men in these tales had to fight many wars, devils and beasts before they could claim the women as their own. And then, of course, 'they lived happily ever after'.

Even as a child, the bodies of women attracted me. I used to fantasize about breasts and what it would be like to touch them. I never got round to doing that, as a kid anyway! There were always these boys around me instead, whom I hardly ever noticed.

But when everyone else started falling in love I guess I too decided to get myself a boyfriend. I went about it in a very cool and calculating manner. I chose a boy who was among the most 'sought after', went to him and announced in a confident voice, 'I want to "go around with you" and do the things that other girls do—that is, if I really want to.' Obviously he had no problem with this plan, and we would often sit under the old banyan tree and talk. I was keen to know what it was exactly that boys and girls did together, and he would tell me. I guess my eagerness to be accepted as a normal adolescent and the naïveté of my queries made him feel more like my elder brother than my boyfriend! Nevertheless, I was relentless in my pursuit. One fine day I declared that I would soon be turning sixteen and wanted to be kissed before then. Surprisingly, he did not immediately oblige. I persevered and, I think in complete exasperation (and to get rid of me), he proceeded to kiss me, after telling me very seriously that I would hate it.

Which of course I did.

After that, I was sure the girls who described a kiss as an earth-shattering experience were all lying. But I never admitted the truth of my feelings to them. I was at that time staying in a hostel and wrote to my father (of all people) that I 'had a boyfriend'. Back came a long letter from my mother warning me about men, saying that they were all scumbags. According to her all they ever wanted was sex, but I should not give in to them. This letter never quite put me off men, but the words stuck in my mind.

After that it was quite a while before I got involved in a relationship. My world turned around . . .

. . . and I fell in love.

That really was like an earthquake. And I still feel like the survivor of one. Never forgot it, cannot ignore it, but have learned to live without—her. Reminds me of that song *With Or Without You* by U2. She represents life to me. She was the first 'person' I could relate to, who cared about who I was, as I was. Unconditional acceptance from her made me lose my inhibitions (though I do not really think I had many to begin with).

She was eager to be with me, every spare moment that I could spend with her. And I went the usual route of 'I cannot live without her', all my thoughts occupied with when I could be next to her again.

She was a bold one, she took the first step in us getting close . . . physically close. We kissed. We touched, and it opened up in me a volcanic response. At night I would sneak out of my home and run down to her room. She lived in the ground floor flat opposite my place. I would gently knock on her window and she would open up her heart for me . . .

Love, pure and complete, had happened to me. I forgot the world outside, but she did not. That was what I admired about her—the ability to align herself with the world, as a confident go-getter. Well, she got me. But then the 'outside' started intruding. For her, what we shared was not love, just an emotional intimacy; she refused to accept or continue what I thought was a relationship.

One fine day . . . she got married. We still met, and once we also made love.

That was a long time ago. She is happy, she has learned to love the man she married. The man who so desperately loves her . . .

I met a man who desperately loves me. It feels good.

Or does it?

What if . . . the question persists. There are no answers. Wishes do not come true in real life.

It is over.

Even as I write it, I cannot accept it. Perhaps some day, somewhere, in the next life . . . We shall meet again. Love lasts forever, it will not be denied.

She lives on in my heart, my body. I feel sad sometimes, really hurt and rejected. I cannot understand the compulsions of the world. But I do continue to live.

I am full of life and vibrant.

On some rainy days, when the storm clouds gather and the skies pour down my tears, I feel her move within me, searching for the rhythm to which we danced.

What more can I write, do I have anything to say?

Reader, I have but one request: do not judge or analyze, just flow with the life inside your heart. Feel with me, and leave the rest to fate.

Songs

Shanti

I

Hiccups torment me
from morning to night—
She is thinking of me, I know.
O, who will carry my letter?
She is in a land so far away.

O, look at the mirror
in the dark of night.
My love is not here with me.
But see, her face beckons me, beckons me
To be, O to be with her.

It pours and thunders into the night.
My love is not here with me.
I am in the arms of a raging storm . . .
O, how do I cross the river,
The clouds in turmoil through the skies?

The evening lies wasted, I wait
for my love who does not come.
She comes, O she comes
in the quiet of the night.
And I offer flowers to the sweetness of
                                          our bed.

(*translated from Hindi by U.S.G.*)

II

Friend, your touch—
A cool dewdrop.
Friend, approach me
slowly, enter my gaze.
Friend, take shelter
in the shade of my love.

Yearning, I watch
the path you will take.
The street is abandoned,
the night is so dark.
Still, we have a tryst,
we have a secret.
Exhausted,
heavy-hearted,
I lean on you.
When you despair
I block your fall.

Two selves united
in sympathy—
this is also
a meeting place.

My mind is ablaze,
yet darkness shrouds my life.
Why is it that my house
and the whole world
seem so desolate?

Let's untangle a new radiance
from these dense, tortured nights.

Friend, your touch—
A cool dewdrop.
Friend, approach me
slowly, enter my gaze.
Friend, take shelter
in the shade of my love.

(*translated from Hindi by V.S.*)

Song for the Angel of Sin

Myque

As you tell your tales of love and magic,
I listen with eyes as wide as pools.
My brain ain't listening, it's lusting for you,
Hop aboard baby, join the troupe of fools.
Your lips are moving, spitting impressive words,
You're looking at me, but your eyes, they can't see
What I'm looking at, what I'm looking for,
I wish you knew I was looking for me.
Where have I gone? Where have I wandered?
I've disappeared somewhere, somehow,
I've crossed the border, jumped the wall.
And it's too late now.
Your hands are spread out like an infallible God,
I'm motionless, angry, lungs drawing smoke.
Your body sways, and I control mine,

This want is no more a joke.
Every night I close my eyes and imagine
The feel of your mouth on my own,
I feel so hot, so hot, that I shiver,
I want to scream but I can only moan.
I dream of a million fires burning,
You're standing in the midst of it all, you're smiling,
Sweet Angel of Sin, I hear you calling,
I'm coming although I know I'm falling!
I feel you, I hold you, I ravish you,
I surrender, I can't fight anymore,
The fires are burning and all I can think of
Is that I want you more than ever before.
Slowly we slide through the minutes, the hours,
So much closer to the sin sublime,
We're almost there, we will be tonight
Again, Angel—same place, same time,
One more time.

Thy Neighbour's Wife

Sheena

My relationship with a much-married woman began in a very innocent manner. I was getting over a broken affair with the first girlfriend of my teens and chose Meera to unburden all my misery and pain to, although she was almost ten years older.

Meera came to our neighbourhood in Calcutta as a newlywed in the family of our neighbour Mr Sharma. She was married to his son Ravi, who has known me ever since I was a toddler. Throughout my teens, I instinctively knew that Meera had undeniably lesbian traits. However I never gave it much thought, although on several occasions my then-lover and I had visited her for tea and casual chat. She might have guessed I was gay but she never said anything.

Over time, Meera and I got physically involved. We would meet at her house in the afternoons—a safe time and place since the servants would be taking a siesta. During the early days, I never took into consideration the fact that she was married, and nor did she feel the need to emphasize the futility of investing in a long-term relationship. The sex kept us going for a long time, but gradually unavoidable problems started cropping up.

I used to go to clubs and discotheques with straight boys and girls; I tried coaxing Meera and Ravi to join us, but it never worked. Ravi is an introvert and his traditional Indian values make him feel awkward at clubs and parties. Gradually, I realized how incomplete I felt being with my straight friends and carrying on the game of pretence, dancing with the boys in our mixed group.

A part of me had stayed behind, and I constantly craved Meera's company. During our five-year relationship we did manage to go away for holidays—with female members of her family and other common friends—where we could spend long hours together without time limitations and social pressure.

After a couple of years I was no longer able to cope with the idea of her going to bed with her husband—the very thought of their being sexual would make my blood boil and my frustrations mount.

I could not accept her heterosexual lifestyle, but at the

same time, paradoxically, I could not blame her, as she was already married when I met her, and I had always been aware of this uncompromising fact.

I could not control my emotions, no matter how much I tried to reason with myself. I fantasized about getting Ravi beaten up by paid hoodlums, or doing the job of punching his face in myself. My obsession with hurting this man became consuming and self-destructive. We competed with each other and there were times when the two of us raced our cars while driving—both gripped by the underlying, unspoken tension revolving around our claims on Meera.

She tried her best to sympathize with me—she would proclaim her 'love' for me but it always came down to her 'duty' to her husband.

Five years went by in this way. I found myself spiraling into profound depression. Meera knew that I felt cheated of my years. I was ready for a lifelong involvement and since she could not promise that, never had and never would, she knew she ultimately had to let me go.

I am at present living with my partner of the last five years. We meet Meera sometimes—I know she is still a well-wisher of mine and she is happy that I have found someone with whom I can spend my life.

When I compare the two relationships, I have just one thing to say.

Commitment can only work between two like-minded single people, otherwise the emotional pain is so immense that no amount of sexual gratification is worth it.

Stealing the Stolen
(extracts from a correspondence)

Samira and Jay

June 18

Dear Samira,

I'm sitting in my car watching the cloud into which your plane disappeared. Now that you're gone, I feel almost foolish. Have I given far too much weight to our pilfered evening together? Will you read this letter and smile with pity?

I try to fortify myself, remembering the first time we met. Oh god, only three days ago, wasn't it? It was my birthday, did you know? Of course you didn't—but you were my unwitting birthday present. Ugh, what a silly thought. But that was one reason why I was feeling self-pitying and misunderstood that night. It was simply that I had wanted to spend my birthday alone with Nandini. But since you got in touch with her through the fabled lesbian network, and you were in Bombay for such a short time, Ms Dyke Responsibility of course felt obliged to spend the evening with you instead. And generously invited me along. But that's not to make you feel bad. If it hadn't been for that, I would not have met you.

Anyway, that's why I was so depressed. Though I'm getting more and more that way in my relationship with Nandini. Her personality is so intense that I fade into the background every time we are together in public. But that's no excuse, is it, for getting tipsy at dinner and quoting Keats! I can't remember exactly what I said—something about the wakeful anguish of the soul? Oh god. But I remember that you looked up from your plate and your eyes met mine and stayed there. And the pointed superior silence of my lover didn't hurt as it usually does.

I am so confused by my feelings for you. I want so much, so much, but how dare I want anything at all, when you belong to Tamara and I have Nandini?

Jay

June 18
Dearest Jay,

I never got a chance to tell you how the fragrance of lilies lingers on long after you're gone and fills me with the most inexplicable longings. I've sat in this plane barely ten minutes and here I am pouring myself out to you, over you, all over again.

It's a prospect almost frightening that this journey is one that will return me to my rightful owner, supposedly. Like a stray cat. I dread meeting Tamara. I know she will be there at the airport, brilliant smile pasted across her mouth, waiting. Waiting for me to come to her. To our home. Although I suppose I should be wracked with guilt, surprisingly I'm not. That, I'm sure, has a lot to do with how you make me feel. Jay, it's been so long since someone wanted me this way. I feel eternity could have come and gone and I'd never have noticed . . . until I met you.

You know I have so little to give to you. Maybe you are content with the pittance and will continue to give as much of yourself as you have. It's what I loved about you.

Samira

June 20
Jay,

I haven't bothered to wait for your reply; the need to communicate was too overbearing. Things are very cosy at the moment. Tammy is busy with her work, and whatever time she gets off in the evenings she spends with that idiotic mare she's bought herself. Needless to say, we've slipped back into out mundane routine. Why, was I expecting something else? I suppose in a way I was, hoping that when I walked out and came to Bombay to get away from my own solitude, it would at least ruffle her feathers. Can you believe, she's never even mentioned it once? She's been unbelievably good to me of late, that's true, but it's all so light and affectionate. She treats me like I'm her niece or something—hardly a lover. She hasn't touched me in nearly a month! Are you amazed? Don't be, it's hardly the exception.

Should I be grateful for this easy, taken-for-granted life I have with her? I should, I guess. We have a lovely home, a kitten we both adore, and work to keep us busy. It sounds like a fairy tale. Still, I'm complaining.

I refuse to admit to infidelity, for neither you nor I are in a position to place a label on what we share. But I know I can't lie to myself. I think of you incessantly and crave the warmth of your body, the touch of your skin, the passion of your lovemaking. When do I see you again?

Tammy's just come in.

Samira

June 25
Dearest Samira,

The postman brought me two letters from you in a single afternoon. I am so pleased I can't stop smiling. I've never seen your handwriting before, but it seems like an old and well-loved friend.

Your life with Tamara makes me almost envious. Not just envious of her for having you, but of you for having *peace*. I do love Nandini, as I have told you. My life before her was a mist. I drank too much, had sex with women who cared nothing for me, lived in my parents' house listening to their continuous urging to get married. I was saved from that life by 'the love of a good woman'. I just wish the good woman wouldn't keep reminding me of how much I owe her. Half of our arguments begin with her saying 'When I remember what you were when I met you . . . ' I miss the sound of your voice. I hear you speaking in the background when Nandini is talking.

It's drizzling in Bombay, and the cool grey beauty of the skies is so calming. When I look up and see those small wet clouds above me, I think of Kalidasa's *Meghaduta*: perhaps I could slip my desire for you into one little cloud and send it south to Bangalore, to drench you with all that I feel. Why does the monsoon bring out such passion in us women? Perhaps because we are so close to the water in our tears, our soft moist kisses and the liquid that is our essence. When we made love, our bodies flowed together like the rain over these city streets . . .

Jay

July 8
Dearest Jay,

I must admit that it has become easier being away from you. I still long for the intimacy which is so absent in my life; Tamara, I have come to accept, is inching her way towards a platonic relationship with me. She thinks that she's doing a wonderful job of concealing her plans. If she is involved with someone else, I am to blame, I suppose. It was understood that she was to have the liberty of 'extramarital' affairs should she desire it. Up until now, I have never suspected it. That might account for her absentmindedness, her decreasing attentiveness, the time spent away from home. But my own attitude worries me. I really couldn't give a shit if she was screwing someone else. I've begun the life of a single woman, and although I don't particularly enjoy it, I see that I have little choice, so why crib? is my policy.

Sometimes I wonder if this is the cross I have to bear as a result of my 'illustrious' past. Innumerable lovers, both men and women. I have had my share of intrigue and lust, of passion and emotion, of escapade and sensation. Then I met Tammy. Beautiful, charming, irresistible and 120% heterosexual. Who would have thought that I, the original wild-child of the '90s, would ever settle into stable marital bliss? Who would have thought it of Tammy? She had one leg in her wedding gown when we met and I swept her off her feet into a whirlwind of sodomy. That's all in the past now. Sometimes I feel guilty for tying her down to me before she could enjoy her freshly-discovered sexuality.

I know Tammy and I could never leave each other but I also see how it's all getting stale around the edges. It leaves me confused and hurt, even more so because I can't admit to her what I feel for you. I miss your very being. I love her, but I stopped feeling in love with her a long time ago.

Jay, you are so difficult to ignore. You've become more and more important to me; although I've learnt to stay away from you I feel you all around me. I wish I could share all my sadness, all my madness and make you realize you're the best thing that's happened to me since the padded bra.

Samira

July 15

Dear Samira,

Your letter reminded that I know so very little about the facts of your life. But that seems not to matter to me. Perhaps the ways I know you are not about facts. Our empathy with each other leaves me wonderstruck every time I think about it: that moment when you looked into my eyes over Chinese food on the night we met and I felt you there with me, living in my skin.

I am listening to *La Traviata*—the drinking song. I should be working on my accounts instead. This moment of listening seems to sum up the waltz of should and shouldn't in my life. The irresistible pull of the booze bottle and the utterly basic need to stay sober. The delight of you and all the love, obligation and desperation that's keeping me tied me to Nandini. Or, under my lover's very nose, reading your letter, tucked inside a dull grey copy of the Romantic poets. My mind

384

reveling in the music of Verdi while my body revels in imagining your touch.

How can I forget that I was never in love once before I met Nandini, not knowing how? Her belief in my ability to love like a human being was my salvation. She patiently put together my shattered self. Isn't it ironic that you should have fallen in love with me, and not Nandini, when all that's best of me is her? Because it's true. She is the yards of bandage keeping me whole. If I escape from her and run to you, I'll crumble at your feet and in your hands.

Will I ever know why she wanted me? And yet she loved me at first sight as you say you did too. She saw me drunken and sick, bent over a rubbish heap vomiting, past midnight, outside a bar. I kept saying I didn't know. Where my friends were. Where I lived. Whether I needed a doctor.

Pardon me for my guilt, my love, but I can't help it.

Jay

July 20

My dearest Jay,

Your last letter to me was thought-provoking. I suppose it's easy to take so much for granted. You and Nandini . . . it's so stark and naked when you write it. Perhaps I spoke in complete ignorance of your relationship. I couldn't bring myself to comprehend the logic of your whatever-you-want-to-call-it. You are indebted, obligated, devoted, committed and feel responsible towards Nandini. Etc. Mine is not a dependency so great. I don't need Tamara to live as much as I need to live for Tamara. Do you understand me, Jay? I hadn't realized the breadth and width of your relationship and now I think I do. I feel confused more than ever now, because for me you were not so much the temporary holiday that I seem to be for you. I don't know if I can give you any of the things you say Nandini does. So why me? And what is it exactly you want from me?

I have someone in my life too. Someone to whom I've been able to confess 'I love you'. I guess it means nothing to some but it meant

Forever to me. Do you think I enjoy deceit and deception? I despise it, Jay. I abhor the lying, the hiding from Tamara. I do it because most of the time I know that what we have is worth it, dammit. But some other times I feel 'Why am I doing this?' I have no right to be messing around with the lives of three other people. I should leave all of this insanity behind me and trudge down the endless road of monogamy. I had such belief in you. But obviously I did not look close enough to see all the baggage you lug around.

I miss you and find it hard to pass an hour without thinking of you. I guess people will always keep coming and going over our lives, passing through like cars on a highway. When you crossed my path, I thought the world had caught fire. When we run parallel to each other, the ashes still smoulder. Your life, my life. These few letters, the sound of your voice, seem to be all I have of you. That scent of yours which is like bittersweet pine and almond milk. You haunt my every waking thought, dream and nightmare.

Now what?

Samira

July 28

Dear Samira,

The half-buried anger and irritation in your letter overwhelmed me. More than I can even begin to tell you.

The image of you follows my consciousness like my own shadow follows my body, beside me, glued to me every single moment. In the neon presence of Nandini, the thought of you—dark, cool, serene—makes her seem garish. My work is falling apart all around me. I look helplessly at stacked papers and neglected deadlines.

What do I want from you, you ask? Well, the answer is . . . nothing. I think that is why I look to you. Our love is free of demands and debts. I write to you, or talk to you in our too-infrequent phone calls in the sweet certainty that there will be no bill presented at the end. No payment demanded—in tears and emotional slavery and wrenching pain—for services rendered. So how can I think of you as a temporary holiday? You're the promise that life for women like us need not be a lonely trap . . . all the women who are with each other because they think they might never find someone else. There's a world beyond twosomes. But where's the realness in all this?

You can't understand my relationship with Nandini? I don't understand it either. Nandini finds me very flippant at times. I can't help it, irony is my only escape from her hammer blows. 'We need to talk,' she said to me a few days ago, in the older-sister tone she uses at times like this. 'The time has come.' '"The time has come, the Walrus said, to talk of many things,"' I quoted, laughing and slightly hysterical. She'd made her attack in front of Mala, her dreadful friend that she always drags into our arguments. Then they both looked at me in frozen silence and shook their heads like Siamese twins joined at the hip.

And this morning after breakfast when we were washing the cups together, she must have known I was thinking about something else, because she put down the sponge and her hands formed fists. She has never hurt me. I always tell myself she never would—never could. But I raised my arms to protect myself anyway, and Nandini took one unbelieving look at me and fled from my fear of her. What have I become? What have you made me?

Surely I have not sunk so low as to blame you. I'm sorry. I'm just sick at heart to see the wreckage of four lives that has emerged from this affair.

Don't listen to me. Just come to me. Come see me. Now.

Jay

August 7
Jay,

It seems only to get harder. Just when I was convinced I could make it on my own. My first and most pronounced principle is escape

387

from an uncomfortable situation . . . the last few days seem to have changed all that.

The weekend with you and Nandini was a mixture of all the best and worst of my life. The time spent with you that is so hard to describe. Yet the canopy came crashing down each time she entered the room.

Don't ask me about tomorrow when I can't bear to look today in the eye. Only gods and saints can exist unafraid. And liars. I'm no liar. I know that I can't bear to be without you completely. 'Why is the measure of love loss?' I read this once and felt an imbecile for not understanding. But god, how I felt the ache each time I had to give you up to Nandini, time and again. And there is so much real in that.

Samira

August 10

Samira, what can I say? Your letter arrived so soon after your weekend with us in Bombay. Addressed to me alone. Nandini looked at it, white and stark on the breakfast table with your big black writing all over it. And that wasn't all. Just before breakfast, Nandini had picked up the paper and gone to sit on the couch—the one where you and I made love the night she went out with Mala. I almost screamed, and actually did put out a hand to stop her. And she just stared directly at me. But this time—with your letter lying between us—I crumbled like old wedding cake.

I told her. Not everything—how could I? But some things. Enough. And driven by her silence I swore to give it all up for her. She just turned and started pouring tea for herself.

I have nothing, Samira, nothing. Except the shreds of Nandini which she might bestow on me, sure that I, the worm under her heel, am kept there by that broken blubbering confession. I am bound to her more tightly than ever.

And you and I are tainted. I can't ever bear to think of 'us' again. I know you must feel the same way. Never write to me again. Let me keep you as a perfect memory, beyond the hideous mess of my reality.

Jay

Facsimile
Jay,

    I am taking the first flight out to Bombay tomorrow. Don't do anything, just be there when I arrive in the morning.

Samira

The Forest Fire

Julia

phallus

pain of love tears me
wets my eyelids
wets my cunt

love wrecks my body
fragments my mind
passion burns me to ashes

in my mind
a phallus struggles to be born
i see it i see it now
legs hitched and spread out

Facing the Mirror

in eager anticipation
a dark triangle
soft wet warm

p a l l a v i
my doorway to the universe!

durga

red sindoor spread
across the parting of your hair
red tikka
smudged by our lovemaking
red lips
swollen by the fire burning inside you
red mouth
reminiscent of meetha paan

red hands
with intricate designs
red feet
painted on the sides
red zari banarasi
covering your bridal body
red toenails
red fingers

red between your thighs

forgive me
my passion red
my inability to be gentle
now my breast is red

with the redness from your hair
and my mouth red
with the redness from your thighs

in my hand i grip
the black beads
chained in gold
to signify the marriage
of love and passion

shaktishunyata

durga said . . .
i fear you

your eyes cut through my resistance
you consume me
in your fire

i am afraid of what you create in me
an open crater
desire burning
hungry cells

what passion! what power!
what impatience to lose myself in you

my nipples traverse your palms
my mind breaks free
and spreads out
to become the universe
my body melts . . .
a volatile kundalini

Facing the Mirror

fire in my thighs
a broken dam
the musk of my love juice
fills the air
your tongue brings home
the taste of tantric concoction
sex   saliva   sweat

i die

a thousand moons burst forth
from my head
flying
my body as light as air

'i' am no more

transformed from
tantric shakti
  to
tantric shunyata

Glossary

kundalini – blissful cosmic energy dormant at the base of the spine
shakti – power; the female principle energizing the created universe
shunyata – the inherent emptiness of phenomena

392

Louse

Soraya Patel

Come baby, come, come. As I lift you, extant but invisible, to my lips, I wonder what part of your body I kiss. You are a tiny louse. Half the size of the nail on my little finger—that's how big you are. I guess I've kissed you completely, head, abdomen and piddly legs. Even though you're unrecognizable as Karen, my beloved girlfriend, I must say you've a rather puffy thorax—the remnants of your 38DD tits? Never will be tasting *them* no more . . .

I remember how you said vanilla was nicer than the hardcore stuff with me. So, just to be sadistic, babe, I drop you by a wriggling leg into my ice cream. Perhaps you shriek—but it's with a voice I can't hear. Do lice speak? Cats mew, dogs bark, you made perfectly asinine noises when you were a homo sapiens, but what sound does a louse make, Karen?

I suppose you can't speak, and maybe it's for the best, my little flailing sensation, for it was your tongue that got you into your unenviable new form. True, I'm not a genius. But it wasn't fair to call me names every time I bungled. One day you rose like a furious wave and lashed out at me. 'Louse!' Then I saw you on the floor.

I could have rubbed you out with my heel. I surveyed the possibilities. Then I scooped you up, studied you, and with mock pity, said: 'No sex for you . . . I can't find "it."' Truth be told, I still desired you. And so I took you to the lab and looked for 'it'. I giggled and blushed.

I also saw your face, in its new form, for the first time. Sheepish, embarrassed and woeful under the microscope. I decided to keep you. I still love you, baby! Besides, now you are no longer a sloppy pig, and I find that quite convenient.

Of course you, much to your perverse regret, are a head louse. 'Live life between the legs' was your motto. You swore by it every day and left me feeling small, humiliated and inadequate. Now you are destined to spend your life sitting on my head—as a homo sapiens, you could only do it figuratively.

But the nice part is, wherever we go, we go together.

You clutch on for dear life to my newly-permed hair—darling, I had it frizzed up specially for you, to give you the illusion that you are the *other* kind of louse—as I ski down the mountain. Speaking of mountains, you'd love to come down on mine . . . I spent the money you were saving for a new car on new silicon upholstery. As you behold the seductive way I unhook my lacy ga-lactic decorations, you raise your rear end. Don't be silly. I explained why there would be no sex. Besides, now *you* don't turn *me* on.

Last night, she came into my room. Look at the reversal of our fortunes; earlier, I was the one who had to deal with 'other women'. As she stripped me of beach wear and licked the salt off me, I began to feel sorry for you as you sat by the bedside table, a pathetic hurt little louse. Didn't you look at her sturdy thighs with envy? Yes, yours *are* a little skinny. Just to titillate you, I'll walk around the room with my new titanic tits. I pick you up with my Passion Pink nails. Ooh, wet paint! Now you're knee-deep. I fish you out and get it all off with acetone. Oh dear, did that sting? I place you on my stomach as I lie down in the sun to get an even tan.

What indecorous urges, Karen! Your knees can barely hold you up as you scramble to climb my silicon. Half a day of puffing and panting and you are sitting bushed at the summit of your dreams. If it's any consolation to you, I'll be just as tired tomorrow, since I'll be spending the night with this busty broad visiting from Baltimore. What a name! Baltimore . . . are all its broads balls and more? We'll find out soon. Actually you look a little tired, so I'll leave you at home. Today you shuffle like an old hag. I look at you under the microscope. You are pouting. Well, Madonna takes her pet chihuahua to an animal shrink. I'll do the same.

Damn. One hundred and twenty rupees down only to find out that you hate my womanizing.

Still, the sentimental fool in me misses you. I'm off to Africa, and this time you can come with me.

The witch doctor sprinkles some stuff on you . . . dried elephant dung, I believe. Chants puncture the air. I wander out of the tent, bored. You emerge later, looking older. You need a face-lift. We are surrounded by bosomy native girls, but you look only at me, blushing.

Shit! I'll have to pay your fare home. But you'll never call me louse again.

Gay Elegies, with Apologies to M. Hacker

Ann Urning

Bibliophilia

You've gone and left a book to me:
Strong but Asexual Bonds between
Contemporary Lesbians. What was the 'scene'
when you bought it? Were we
still chaste then? Or was this after our ice-age
fossilized the blood, and the frozen heart seeking courage

from those like Beth (single, plumber, femme, 48),
grew stoic on reading her love for Liz—late
master-mistress, lately like family.
So too, Pam (amateur mesmerist, touching 30)
prophesies, 'Lesbians don't break up.' Why? Because they
                                                    break in
like that piece of glass losing brittleness under skin,
where you, dear girl, are lodged—vexing and vexed,
as also inscribed (love, xxx) between the sheets of this pious
                                                    text.

Copula

(i)
Your face is figured in the mortar
Such as it is. The peeling walls weather
Extremity, the shallow bricks hold true,
But you don't live here any more, and I do.
(ii)
At sundown our city stretches her smoky limbs.
I envy her ligaments—even the broken roads,
The rusty girders, creaking as I made my way to you
Once, when we lived here, more than we do.
(iii)
Then, too, this copula was forbidden—
We were fugitive, even from those who knew
Some bending in the sequence of desire.
Now I don't live here anymore than you do.
(iv)
Or rather, you've flown and I've become the girl-next-door,
Keeping home like Dido and that lot before,
An elegist. If I stayed on any more than I do,
Perhaps you'd come back too?

Variations

Would you come back to a late night movie
at Anupam? 'PVR . . . ', you'd say, streetwise from your year
of marriage, Minnesota and reckless outré-
ness. Later, only because the rhyme demands, some tea,
although I'd prefer something stronger than
civility, the weekly phone call, weekend plan
with mutual friends on neutral territory.
As if there's such a place for those whose layered history
adheres, stubbornly, to the vivid bias of a double bed,
much remembered, much shared. We've coveted
each, our neighbour's girlfriend: you know I've known you
well, you've known me too, as much as any-
one. Can four such dykes and two
bichon frisé pups make up a family?

Meri Jaatwali

Inaiyat Moosa

When I was a child I had perfect teeth.
No jokes, they were straight and white like
you, and no one would guess that now.
But they were perfect way back then before I
started gritting them and grinding them and
drowning them.
I was told all the time,

smacked, pinched, spanked all the time
to stop because then I would look like a rabbit
but they were my way out and they were so
faithful, they still are, they still do the best
they can for me.
Only they were all alone back then
now I have given them something back,
now they have the rest of me for company.
I have given them my all because I need
them to be okay soon to take you out of my
blood.

My blood. I remember you so clearly, so
starkly, I can still see you standing on your
rock with the house of your Lord.
Your smile is as beautiful as the orange on
the water and the joy in my eyes.
I can still see my hand stretched out to you,
demanding, pleading,
with such a big smile on my face,
such a big victory smile and
I see the tears in your eyes, the tears my
victory brought you.
So proud, so proud to see your baby big and
strong.

So good to see my mama smile. Everything
is so good, just like you and me,
we are so perfect what does it matter that our
hands have not yet touched over the water.
I wear you on my sleeve and preen and look,
look at you so happy to see you inside me,
making me so big and strong.
So proud of my little world around me,

come I want you to see what we have made
out of no choice but because we had to and
oh how much we love it.
Wait till you come and see how beautiful we
have made it, just for you, so lost in yours.
This will never do it will never be good
enough for me, I must stop preening and pull
you over to my world because
you would be amazed to see how full of
light it is this thing of ours,
and how much Jesus we have even here you
don't know what to say? Who'd have
thought we'd even have Allah on our side
though admitted He may be a bit harder to
find, not so obvious because of course we
cannot openly display Him.
We have darkness too like on your side of
the sea but we don't notice it because we are
so busy being happy you must not waste any
more of my time like this, you just catch my
hand and allow me to save you like you
saved me.
Of course you knew that late at night with
sweat dripping off me worth to fill buckets I
was so happy walking on the main road at
11:40 wondering where to go, where will
there be peace tonight?
And when I heard those stories, those
amazing stories of how hard it really is,
remember how we laughed at them together
because that could never happen to baby, no
way, not on your life, baby.
I knew you'd smash them all, baby.
They are mere ants on your rock like the ants

that are biting my neck and arm just now,
reminding me that I never really did catch
hold of your hand.
And now they're coming to get me and they
will be relentless and they will tear me to
pieces in front of your raasta-ka-maal
sunglasses that you never could see me through
only when you allowed me to snatch them
away from you
now how will you see me
who we only wanted to be the biggest,
strongest, toughest, meanest
how will you see me now through your dark
glasses when it is fast becoming obvious that
without you blocking my sight there is more
darkness in my world than I ever saw.
My world full of perfect, perfect women
who gape when I pass by and feel oh so
sorry for me,
how will you see them laugh at me now
when you wear your glasses even outside the
light?
Did you see the darkness on my rock when
you refused to take my hand?
I thought it was merely your fucking glasses
that were making you see less of the light,
this wonderful white light that we have made
because we had no choice,
see all the perfect women over here, all the
happy women who have nothing wrong with
them
they sleep, breathe, eat and fuck perfection
all the time how can you point at them like that
it is not polite please stop they are not going

to harm me they are my people and they can
see me so big and strong,
full of you,
so why are you screaming at me to let you
turn away,
you are not even offering me someplace else
to go so isn't this a bit rude?
Come on now, mama, take my hand, take
hold of my fucking hand and come here
stop looking so afraid what is it behind me
that is making you so scared? Which miss
perfect life is terrifying you so
I'll snap my fingers and she'll die, don't you
know I'd do it for you in a second
now take hold of my hand
it does not have
the patience or the grit of my teeth, don't
make me cry now don't make me cry we
must not let our children cry let them not eat
their veg but we cannot make our children cry
take hold of my hand dammit
these ants are
biting, biting I am starting to swell I'm
starting to hurt
just take hold of my hand
what do you mean you can't why are you
standing here you should be there trying to
let me save you
why are you standing here
on my rock
watching these ants bite into my heart and
these perfect lives gape at me and say poor
thing she was so big and strong so sad to see
her whimpering what a shame.

Facing the Mirror

What a shame, mama, what a shame your
cuts look as deep as mine,
your face is whiter than I ever knew
you cannot have me watch you standing here.

You cannot tell me you took the boat across a
long time ago,
but can I not see you through the darkness of
my world because I don't have any
sunglasses,
can I not just see you and tell you now your
baby can be even bigger, tougher, stronger,
meaner?
Why can I not see you in my own world
through all these perfect women who I am
almost taller than
surely we did not build a place so dark
because we had no choice,
surely there is no corner of my world so dark
that you could disappear,
that you could not even glance at my eyes for
us to say my blood, my blood, what a terrible
death you have died.

Glossary

Meri Jaatwali – Woman of my Tribe
raasta-ka-maal – (lit.) goods from the street, i.e. cheap

For You

Maya Sharma

Who are you,
    sitting so close to me?
    My eyes swell with tears
    as you touch my fevered head.

You, draped each day
    in widow's white.
    How could you know
    the magic of touch,
    so light, so strong?
    Tell me!

How can I bear
    the weight of you
    so near to me?
    I, who am so used
    to carrying bricks,
    stones, mud.

I turn my face,
    push your hand away.
    Even then, you sit so near?
    Is the shelter you offer
    the truth or a dream?
    Tell me!

Why should I believe?
    Why should I dare

when the gods themselves
in their temples
have never granted me a boon?

Tell me truly, who are you?
In your own voice, tell me—
all that you have known
all that you have won
all that you have felt—
and I will ask no questions.
Tell me!

Bound to my home and hearth,
should I tell you
my hidden truth
of years and centuries?

Holding you, then,
should I cross the black fear?
Should I say it in words?

I was smothered within the bride's red chunni,
then I was bound to the yellow for my son.
Holding him, the family's lamp,
I melted away, turned to froth
and overflowed.
Only burnt dregs of me remain.
Should I knot myself into a bundle
and find my way to you?

(translated from Hindi by Maya Sharma)

ॐ

Always in Due Course

Barley

How I used to enjoy the poetry readings at the Literary Society in my college! I spent a lot of time there in my first year, because my cousin Shanta would recite. She sometimes chose Lord Tennyson, whom I liked tremendously. His poetry was full of unhappiness and the failure of love. '"My life is dreary, he cometh not,"' Shanta would declaim, looking sadly into the distance. '"I am aweary, aweary, I would that I were dead!"' She would lower her gaze at the end and walk off the stage before the clapping was over. And because she read so well, there would be a lot of applause.

This poem which I liked so much, by sheer contrast made me think of everyone and everything I did not want to be in my life. The couples walking together in the park and then getting into their old white cars with the dusty windows. The neighbour's wife, hanging washed clothes on the balcony. I would see the same white sheets and shirts every Friday. The woman that I saw on the train every morning, turning the pages of her ladies' magazine. I could tell she was reading each article from beginning to end with such thoroughness, waiting for her stop to arrive.

'What do they know about longing?' I would say to Shanta as we went looking for tea after the Literary Society meeting. 'Or about passion?'

In my head at least, I knew passion and longing very well. I was always bursting with desire, first for one girl, then another. Glowing from within with all of that wanting, I would carry my secret as carefully as a stolen egg. In class I took to sitting at the very back, on one of the raised wooden benches.

Crouching there, I had a sweeping view of the whole room and of the women I craved. I could hear them gossiping, even from where I was, the whispers rushing to and fro between them like the sound of a breeze among leafy branches. In the canteen I would stay as far away as possible from my many loves, but I would watch them.

I always sat alone, sealed into the bubble of my yearning, desperately loving but knowing almost nothing of what it is to act on love.

After all, true passion is an action. It is not felt inside, but consciously put into practice. I am not so cynical as to believe that love refers only to the physical act of sex. Affection is an accumulation. When enough sweet words have been said and caring gestures exchanged, you will have built the house of love around you, and you will literally be 'in love'.

But I always lacked the patience needed to construct love, to tell you the truth. I perpetually left it half-finished. What did it matter? I knew I was not like the birds by the window. Chittering, beaks full of straws, they built and re-built nests for their little ones. In their bright eyes was a heavy misgiving about all intruders. The grey cat prowled under their tree, looking up at them without much interest. I always fed him well, you see.

The years passed quickly, the girls around me fell in love one by one and got married. 'Let love come to her,' my dear father would say whenever anyone nagged him about my future. Poor man, he did not know how I was made. Everywhere around me, by the hundreds, women found men and men found women—sometimes, I am certain, women found each other. But I was proud that such was not my destiny.

Once, memorably, a woman in my law college caught me looking at her and came up to me. Brown-eyed and purposeful, Priya held me by the shoulders in an empty classroom and gave me one happy kiss after another, until I was breathless and my head was spinning. For a week I was full of a longing to follow the course of this love to its proper end, but as usual I ran from it.

She tried to get me to see her and called me constantly, saying that she wanted to be with me forever, forever. My father pretended not to know what was happening. I just shut Priya out of my life, numb with the fear of love becoming something dull and common if it were made into a rock-solid structure. For many weeks after that, my mother would be full of smiles whenever she looked at the telephone and saw that it was quiet.

Ten years on, I am still not sure of the proper way to go about 'making love'.

This, even though I once lived with a lover for three years as her 'housemate', enjoying each day a loud, smacking kiss in the morning before work, another one after work in the evening, a third one before bed.

And several times I have secretly followed strange women in the street when they did not know who I was or even that I was there, leaving them in peace after an hour of watching and longing . . . That was closer to my idea of perfect love.

Is there something between 'never' and 'forever', I think as I sit and watch a beetle fallen into a flower pot, struggling through clods of dirt mixed with dried rose leaves.

It seems unlikely.

Vande Mataram!

Qamar Roshanabadi

On the solemn occasion
of the fiftieth year
of Indian independence
I salute our motherland,
home of the most beautiful women
on this stubbornly-spinning globe,
luminous as the final tear
in god's unshuttered eye.

Ask me, and let me ask you how it feels
to be so draped with living necklaces,
to stalk the tigers crouching in your veins,
to blink back tears, to bite down joy
as sudden seething forests moan
in the desert of your aching arms.

And let it be proclaimed to those
among, between and all around us,
sweating their ignorance
from each unyielding pore—

we have been acquitted
by none other
than the great
Vatsyayana himself,
for in his Kama Sutra
he has inscribed
and the world has read

what our bodies and minds
have always known:

The calf's mouth is pure when it drinks milk;
the dog's mouth is pure when it seizes game;
as also the bird's beak when it makes fruit fall;
and the mouth of a woman in the act of love.

READ MORE IN PENGUIN

In every corner of the world, on every subject under the sun, Penguin represents quality and variety—the very best in publishing today.

For complete information about books available from Penguin—including Puffins, Penguin Classics and Arkana—and how to order them, write to us at the appropriate address below. Please note that for copyright reasons the selection of books varies from country to country.

In India: Please write to *Penguin Books India Pvt. Ltd. 11, Community Centre, Panchsheel Park, New Delhi, 110017*

In the United Kingdom: Please write to *Dept JC, Penguin Books Ltd. Bath Road, Harmondsworth, West Drayton, Middlesex, UB7 ODA. UK*

In the United States: Please write to *Penguin USA Inc., 375 Hudson Street, New York, NY 10014*

In Canada: Please write to *Penguin Books Canada Ltd. 10 Alcorn Avenue, Suite 300, Toronto, Ontario M4V 3B2*

In Australia: Please write to *Penguin Books Australia Ltd. 487, Maroondah Highway, Ring Wood, Victoria 3134*

In New Zealand: Please write to *Penguin Books (NZ) Ltd. Private Bag, Takapuna, Auckland 9*

In the Netherlands: Please write to *Penguin Books Netherlands B.V., Keizersgracht 231 NL-1016 DV Amsterdom*

In Germany : Please write to *Penguin Books Deutschland GmbH, Metzlerstrasse 26, 60595 Frankfurt am Main, Germany*

In Spain: Please write to *Penguin Books S.A., Bravo Murillo, 19-1'B, E-28015 Madrid, Spain*

In Italy: Please write to *Penguin Italia s.r.l., Via Felice Casati 20, I-20104 Milano*

In France: Please write to *Penguin France S.A., 17 rue Lejeune, F-31000 Toulouse*

In Japan: Please write to *Penguin Books Japan. Ishikiribashi Building, 2-5-4, Suido, Tokyo 112*

In Greece: Please write to *Penguin Hellas Ltd, dimocritou 3, GR-106 71 Athens*

In South Africa: Please write to *Longman Penguin Books Southern Africa (Pty) Ltd, Private Bag X08, Bertsham 2013*